THE HISTORY OF UNILEVER

VOLUME III

THE HISTORY OF
UNILEVER

CHALLENGE AND RESPONSE
IN THE POST-WAR
INDUSTRIAL REVOLUTION
1945-1965

BY

CHARLES WILSON

IN THREE VOLUMES · VOLUME III

FREDERICK A. PRAEGER, *Publishers*
New York · Washington

BOOKS THAT MATTER

Published in the United States of America in 1968
by Frederick A. Praeger, Inc., Publishers
111 Fourth Avenue, New York, N.Y. 10003

Printed in Great Britain

PREFACE

The History of Unilever (1954) described the growth and development of the business from its beginnings down to the final merger of 1929, and, in more general terms, to 1945. This volume takes up the story where Volume II of the *History* left off, and describes the developments of the next twenty years.

Inevitably, the treatment is somewhat different from that of the preceding volumes. The 'managerial revolution' has certainly not destroyed the importance of the individual contribution to business growth. But for obvious reasons the author writing virtually contemporary history cannot attempt to assess the individual contributions of those who are still in office or have only vacated it very recently. Sadly, the story of these twenty years must be largely anonymous. After much thought, some trial and more error I decided to divide this volume into two halves. In Part I, I have tried to identify and analyse the forces making for growth in a period of unprecedented expansion and change. In Part II, I have recorded some of the historical evidence on which the analysis of Part I is based. To have combined the two in a single essay would, in my view, have strained the patience of the reader and the capacities of the writer. The distinction between analysis and chronicle is not absolute. Part I contains some evidence; Part II develops some analysis. But broadly, Part I is designed for the reader with a general interest in the problems of business development; Part II forms an appendix of further reference for those who want to carry their enquiries into more detail.

That said, I will let the narrative speak for itself; except to say this: there is an influential school of thought amongst economists which holds that 'the market economy' of former times is disappearing, if it has not already disappeared; and that the great corporation is in itself a major reason for its disappearance. According to this school of opinion, the great corporation has become an autonomous economic force, virtually independent of the forces of the market, monopolistic, making price systems rather than following them, dictating to consumers rather than meeting their needs, living within a closed economic system facilitated by the availability of capital saved from profits. As an historian I believe these views, with their implication of a sharp, total break with older forms of industry, to be much exaggerated. Competition never *was* perfect. The initiative towards new products has always come in large measure from the *entrepreneur*. Whether capital comes from the money market or from undistributed profits makes less difference to business policy than is assumed. To those who know no history, life seems a series of revolutions. The historian uses the term 'revolution' sparingly. There is, even in the turbulence of the mid-twentieth century, much continuity in our economic life and institutions.

The profile of Unilever that follows seems to me to bear out this view. The *nature* of competition has certainly changed, but competition itself remains the spur to enterprise. In these two decades the outstanding features of the expanding enterprise of Unilever have been, first, its *organic* character. Capital investment has been deployed in carefully selected fields for which Unilever felt itself particularly fitted by experience: there have been no indiscriminate forays into unrelated enterprises. Secondly, the period has seen a growing realization that the successful organization of the concern requires constant and continuous blending of the skills of scientist and salesman. The one without the other would certainly be inadequate and could well be disastrous.

If the history of Unilever in the first two decades after the Second World War has any general lessons to offer, these are amongst them. If I am correct in believing that market forces are still important (though doubtless assuming different forms in the world), Unilever's experience has (I believe) some general application in industry at large.

One important episode in the very recent history of Unilever is not dealt with in this volume. In 1963 the Government referred the detergents industry to the Monopolies Commission. The Commission reported in 1966, but the final negotiations between the Government and the industry were not completed until 1967. Indeed, in some ways the story may be said to be continuing. It has not been dealt with here for the simple reason that this volume ends at 1965. I have therefore resisted the temptation to include any comment on the investigation and its results; the whole matter will be the subject of a separate study in due course.

At the end of Volume II of *The History of Unilever*, I compiled a list of those who had in one way or another helped me to complete the first two volumes, and a list of sources from which documentary material had been obtained. I concluded that neither list is possible on this occasion. The number of those who have, formally or informally, given me the benefit of their knowledge and experience is far too large to be printed. Indeed, there are few Unilever businesses in the world from which I have not had some personal information in the course of research. Reluctantly, therefore, I must confine my specific acknowledgements to a very short list of those who have been most constantly in touch with the progress of this work. To the Chairmen holding office during the period of my research—Lord Cole, Mr F. J. Tempel, Mr Harold Hartog—and the other member of the Special Committee, Dr Ernest Woodroofe, I am grateful for much expert and patient advice. To the Board as a whole I am indebted for giving me free access to all the evidence I needed and full discretion as to its use. To the Secretary of Unilever Limited, Mr P. A. Macrory, I owe a debt that cannot be repaid, for he has at all times made himself available for help and advice on every aspect of my problems. To Mr K. A. Bayley and his colleagues in Information Division I am indebted for all kinds of practical help most willingly provided. For Continental affairs Mr E. A. Hofman has, as with the former volumes, given me unstinted help. I also had the benefit of the valuable assistance of Mr Alan Watson, who collected much of the evidence, verbal and written, on which the book is based. In Rotterdam, Mr J. Schim van der Loeff and Mr Arie Braakman have been my vigilant guides through the problems of Continental Europe. To Professor H. Baudet, of Groningen University, who is responsible for the Dutch version of the book, I am indebted for valuable constructive criticism on a number of points. To the many others whose conversation helped to bring Unilever and its problems to life I offer grateful thanks. I hope they will regard this volume as a fair interpretation of the information they gave me.

The primary sources from which the material in the book has been drawn are internal to Unilever (Board Minutes, Committee Minutes, memoranda, correspondence, statistics, accounts and the like). They have been carefully recorded and preserved for future reference, and there would be little point in listing them here. So have all the hundreds of interviews and opinions I have used. Secondary material that is specifically relevant to the text is quoted in footnotes.

CHARLES WILSON

CONTENTS

PART ONE : THE DYNAMICS OF GROWTH

Chapter   *Page*

1 Challenge and Response   3

2 Management: Its Ends and Means   27

3 Men   45

4 Research and Technology   64

5 Markets   90

6 Capital and Finance   108

   Summing Up   132

PART TWO : THE CHRONICLE OF GROWTH

   Introductory: The Patterns of Growth   149

7 The United Kingdom   155

8 The West European Continent   183

9 Africa   213

10 Overseas Markets   227

The Unilever Board   271

Index   275

MAPS, CHARTS, Etc.

Figure		*Page*
1	The Unilever Structure in 1949	34
2	The Unilever Structure in 1965	35
3	The Unilever Structure in 1967	36
4	Unilever Research Laboratories 1965	68
5	Research arrangements at Port Sunlight	75
6	Return on Capital Employed 1954–64	115
7	Unilever: Employment of Capital 1949–65	120
8	Unilever Limited: Capital Employed 1949–65	128
9	Unilever N.V.: Capital Employed 1949–65	129
10	Unilever Limited and Unilever N.V.: Capital Employed 1949–65	130
11	Unilever: Capital, Growth and Diversification 1951–65	131
12	Unilever Total Third Party Turnover 1938–65	153
13	Unilever Sales of Detergents 1950–65	154
14	The Transformation of The United Africa Company's Operations in Nigeria 1949–65	222/3

PART ONE

THE DYNAMICS OF GROWTH

CHAPTER 1

CHALLENGE AND RESPONSE

'FIRMS' Lord Cole, the Chairman of Unilever Limited, once remarked, 'are often compared to ships. Well, Unilever is not a ship, it is a fleet—several different fleets, several hundred subsidiary companies—and the ships many different sizes, doing all kinds of different things, all over the place.' Some carried cargoes of their own manufactured products, others raw materials. 'Different histories, different backgrounds, different beginnings.'[1] The assembly of the Unilever 'fleet' over a period of more than three-quarters of a century down to 1949 was described in the *History of Unilever*.[2] It showed how the twin processes of concentration and expansion had jointly produced a proliferating business on a world scale. Out of the little town of Oss in North Brabant and the Victorian model village of Port Sunlight rose the Unilever of 1929, comprising a sizeable part of Europe's oils and fats industries. Already this European manufacturing organization had widespread interests in Africa, Asia, Australasia, and North and South America. Although it was still mainly concerned with the trade in oils and fats and the manufacture of products from those raw materials, Unilever had already shown signs of interesting itself in other related products, particularly in foods other than margarine. Nevertheless it remained principally a complex of oils and fats industries. These had come together for a variety of reasons—the pressure of competition, the interplay of personalities, the desire for mutual advantage and the exchange of knowledge, and the pressure for expansion. Broadly, Unilever's history justified a remark of William Lever's in 1903: '. . . if combines result in cheaper production and more abundant supply these undertakings will be successful; if not they will be failures . . . [they] will be simply putting off the evil day . . . simply drag each other down, down, down until they disappear.'[3]

[1] In a discussion with Kenneth Harris. *The Observer*, 6 and 13 January 1963.
[2] *The History of Unilever: A Study in Economic Growth and Social Change.* Charles Wilson, Cassell (2 vols), 1954.
[3] William Lever, addressing a Men's Meeting at Port Sunlight, 11 January 1903.

3

Unilever had had its ups and downs, but its fundamentally progressive policies endorsed by Dutch and British alike after 1929
had ensured not merely survival but expansive success.

This study continues the history into the two decades after the
end of the Second World War, a period that has been described,
with more justification than such labels usually deserve, as 'the
age of the second industrial revolution.'

In 1948 the Unilever 'fleet' included 402 operating or administrative companies. They were making and selling goods to a value
of over £600 million a year in 50 different countries. By 1965
the 'fleet' had grown, especially in Continental Europe: in all, over
500 businesses were now operating in more than 60 countries,
with a turnover of more than three times that of 1948—to be precise
£2,326 million. Briefly, the change can be summarized: more and
larger component firms carrying on a larger volume of business,
and business of a more highly diversified character.[1] They were
operating over larger areas of the world's surface and they were
employing new and often revolutionary methods to manufacture,
advertise, distribute and sell their goods. They were operating in a
context where not only economic conditions but the political
institutions of the world had been transformed.

To take first the political and economic changes in the world in
which Unilever found itself operating after the Second World War.
The war itself had brought destruction and devastation on an
apocalyptic scale. Estimates of the number of people killed have
varied from twenty-two to fifty-five million; of wounded from
thirty-four million upwards. Houses, factories, industrial plant
worth £1 trillion were destroyed. Much of what was left in Europe
and Asia was poorly maintained. Stocks of food and raw materials
were run down. Channels of commerce were disrupted. Europe's
investments had had to be liquidated to pay for the war. Public
expenditure was enormous and all the belligerents suffered from
inflation. To anyone who remembers the war and post-war years
the agony seemed at the time intolerably drawn out, never-ending.
Shortages, rationing, regulations, bureaucracy in all its petty and
restrictive forms seemed to go on for ever.

Yet after twenty years the picture had changed, the human

[1] As Part II demonstrates, a number of factories and businesses were closed
under plans to concentrate production. In some cases these were put to different
uses. But in any event, closures were exceeded by newly built or newly acquired
units, especially in Spain, Italy, France, Sweden, Greece, etc.

agony already apt to be dismissed summarily, almost cynically, as a passing moment of history. As if to compensate humanity for the war horrors wreaked upon it in the name of scientific progress, science itself set about the restoration of material prosperity. Almost all the progress that began to be apparent after five or ten years of peace could be traced to the development of scientific concepts and methods once harnessed to war, and now harnessed to the tasks of peace. The jet engine, prefabricated buildings, new techniques in engineering and metallurgy, medical (including nutritional) discoveries, atomic power, automatic methods for saving labour, even the development of the psychological and social sciences in connection with the problems of armed forces—all were transferred from the waging of war to the enjoyment of peace. Thus, within an astonishingly short time, the rise in the general standard of living which had been a feature of the half-century before the war and had been interrupted for six years was resumed.

Just as the first industrial revolution of the eighteenth century had seen the output of industry rise dramatically with the application of machinery and steam power, the structure of industry transformed and social life itself revolutionized, so this new industrial revolution saw another leap in the quantity and quality of industrial output. In the 1950s and 1960s the activities of Unilever were transformed under the influence of this new surge of scientific enquiry and application. Before the war it could hardly be said that research or scientific method was strong in Unilever. It is true that Unilever comprised much technical knowledge of a practical kind, but in general it was orientated towards salesmanship rather than towards science. Now, at every point, scientific method rapidly began to take control of activities formerly operated by traditional or customary methods. It was significant that by 1957 the Chairmen's speech at the Annual General Meetings could be devoted to research in Unilever.[1] 'By research' the Chairmen said, 'we mean a quest for new knowledge which can find immediate commercial application or provide the basic scientific information we hope will ultimately lead to new and improved products

[1] See Volume I of *The History of Unilever* for an explanation of the dual organization of Unilever. The Chairman of each company being the Vice-Chairman of the other, each delivered an identical annual speech. To quote the Prologue to Volume I: '. . . since the purpose of the fusion was single, not divided, direction of policy, nothing was left undone to diminish the effects of dualism in practice.' The speeches by the respective Chairmen were delivered at Annual General Meetings taking place almost simultaneously in London and in Rotterdam.

and processes.' They went on to say that the translation of research into production was the function of *development*. Moreover, because scientific research in the narrow sense was not enough, it had to be accompanied by social research into the changing habits and needs of people in different countries; the process known as 'market research'. 'The grocer's shop', as Unilever had sometimes been described, was rapidly turning into a scientific laboratory. The following chapters will describe how not only manufacturing processes but also the economics of advertising, the selection and training of management and the diversified working of the whole business itself became in these areas the object of methodical enquiry on a scale never previously contemplated. Chemists, biologists, psychologists, sociologists, economists, were all recruited to help guide, measure and control the expanding, changing activities of Unilever.

It had long been recognized by a handful of far-sighted industrialists and scientists that the function of industry did not necessarily consist only in supplying the 'felt wants' of society: that the inventor was sometimes ahead of the 'wants' of his time, creating new wants, not merely supplying old ones. 'The steady methodical investigation of natural phenomena' Ludwig Mond, a great Victorian industrial chemist, had said in the 1880s, 'is the father of industrial progress.'[1] But such scientific initiative had played a limited part only in the history of the industries that had become Unilever. The scientific knowledge they deployed was for the most part simple. The invention which enabled liquid oils to be turned into solids (dating from about 1910) was a major step forward in the scientific history of oils and fats in the twentieth century. But in general the successful manufacturers had progressed through skill in distributing and selling methods as much as through skill of manufacture. William Lever himself had made his reputation as a master of salesmanship. The new men coming into the industry after the Second World War increasingly realized that the new economic and social conditions in the post-war world demanded a combination of science and salesmanship. Dr E. G. Woodroofe, a Vice-Chairman of Unilever Limited and himself a scientist, put the matter succinctly: 'There are two essential elements of success in innovation in the consumer goods industry. The one is a clear recognition of the existent latent or creatable desires of the public, the other the harnessing of technical

[1] Ludwig Mond. *The Life of Ludwig Mond.* J. M. Cohen, Methuen, 1956.

means to satisfy these needs. Understanding that these are not separate elements and that they must be combined into a single force is the heart of the matter.'[1]

History reinforced this contention. The old and famous partnerships on which the first industrial revolution was founded invariably consisted of one partner skilled in the arts of commerce and another skilled in the technical means of production. Such were Boulton and Watt, such were Wedgwood and Bentley and scores of others. This classic partnership between salesmanship and a sort of science had often become weakened with time in Britain. The immediate post-war years had found Unilever itself sadly lacking in the necessary scientific resources for research and development to keep it competitive and expanding. In a world where traditional products like soap were giving way to more efficient but more complex synthetic detergents, and where, throughout the whole range of food products, methods of manufacture and preservation called increasingly upon the knowledge of chemists, biologists, engineers and others, the beginnings of change were slow and uncertain, but by the second half of the 1950s the scientific movement was steadily gathering momentum.

But if Unilever was undergoing an inner revolution, it was also facing a revolutionary world outside. In Europe, Asia and Africa especially, the war years had so changed the balance of forces and ideas that it was not long after the war before the basic political and social institutions of these continents were all transformed. Most immediately important to Unilever were the changes in Europe. The Napoleonic Wars, when Napoleon's armies had occupied large areas of Europe, had had as their aftermath radical changes in the structure of Europe, especially the unification of Germany and Italy. From customs unions and new railways had come the new and unified Germany of Bismarck. The twentieth century operated on an even larger canvas. The Second World War had shown up the obstructive irrelevancy of a Europe divided into conflicting national states. Its absurdities became clearer as methods of transport, themselves revolutionized by wartime advances, drew the world ever more closely together. Hence the move towards economic integration in Europe—the Benelux Pact of 1944, the European Coal and Steel Community of 1952; the European Atomic Energy Commission of 1957, the European Economic Community under the Treaty of Rome in 1957, and

---

[1] 'Science and the City', *New Scientist*, vol. 20, no. 366, 1963.

finally in 1959 the European Free Trade Association between Britain, the Scandinavian countries, Switzerland, Austria and Portugal. The prospect of the economic unification of a large part of Western Europe—Belgium, France, Germany, Italy, Luxembourg and the Netherlands—was a matter of the first importance to Unilever, for (as the Chairmen told shareholders) 'Nearly two-thirds of your capital is employed in Europe; 61 per cent of the third-party sales and 72 per cent of the profit are made there, and when you read that 68 per cent of the capital expenditure approved in 1962 was for Europe you will realize that we expect this pattern to continue. In broad terms it comes to this, that about one-third of our business is in the countries of the European Economic Community and one-third in those of the European Free Trade Area.'

The claim was not unjust that from the beginning Unilever had welcomed the Common Market. In January 1958 the Board had said: 'We welcome the institution of the European Economic Community for the part it seems about to play in raising the standards of living in the member countries.' Almost alone amongst the ten largest companies in the Western world, Unilever was a European-based business, with over a hundred factories in Continental Europe alone, of which more than forty were in West Germany. For such an international business the Common Market created both opportunities and problems. Obviously a larger free trade area would in the end be to the advantage of producers and consumers. Historically there was no doubt about it. What the Act of Union of 1707 had done for trade between England and Scotland, the removal of internal customs and tariffs had done for France in 1789, the Zollverein in 1834 for Germany, the Common Market promised to do, but on a much vaster scale, for Europe. Moreover, the Common Market was not merely to be a customs union. It was (in the words of the Treaty of Rome of 1957) 'to promote throughout the Community a harmonious development of economic activities, a continuous and balanced expansion, increased stability, accelerated raising of the standard of living, and closer relations between its member states.' There was a 12-year programme for attaining these ambitious ends. Manufacturing standards, agrarian policy, taxation, monopoly policy, labour and social programmes, and transport policies, were to be co-ordinated and improved.

The opportunities created by this vision of a new Europe for

Unilever seemed limitless. Yet if they were to be realized Unilever had to adapt itself flexibly and swiftly. For the structure of Unilever as a manufacturer had been largely dictated by the existence of those very national boundaries and national tariffs which it was now the function of the Common Market to obliterate. Both Lever and the Dutch margarine manufacturers had set up their factories in other countries in Europe and elsewhere because the tariff walls which began to rise against imports everywhere in the late nineteenth century had made it virtually impossible to do business economically and profitably on the basis of an export trade from British- or Dutch-based factories.

Hence the Unilever inheritance of factories in Germany, France, Belgium, Scandinavia, North America and elsewhere. Unilever's products had come to be manufactured on those sites that were most economical under the conditions of the economic policies pursued by the nations before 1939. But where now within a Common Market would the best place be for production? Even under the old conditions manufacture within the national boundaries had become increasingly concentrated in the largest possible factories. This was particularly true of margarine production. How far would it be wise for Unilever to concentrate its entire production for Western Europe in one or two factories? To study such problems two Unilever Common Market conferences sat in 1962 and 1963. Some four hundred experts set to work and produced twenty reports which dealt with marketing, factory location, tariffs, cartels, transport, etc. They represented about a hundred Unilever companies within the Common Market and making a wide range of products. Some of the recommendations— for example, affecting the standardization of brand names—were put into effect almost at once. A third conference met in 1966. It still faced major problems, particularly those of the location of factories. Here the problems are obviously enormous and fundamental and the location studies influenced new investment decisions. The decisions, however, must be taken; they cannot wait indefinitely. For the rising competition of newcomers (especially powerful competitors from America) who are starting from scratch, with freedom to choose their own most advantageous factory sites in Europe, makes the matter urgent.

There was another side of the coin; the post-war pattern of Europe imposed great sacrifices on the Unilever of 1929. For the Russian advance into Central Europe and the final dropping of the Iron Curtain on markets like Poland, Czechoslovakia, Hungary, Rumania, Bulgaria and Eastern Germany severed a large part of those industries which had been in part the contribution of the former Schicht group to the 1929 combine. Negotiations, long-drawn-out over many years, were to continue—and still continue—but though some terms of compensation were here and there achieved, the fact had to be faced that Unilever's properties beyond the Iron Curtain had been lost. Formerly centred in Aussig in Czechoslovakia, the great complex of Schicht businesses, built up to serve the territories of the Austro-Hungarian monarchy, dissolved. Only a rump remained in Vienna. Yet here in Austria another Phoenix was to rise. The old bastion of Europe against the Turk steadily became a peephole through the Iron Curtain. Small though its markets were by comparison with the old days, Austrian Unilever became a very lively and expanding group of operating companies.[1]

In the period with which this book is concerned Europe meant Western Europe and such eastward areas in European Turkey, Greece and the Middle East as remained outside the Russian sphere.

There were many other problems. One was the relationship of the two halves of the Unilever body, Limited and N.V., left in suspense by the failure of the negotiations of 1961–63 to bring Britain into the Common Market. 'Unilever' (as Lord Cole remarked in 1963) 'is a child of Europe.' Whether Britain entered the Common Market or not, Unilever was, as he said, 'in'. 'We were in Europe before they started the Common Market . . . we hardly notice the Channel. . . . The issue is not whether we go in or not, but what kind of relationship we have with the Six with whom we are already tremendously involved.'[2]

Whatever the ultimate outcome, it was evident that from the beginning the Common Market provided a tremendous stimulus to the Netherlands. The physical chaos of 1945, the loss of the entire Dutch Eastern Empire, the burdensome problem of the refugees from Indonesia—all these apparently overwhelming disasters were mastered. The whole Dutch economy was re-oriented towards the new Western world that arose from the ashes. A new, forward-looking society saw itself as part of a great free trade area rich in opportunities. Nowhere was the stimulus of the

[1] See pages 79, 210.
[2] In a discussion with Kenneth Harris. *The Observer*, 6 and 13 January 1963.

Common Market more visible than at Rotterdam, which began to assume its natural role as the shipping centre for the new Europe, and in fact the largest port in the world. These freshening breezes were felt not least at Unilever's headquarters there.

The location of factories was not the only problem posed in the new Europe. The common agricultural policy was another one. Relations with the world's farmers had always been a major concern for Unilever. Often in the past, Unilever, like other margarine manufacturers, had faced hostile legislation in many countries of the world which was the result of the powerful lobbying by dairy farmers defending their market for butter. The post-war years saw this legislation generally (though not universally) modified and relaxed; in some cases it was completely abolished. The most remarkable change was in the United States. As late as 1950, the farmers' lobby still maintained discriminatory laws against margarine. After that came a change in attitude and a steep increase in margarine consumption. Behind this lay an important change in the relationship of the manufacturer and the farmer. New technology made it possible to use soyabean and cottonseed oils on a scale which had previously been impossible, and these were grown precisely in those areas (like Minnesota) where the dairy interests had previously been strongest.

Thus North America became a large-scale exporter of edible oil, supplying four-fifths of the world's needs of soyabean oil. Europe, on the other hand, was importing more soyabeans and soyabean oil than any other single raw material. Within the Common Market Unilever was a great buyer of oils and fats for margarine and to a lesser extent for soap manufacture. In most of the West European countries, Unilever had been able to buy the oils and fats it needed in the best markets and import them free of or at low duty. Now it was faced with the Common Market agricultural policy, based mainly on the system of increasing the prices of imported products up to the level of Common Market producers' prices. If this system had been applied in the case of oil seeds and vegetable oils, the margarine price would have to be increased considerably.

The strong farmers' lobbies not only demanded protection for the olive oil producers of Italy and the rapeseed growers of Germany and France, but they also wished to have a link between the margarine and butter market. This would take the form of a levy on the margarine industry with the object of stabilizing the relationship between the prices of margarine and butter, thus protecting the dairy farmer.

Behind such demands lay the biggest danger threatening the future of the Common Market—that it might become, under the influence of restrictionist lobbies, an inward-looking organization, heavily protected against the outside world and dedicated to the protection of its own powerful vested interests rather than to the expansion of trade with the rest of the world. The Unilever view was (and remains) that the Common Market will benefit the world and itself in so far as it is dedicated in the end to the freeing and enlargement of world trade and industry.

Meanwhile a new technology was constantly introducing new balancing elements into the relationship between Unilever and the farmer. One was the new technique, already mentioned, which enabled soyabean and cottonseed oil to be used more extensively in the manufacture of margarine and thus gave the North American farmer a stake in the prosperity of the margarine industry. Other quite different developments in food preservation had created a stake for the farmer in some parts of the European Continent in the prosperity of Unilever as a food manufacturer. New techniques of quick-freezing and quick-drying foods were developed in the post-war years.[1] It became clear that it would not pay to preserve foods by such methods unless the materials were of the highest quality. As Unilever became a food processer on a vast scale in the 1950s close relationships had to be established with the farmers so that the whole process of growing—the quality of the seed, methods of cultivation, the moment and the method of harvesting—could be designed to produce the desired qualities of vegetables and fruit. Hence the growing network of relationships with farming in Great Britain and some areas of the Continent. These helped to bring a more scientific approach to the business of agriculture and horticulture, to improve the quality of crops and provide the farmer with a secure outlet and a buffer against the vicissitudes of the market.

To this growing business as a buyer of vegetables, fruit, milk (for ice-cream), meat (for canning, sausages, pies and bacon), Unilever joined a growing complementary trade in animal feeding-stuffs. And here again the Unilever businesses which specialized in selling cake and compounds for animal feeding to the farmers made it their business also to organize scientific services for

[1] See Chapter 7.

the technical assistance of farmers, particularly those who bred stock. For some proportion of farmers, at any rate, there was a growing realization that the link with Unilever through contracts and technical assistance could promise a better prospect of profit and stability.[1]

The history of Unilever, bound up as it had always been with the development of industrial urban society, was predominantly centred in Europe; but it had other interests in the developing economies outside Europe. The size of the individual investments must not be exaggerated. Hindustan Lever, a large and successful enterprise with sales in 1964-5 ranking second amongst India's large companies in the private sector, accounted for less than three per cent of Unilever's total turnover. Unilever's demand for oils and fats as raw materials for margarine and soap would in itself have ensured close relations with those African and other overseas territories which were the great producers of oil-bearing seeds. Over and above these general needs was the historical presence of William Lever. Hawk-eyed for business and profit, ever wary of what he called 'the danger of being squeezed on raw materials', Lever had burrowed his way into the African trade—hence by the 1930s the giant amongst the African traders called The United Africa Company. He had likewise discerned markets amongst (as he characteristically phrased it) 'the washing needs of the teeming millions of India' and numerous other developing economies. Thus Unilever had come to have great component firms growing and buying raw materials in Africa and Asia, and other local manufacturing companies which had grown out of the old export trades operated from Britain and from Holland.

Upon all these fell the abrupt ending of the old colonial empires, the shock of political independence and all the political, economic and social upheavals connected with it. The conditions of life and business in these extra-European areas where Unilever had put down roots varied widely. They shared only one common characteristic: a generally low standard of income for most people compared with European standards, and ever-present poverty on a colossal scale. The newly independent governments in the post-war period all took up the challenge of poverty where the colonial governments had left off, and with renewed energy, not always directed to the best advantage. The curse upon material progress in most backward areas had been that effort invariably tended to

[1] See Chapters 7 and 8.

diminish as soon as the rudimentary needs of life were satisfied. Throughout all the developing economies there was a tendency for numbers to outstrip economic growth. The faster numbers grew, the slower was the growth of income per head, and each success in satisfying an elementary want seemed to be followed by a fall in productivity. Where there was little or no surplus of production over consumption, how was the spiral to be turned upwards? Everywhere the orthodox answer came: by planning consciously the economic life of the country, and particularly by restraining 'unnecessary consumption' so that necessary investment could be provided out of savings from income. Hence everywhere Unilever had to accept arguments and plans in part Keynesian, in part Socialist, designed in large measure to restrict consumption, tax incomes, control imports and stimulate exports in one way or another.

Like all Western capitalist businesses, Unilever also faced in many places antipathies which further complicated the normal running of a business. Quite apart from such hostility as faced Dutch operators in, say, Indonesia, or the Belgians in the Congo, or the British in Egypt after independence, there were often deeper tribal and communal traditions which made Western individualism seem alien and inappropriate. Private capitalism, the norm of economic expansion in Western Europe, often seemed merely an instrument of exploitation and a symbol of oppression to Asians and Africans. Hence some instances of outright obstruction, expropriation and the like. 'Our interest in Egypt' the Report and Accounts for 1963 had to confess, 'is now limited to a fee for specialist assistance and the use of trade marks which we receive from the business of which we formerly had a 50 per cent share. This business was finally taken over by the State in August 1963, compensation being payable in Egyptian State Bonds.' Elsewhere there was confusion and uncertainty. The next year saw the Indonesian business put nominally under the supervision of the Ministry of People's Industry. In the Belgian Congo the Unilever plantations and all the housing and welfare services that went with them, perhaps the most precious of Leverhulme's industrial nurseries, were threatened with reversion to the jungle by 1965.

Such disasters apart, Unilever through its local managements has usually managed to achieve a *modus vivendi* with local government by which it was able to carry on its business. Local managements often had to face interference, uncertainty, hostility, which severely taxed their diplomacy and nerve. The apparatus of 'economic planning' often seemed little more than a process of petty obstruction and ignorance. But in general Unilever managers were brought up with a proper respect for local traditions and a realization that business could only be conducted if local traditions were respected. The Chairmen put it thus in 1959: 'Industrial development, we feel strongly, must be related to the general development of ways of thought and methods of upbringing and education in the community, otherwise very great strains will be set up—after all, our own society is by no means free of those strains yet and it is nearly two hundred years since modern industrial development began.'

This recognition involved many important consequences. First of all, it meant everywhere a rapid development of schemes of education and training to increase the number of managers of local origin. In West and East Africa this process had already gone a long way.[1] Likewise the business in India, one of the brightest stars in the Unilever galaxy, had been almost completely entrusted to local managers.

The new managements inherited from their predecessors the responsibility of ensuring that local development was concentrated on those markets and products suited to the country in question. In India, for example, where only a small proportion of the total population of over 400 million have money for more than the bare necessities of life, it would be folly to ignore the limiting factor that even by 1960 the real national income per head had risen to only about £25—amongst the lowest in the world and only one-fifteenth of that of the United Kingdom. Equally, the changing face of Africa demanded a radical shift in the operations of The United Africa Company. Here the emphasis had moved first from retail to wholesale trading, then from general trading into specialized trading and most recently into manufacturing—timber, coach-building, furniture, beer and so on.

The job of the top management at European headquarters was on the one hand to recognize the limitations on Unilever's freedom of action in such areas, while ensuring that local operations conformed to a pattern suggested by the marketing and technological experience with which Unilever was best supplied. 'In countries like these' said the Chairmen in 1959, 'we cannot do a very great deal to improve matters because the development of

[1] For details see Chapter 9.

patterns of society and ways of thought is part of a nation's historical development which no single firm can massively influence.' Such were the limits, but within those limits it was headquarters' job to control major expenditure and the placing of senior managers. If this central guidance were lacking, 'Unilever would cease to be an operational company. It would become an investment trust and most of the justification for its international activities would disappear.'

Overseas companies provided a rich crop of problems. Yet the contribution of Unilever to the economic development of such underdeveloped areas was probably most valuable just because it was a strictly economic relationship. ('The relationship between the United Africa Group and Unilever as sellers and buyers of oils and fats is strictly businesslike.') In this respect it could be argued that it was fundamentally of more value than, certainly different in kind from, those government loans or gifts that were subject to less strict supervision and accounting and brought less in the way of direct training for business or manufacture. Contrariwise, Unilever was very ready to acknowledge that the new areas were of great value to the business in helping it to find solutions to the problems of higher management. 'Unilever' said the Chairmen in 1954, 'produces industrialists. The United Africa Group produces merchants, men with a quick sense of what the market requires, a desire to keep prices low enough for further expansion of sales and a wholesome fear of overhead expenses. Both types are needed in a large business, the long view and systematic planning of the industrialist, the market sense and quick response of the merchants.' It was this broad exchange between Europe and the extra-European world that gave Unilever one of its greatest assets: the cross-fertilization with a multi-national outlook. 'In a world where narrow nationalism is not the least nor the most distant of dangers, that is something worth doing.'

Such imponderables complicated even further the infinitely labyrinthine problem of overseas investment. How much should a European-based business invest overseas, especially in the new economies? What return should it expect? In 1949, over the whole range of Unilever industries, every £100 laid out in turnover returned roughly £4. 15s. in gross profit. Of this, just under one-half was paid out in taxes to governments. In 1965 each £100 returned just over £5 gross profit, of which just under one-half went in taxes. But in the developing economies the corresponding figures in 1965 were 75s. gross profit, of which just over one-half went in taxes to governments. Clearly, no prudent manager with a proper regard for his responsibilities to the shareholders or the business would be in any tearing hurry to rush into overseas investment on the basis of such figures, especially when added to them were the risks of political trouble, expropriation by hostile governments, wild inflation (as in South America) and the like. The greater likelihood remained (as Lever had reminded his shareholders in 1906) that popular opinion would shy away from such investments as unbusinesslike and unprofitable. He was speaking then of investment in European societies, which seemed in the early twentieth century as dangerous a jungle to the average British investor as the developing economies sometimes seem to his descendant of the 1960s. In such situations the economist could give only limited help to the businessman in reaching his decision to go in or stay out. The economist could measure the existing situation and suggest its probable evolution but, where major decisions of a once-for-all kind are involved, human judgment and intuition were still the final arbiter. All investment involves risk, political as well as economic. Nearly all new investment goes through a period of low return. It takes judgment born of long experience to balance all the ponderables and the imponderables and decide whether the business is worth the candle.

During the past century the evolution of the oils and fats industries, along with that of a number of other modern industries, has been closely associated with the changing and growing needs of the people in the industrial cities of the West. It was the conditions of town life which largely created the demand for soap and detergents and for additional supplies of food beyond what had once been obtained from the countryside. As the income of industrial society rose, so did its ability to buy the factory-made products which it needed to translate rising standards of living into the realities of everyday life. Unilever, in short, was itself part of the new pattern of an industrial society increasingly concentrated in towns, and its prosperity depended upon the continued rise of living standards.

This continued to be as true in the 1960s as it had been in the 1880s when Lever was himself ministering to the needs of the new working- and middle-class England. 'There is only one thing' remarked Lord Cole succinctly in 1963, 'that would really put the breeze up us here—the prospect of the general standard of living standing still or declining.'[1] The pessimistic eye might sometimes find it difficult to detect any perceptible rise in living standards in the new societies of Asia or Africa, where the struggle with poverty seemed unabated and progress to consist of one step forward and two steps back. Yet even here, progress, even measurable progress of a material kind, was visible.

Western Europe itself still had its dark patches of sheer poverty. Spain, with large underpopulated and backward areas, relatively poor communications in many places, primitive methods of distribution and a conservatively inclined people, presented a strong contrast to the new-world affluence of Sweden, where Unilever operated in Europe's most sophisticated market. Seven million Swedes enjoyed a national income of £500 per year per head, against 31 million Spaniards with an average income of £125 per year. Most of Western Europe came between these extremes, but moving nearer to Sweden than to Spain.

The larger volume of improved products—detergents, prepared foods, cosmetics, toothpastes, cleaning agents and the like—which Unilever produced was not only linked to rising money incomes, but to changing social habits and the use of other products which were themselves the result of new technologies.

Everywhere increasing numbers of married women in Europe and America continued to work after marriage. By 1958 in Britain 40 per cent of married women between 30 and 34 years of age had jobs. This kind of situation, joined to the virtual disappearance of domestic help, created an entire new crop of demands. An important one was for so-called 'convenience' (i.e. prepared) foods which could be quickly made ready for eating without elaborate work or fuss. New and more delicate textures (especially of synthetic fibres) in clothing demanded new and more delicate types of detergent. The value of a washing-up detergent was more immediately apparent when one had to do the washing-up oneself.

These social changes were not wholly dependent on spectacular affluence. They had continued even during the bad times of the 1930s when Unilever had doubled its output of soap flakes to correspond with the growing sophistication of feminine dress. But of course they were more rapid and startling in the times of affluence of the 1950s and 1960s. They were also closely connected with other new technologies; sales of frozen foods might not

[1] In a discussion with Kenneth Harris. *The Observer*, 6 and 13 January 1963.

depend entirely on the numbers of refrigerators in use in a society, yet unquestionably the refrigerator was an integral part of the process which made frozen food a feature of everyday life. Mass advertising preceded the wireless set and the television set. But it was television which created the largest advertising budgets in history, fashioned new techniques for launching new products on a mass scale and radically changed the relationship between technology and marketing once and for all. Surfaces made from new materials combined with the absence of domestic help to create a new demand for waxes and cleaners for furniture and floors. More widespread use of carpets created a demand for new shampoos. And all these new products needed their own special packs and containers to preserve their characteristics of flavour or effectiveness.

The Swedish and the Spanish housewife might still be separated widely in their habits and preferences, but both were exposed in different degrees to the same pervasive influences from which no individual or society was immune. However much an observer might deplore the passing of the old social order, and the impact of much of what passed for material progress, the change was here and it had come to stay. At bottom it sprang from a new technology of communication and the essence of this was that it was irresistible and all-pervasive. The task was not to try to stop it, but to try to ensure that it was applied to the best social advantage.

Amidst the abstractions—the standards, the trends, the patterns and the cycles—one concrete monument to the new age was the institution generally known as the supermarket. Ignoring the technical differences and gradations between different types of supermarket, let us say that its characteristics were its large size, the great variety of goods sold, and the help-yourself method of service. All these reflected both the greater economy of such stores over the older and smaller grocer's shop, and the growing shortage of shop labour. Self-service food stores had developed slowly in America during the 1930s. By 1950 they represented over one-third of the grocery trade in North America, by 1960 well over two-thirds and by 1965 95 per cent. In Europe the change was slower, but against all the prophecies of experts who predicted that this was a purely American phenomenon, the number of self-service stores in Britain trebled between 1954 and 1960. A similar revolution took place in Germany, in the Netherlands and other Continental countries.

c

This new pattern of large groups of powerful retailers revolutionized the relationship between the manufacturers of the products sold in supermarkets and the retail trade. Ever since the Industrial Revolution, the normal relationship had been one which allotted superior strength to the manufacturer. Large-scale advertising had confirmed and underlined the dominant position of the manufacturer, or at any rate the manufacturer with the initiative and enterprise to take advantage of his position. The retailer's task was to meet the needs of consumers who knew what they wanted because they were familiar with the quality of the manufacturer's products and had probably been further persuaded of their merits through advertising. This had not always been so. In earlier centuries it had been the merchant who had dictated to the manufacturer. In the social scale a merchant might pass for a gentleman; a manufacturer remained more on the level of the superior artisan. Now the balance seemed to be tipping again. The largest American group of supermarkets had a turnover comparable to, for example, the whole world turnover of Unilever itself. This was exceptional, but even the European supermarkets of moderate size wielded an economic bargaining power never possessed by the old retail stores. Alongside many other manufacturers Unilever swiftly found itself faced with the need to adapt to the new conditions of retail distribution.

Advertising by the manufacturer through all the various media available still remained of prime importance. This was the manufacturer's direct link with the consumer and the means by which the general merits of his products were brought most vividly to the notice of the housewife. Yet the retailer could now bring considerable influence to bear on sales by the prominence or the lack of prominence that he chose to give to a product in the supermarket. His willingness would be influenced by the manufacturer's ability to produce packages which stood easily on narrow shelves and advertised themselves by designs which might catch the eye of the customer walking round a supermarket. Packages needed to state clearly by print or picture the exact contents of the package. In short, the apparatus of packaging was no longer merely to protect or to preserve but also to sell. 'If your goods are to be sold by self-service' the Chairmen told the shareholders in 1965, 'your package is fighting for you against every other package directly or indirectly competing. You cannot expect it to get much help—at least in self-service stores and supermarkets—from the people running the shop.' Bulk packaging had to be done so that a new consignment could be quickly and easily opened behind the store. The older type of salesman, moving from shop to shop persuading the shopkeeper, disappeared. Now the crucial negotiations between manufacturer and retailer took place at the highest level. At most the salesman's job was to help the supermarket manager to present his merchandise.

The shaping of a new and more flexible relationship was not only important but urgent. For the bargaining power of the new retail organizations was such that if their needs were not met by the manufacturer of the advertised product, there was a risk that they might try to negotiate for the manufacture of their own brands under their own names. The manufacturer had thus to rethink the whole of his market diplomacy afresh, to try to consolidate his position with the retailer by developing to the utmost those manufacturing advantages based on superior technological knowledge and experience, and by the skilled advertising through all the available media of the special merits of his own products.

The new retailing system had thus renewed the competitive struggle for the customer's goodwill with a vengeance. Then there were the problems of Unilever's own interests in the British retail trade—Mac Fisheries, for example. Here was a legacy from another of William Lever's adventures in the shape of a large group of small retail shops dealing largely in fish. One curious result of rising living standards in Britain particularly proved to be the decline of sales in fish. In the 1950s Unilever began to modernize the Mac Fisheries retail shops. They were no longer to sell only fish but fresh fruit, vegetables, cheese, meats and so on. By 1964 the policy had taken a new turn. Through Mac Fisheries a group of 40 large Premier supermarkets was acquired. Thus Mac Fisheries became one of the largest marketers of fruit and vegetables in the United Kingdom, with a turnover of £32 million.

In Germany Nordsee, the fishing/trawling company in which Unilever owned an important stake, faced different problems. Nordsee had one of the most modern trawling fleets in the world. Their trawlers, equipped with new techniques of filleting and freezing at sea, were able to harvest larger and larger areas of fishing grounds. Nordsee too owned a large chain of retail shops and, like Mac Fisheries, they expanded and improved their shops and turned them over to self-service, although they did not feel the need to widen the range of products in the same way. They also introduced fish restaurants and opened one in a large shopping centre outside Frankfurt-am-Main. Like similar out-of-town centres in the United States, this one was designed primarily for week-end shopping by motor car.[1]

Even in Africa new retail techniques were coming into play. Since the Second World War, The United Africa Company, while moving out of the traditional retail business, had developed large department stores in British West Africa known as the Kingsway Stores.[2] They offered to the African consumer products of a range and quality equal to those which could be bought in similar stores in Europe and America, and they were housed in air-conditioned modern buildings, containing large self-service food departments comparable to those of the Western world.

Thus, in the new societies as well as the old, Unilever faced and grasped the problem of adapting itself to the consequences of a revolution in transport and distribution and in the social habits of the consumers.

Providentially for Unilever, its great constituent firms were rapidly passing, or had already passed, through the trials of the 'managerial revolution' by 1929. Its two principal architects, Francis D'Arcy Cooper and Paul Rijkens, professionals both, had already established unquestioned authority in their respective businesses. Thus the transition from owner-management to management-without-ownership had already gone a long way. It was a great thing that it was achieved without loss of continuity of men or principles, and without any of those upheavals which often scarred businesses at this crucial juncture in their affairs. By good fortune and good management the old order gradually gave way to the new. The new men in Unilever had stood close enough to their predecessors to appreciate that both its strength—its dynamism—and its weakness depended on control by individuals. Now their efforts were to be directed also to countering the dangers inherent in the new order.

D'Arcy Cooper died in 1941. His achievement had been to set Lever Brothers on sound foundations, and to create a management team that had already streamlined Unilever for a competitive future. His successor, Geoffrey Heyworth, had served his apprenticeship with both Lever and Cooper. Four years earlier, Paul Rijkens had become Chairman of Unilever N.V. He had helped to bring Unilever safely through the international economic

[1] See also Chapter 8.   [2] See page 219.

confusion of the 1930s. Now in a remarkable partnership which was to last for the greater part of two decades, the two men were to see Unilever through the trials of the war years, reconstruct it in the post-war years and lead it to unprecedented expansion and prosperity thereafter.

Their talents were in a remarkable degree complementary. Rijkens was above all the diplomatist of business, master of the intricacies of international monetary problems, the tireless negotiator, of endless patience, architect not only of the great merger of 1929 but of a score of lesser ones before and after 1929. Unlike Rijkens, who confessed once that he had never sold anything, 'not even a pound of margarine', Heyworth had from the beginning been concerned with the commercial aspects of the Lever business, whose recovery in the 1930s was based on his brilliant rationalization scheme for the soap trade. Whereas many schemes in that era of rationalization smacked of monopoly, this one was designed to bring genuine competition back into the soap trade. For if Geoffrey Heyworth acquired one conviction during his early business career in Canada it was a belief in the ultimate economic importance of competition. Many years later he summed up his own philosophy in an interview with an American journalist. 'We run our business positively, keep it healthy and growing, and let the chips fall where they may.'[1] An empiricist, he was never content with mere empiricism. On the contrary, his was a mind that took a particular relish in probing out the logical consequences and philosophical implications of business decisions.

Heyworth and Rijkens shared two convictions that were essential to the progress of Unilever during their long joint stewardship. To neither was Unilever merely a shrewd international marriage of business convenience. It was also a great experiment in international relations. If it was to fail it would show that like other political animals, businessmen were slaves to the sentiments of the parish pump. If it succeeded it would be a victory for good will and good sense with consequences beyond its own boundaries. For Rijkens, a man of wide culture, the things which united Europeans were more fundamental than the political accidents that divided them. A passionate European, Unilever was for him a mirror of European unity. Between his retirement in 1955 and his death in 1965 his main concern came to be the progress of European cultural and economic unity. For Geoffrey Heyworth, whose

[1] *Fortune*, January 1948.

early career had been spent in North America, Unilever likewise offered a fruitful field of Commonwealth and American co-operation, linked with an expanding area of the European economy.

On a second basic principle there was similarly complete unity of view. Both men were, by nature, liberal in outlook. Both apprehended clearly a danger that in these still early days of unification, Unilever might become over-organized, over-centralized, over-bureaucratized. The risk was specially acute just after the war when the operating companies in Europe and overseas, still sadly depleted of men and resources, were apt—as Rijkens often remarked—to look to London or Rotterdam on every occasion. Against this, both men resolutely set their faces. Unilever could only be set on the road to recovery and expansion by exploiting all the self-reliance and knowledge represented by the local managements. The parent companies were there to advise, guide, encourage, not to bully, nag or issue more than the basic minimum of orders. Circumstances would doubtless vary the relationship of the parents and their numerous family's varying needs, from time to time. But the need for self-help and self-criticism was unchanging. This was their great legacy to Unilever.

Although they both insisted on the paramount importance of the *collective* responsibility of the management team, its third man in the post-war decades, Sir Herbert Davis, was by experience particularly qualified to handle a different range of problems from his two colleagues. While they could, very roughly, be said to represent the British soap and Continental margarine industries, Davis was an Englishman who had become Jurgens's leading authority on oil-milling and raw materials. One of the comparatively rare graduate recruits to industry before the First World War, he had studied economics at Cambridge under Keynes. He became one of Lord Woolton's most valued lieutenants in the wartime Food Ministry, being knighted in 1943 for his services. After the war he returned to Unilever and in his own person represented yet another link between the British and Dutch groups. To the calculations and decisions of the Special Committee he brought his own highly personal contribution. Always receptive to genuine initiative and enterprise, he was crisp in thought, laconic in speech, merciless to anything that savoured to him of loose and sloppy thinking.

The quality of the leadership in these years could be left there, to rest on its own demonstrable results. Yet this would not be quite the whole story. For its services were to be sought, and freely given, outside as well as inside Unilever, in a dozen government enquiries and Commissions on taxation, planning, the organization of the public sectors of the economy, on higher education, social welfare, etc., both in Britain and Holland. Here Heyworth and Rijkens were pointing the way to a new relationship between industry and society. If industry was becoming more conscious of its own need for wider social experience, society was becoming aware that a new type of industrial management was developing a new kind of experience indispensable to its own self-knowledge. A society and a capitalism both in transition were forging a new kind of mutual relationship.[1]

The men who succeeded the long partnership of Geoffrey Heyworth and Paul Rijkens had much in common with their predecessors and with each other. Like them, both were graduates of what William Lever liked to call the University of Hard Knocks. George Cole (created Lord Cole in 1965) had seen service in a variety of commercial business appointments in Africa and in Britain; F. J. Tempel's career was essentially a European one— in Holland, France, Italy, Germany and Britain. Both were empiricists, both shared a suspicion of theory in business and a dislike for the idea that the responsibilities of the chairman of a large corporation had become in essence a public relations matter. In short, both were practical exponents of the art and science of industry. Although both were believers in a firm government, they were ready to see their ideas modified by changing circumstances, but neither was likely to change tack for the sake of doing so. The principles that had proved successful under their predecessors were not likely to be discarded save for good reason. Their presence on the Special Committee symbolized the continuing demand of the 1960s for commercial experience and enterprise.[2] That they were joined in 1960 by J. A. Connel, and, on his premature death the following year, by Dr Ernest Woodroofe, both scientists by training, was a recognition that new technology and diversification based on scientific knowledge and measurement were now equally essential to Unilever's competitive strength and continuing expansion.

[1] See Chapter 2.
[2] In 1966 Mr Tempel was succeeded as Chairman of Unilever N.V. by Harold Hartog. For his views on Unilever organization see page 41. The early history of the Hartog business (later merged with Unilever) is told in *The History of Unilever*, vol. II, pages 250, 251, 252, 255, 258, 265, 283, 284, 285, 286.

Indeed, if the major characteristics of the post-war decades had to be summed up in a phrase, it could best be done in a sentence from George Cole. 'You should try' he said in 1963, 'to *reduce* the element of luck.'[1] In the post-war world, where the welfare of more than a quarter of a million managers and employees was at stake, where investors' capital running into hundreds of millions of pounds was at risk, and where each new venture introduced a bigger element of responsibility, the role of hunch, intuition and luck inevitably diminished. This was the fundamental reason why scientific method in all its varying forms came in these years to be built more into every operation of Unilever.

---

[1] In a discussion with Kenneth Harris. *The Observer*, 6 and 13 January 1963.

CHAPTER 2

MANAGEMENT: ITS ENDS AND MEANS

'IT is not from the benevolence of the butcher, the brewer or the baker that we expect our dinner, but from their regard to their own interest.' Even after half a century of growing public economic enterprise, including the New Deal in the United States, a succession of Soviet economic plans, the schemes of Dr Schacht, India's five-year plans and a score of Welfare States strung round the Old World and the New, there was still something to be said for Adam Smith's dictum. But nobody could pretend that things had not changed. Brewers, butchers and bakers were no longer the same men they once were. The 'managerial revolution' had supervened, and with rapid effect. As lately as the 1920s, the affairs of Lever Brothers, already a business on a world scale, had still been managed in detail by the sole ordinary shareholder in person. Similarly, but perhaps with less *panache*, the affairs of Jurgens', Van den Bergh's and Schicht's had been controlled by their owner-managers. Forty years later the owner-ship of Unilever, as of most large businesses, was entirely divorced from its management. The new managers were a salaried, quasi-professional class with little or no financial stake in the business other than their salaries. (For Unilever did not generally favour the growing American custom of rewarding its top management with a slice of its own capital.) '...The plain fact is' said Lord Cole on one occasion, 'that they *can't* become capitalists in any relevant sense of the term because of the pattern and levels of taxation.'

This further division of function between ownership and management nevertheless raised important new issues for industry in general and for Unilever in particular. What were the responsi-bilities of the Unilever directors and managers, and to whom were they owed? Although throughout industry in general conflicts of interest between managers and shareholders were rare, the *possibility* of conflict was something of which account had to be taken. And enough cases had come before the courts to define at any rate some of the issues. Judges had on many occasions laid down their view of the duties of a company director, though they had understandably been more explicit on general principles than on specific ways and means by which these duties should in practice be discharged. The point had nevertheless emerged clearly that the first duty of a company director was to the entity known as the company—the incorporated body. It was always possible that circumstances might arise in which policies which the directors might conceive to be in the interests of the company might clash with what the shareholders conceived to be their immediate interests. Fortunately, such cases were uncommon (and had not so far arisen in the case of Unilever itself). But were such a case to arise, the interests of the company would, in the eye of the law, come before the immediate interests of any shareholder. This did not alter the fact that *normally* a director could regard himself as there to promote the interests of the shareholders. Yet what *were* the interests of the shareholders? And who *were* the shareholders? Those who held the shares today, or yesterday, or tomorrow, or in twenty years time? The answer that emerged, empirically and in practice, was that the company's interest was the continuing profit accruing to the continuing body of shareholders over a period of time. It was to maintain this continuous interest that the management's duty was pledged.

Some critics might think such a view was a narrow, legalistic and a-social, if not positively anti-social interpretation of the social responsibilities of the business world. As the great private patrons of the past disappeared, should not the great new business corporation take over their functions with regard to the arts, culture and good works of charity? The alleged niggardliness derived in part from the company constitution. Plainly the management had no right to distribute the shareholders' rights in an indiscriminate bonanza. Yet Unilever, comparatively conservative in its attitude, made large grants to what it conceived to be educational purposes relevant to its affairs. The last quarter-century has seen private capitalism developing into a series of parochial welfare states living within the National Welfare State itself. Paternalism—the model village, for example—had largely disappeared. But pensions, medical assistance, sports clubs, luncheon vouchers, and so on were pretty well universal. Some, indeed, of the old guard in business held that the greater threat to the ability of capitalism to contribute to social wealth came from the propensity of businessmen to assume postures of well-meant but misdirected benevolence. Probably the majority of business-men would nevertheless have defended their policies on the grounds that good relations with employees and with the public, reputation *vis-à-vis* governments, an enlightened attitude towards cultural and charitable benefactions, etc., in fact all those actions which the modern business undertakes of a welfare character, could be justified because they contributed to the long-term stability and prosperity of the business (those who knew their Adam Smith would no doubt observe that even the *Wealth of Nations* adds that self-interest must always be modified by what it calls 'sympathy' or what the twentieth century would probably call human decency).

Be that as it may, the power to do what was conceived necessary in the general interest in any company would rest theoretically in the last resort with the general body of shareholders who had invested their money in the company. In them was vested the right to elect the directors of the company. And the relationship between the shareholders and the company was governed partly by the general law, and in particular by the Articles of Association of the company. These Articles gave the directors the power to run the company. From the beginning Unilever had consisted of two parent companies, and so it continued in this period: Unilever Limited (the British company) and Unilever N.V. (the Dutch company). These two parent companies had identical boards of directors and their constitutions were as similar as the legal systems of England and the Netherlands would allow. The maximum number of directors was twenty-five, but there was no stipulation that any particular number of the total should be Dutch or English. The object had become (as Lord Heyworth observed in 1949) 'to produce an Anglo-Dutch team and not two nearly balancing factions'.[1]

All the directors were full-time working directors holding managerial appointments in the business, and they were paid not as directors but as managers. A body of twenty-five men was too large to deal regularly with policy questions, or detailed operations, or to act with the speed and flexibility necessary in a world of rapid change and turbulent competition. The Articles of Associa-tion empowered the directors to delegate their powers to com-mittees consisting of such colleagues as they thought fit. By

[1] In an address to the Institute of Public Administration, entitled *The Organ-ization of Unilever* (reprinted 1955), page 5.

formal resolution they appointed annually a Special Committee consisting of the Chairman of Unilever Limited, the Chairman of Unilever N.V. and a Vice-Chairman of Unilever Limited. This was really a kind of Cabinet to which were delegated all the powers of the whole Board of Unilever Limited, except those special powers which the Board reserved to itself; for example, to issue new capital, declare a dividend, pledge the company's assets, or co-opt individuals to fill emergency vacancies on the parent Board.

No matter that has to be settled at the top is decided without the participation of the Special Committee. The Special Committee reports to the conference of directors at the weekly Board meeting, and the Board in its turn reports annually to the shareholders. The Special Committee may therefore be said to be somewhat like a Cabinet or Government; the Board somewhat like a Parliament; and the shareholders somewhat like an electorate. Always provided it is remembered that the Unilever electorate can reject or confirm the Members of Parliament once a year at the General Meeting, when the whole Board resigns and comes up for re-election; and that there is not in Unilever a Shadow Cabinet in opposition, urgently promising that if they get a majority they will do better than the resident incumbents.

In 1949 Lord Heyworth described the rest of the organization (see Figure 1, page 33) through which the Special Committee and the Board operated the daily business of Unilever.[1] Below the Board came four management groups. One was responsible for the conduct of the business in Continental Europe, one for the United Kingdom, one for countries outside Europe, and one for the affairs of The United Africa Company. These controlling groups included members of the Board as well as other members drawn from the general management.

Alongside these main control groups was a series of specialized departments which provided advice or services for the regional managements, the factories, and the men who sold Unilever products. They included such services as accounting, auditing, marketing, buying, staffing, research and technology, insurance, legal advice, finance, international affairs, economics, etc. These services existed for the benefit of the policy makers at the centre and the managers in the many countries who were responsible for local Unilever activities. In most countries on the European

[1] *The Organization of Unilever*, page 5.

continent this operational management fell to the so-called National Management. In the United Kingdom a rather different system operated. The functions which were performed in Continental Europe by National Managements were undertaken in the United Kingdom by four 'executives' who were responsible for the four principal sections of the business—soap, margarine, oil milling and food. Below these National Managements, or 'executives', came the individual operating units; sometimes they dealt both with manufacturing and selling, sometimes with only one of these functions.

The major problem of the top management in Unilever was to determine the balance between these two parts of the Unilever organization, between the central headquarters and the operating companies in the field. For it must never be forgotten that Unilever had come together centripetally—through the fusion of what had at one time been many independent companies. Their local knowledge and expertise was one of the most valuable assets Unilever possessed. It was not to be squandered or squashed out of existence by over-centralization, or executive bureaucracy. There had been times when it had been necessary to emphasize the responsibility of the centre. In the post-war years the movement was away from centralization towards utmost decentralization. This was partly because the war had necessarily left many companies in Europe to their own devices and revealed capacities for independence which it would have been folly to try to deny. But in the era of reconstruction, also, local freedom was necessary to restore morale and the physical strength of the operating companies. The immediate need was to ensure that the man on the spot was given the maximum help to discharge his responsibilities with as little interference as possible.

Basic control was, of course, essential. It rested upon three instruments: The Annual Operating Plan, The Annual Capital Expenditure Budget, and The Annual Review of Remuneration and Selection of Top Management. The first enabled the operating units to estimate their prospective sales and costs and discuss them with the controlling groups up to the Special Committee. Once the estimates were accepted, it was the job of the operating unit to carry out its plans. The provision of new plant or the renewal of existing plant came under the Capital Expenditure Budget. This demanded discussion with the advisory departments and acted as a means of focusing longer term policy. Each budget had to be approved by the Special Committee. So, in the last resort, did the decisions about the pay and selection of senior managers.

The emphasis was all on flexibility, voluntary discussion and persuasion, rather than coercion. 'The centre' said Lord Heyworth, 'must resist the temptation to add to control.' Headquarters should be sparing in reproof of mistakes. Its job was to foster initiative and encourage the man on the spot. The function of the advisory department was to advise; not to give orders, but to 'suggest, recommend or persuade'.[1] Amongst the constantly changing group of about two hundred men who took the vital decisions, personal contact and discussion were more important than functional charts, blue prints, or written definition of duties. Technologies and market situations changed rapidly. If bureaucratic rigidity crept in it could end by being *rigor mortis*. The advantages that might accrue to Unilever through its internationalism and its size would become only fatal hindrances.

Such was the chain of command through which management was to discharge its responsibilities to the company and the shareholders in the early post-war period. Fifteen years later the organization was still basically the same. Certainly the spirit and the aspiration remained the same. It was summarized briskly by Lord Heyworth's successor in 1963: 'With such a big, scattered, diverse conglomeration of units as ours' said George Cole, 'you delegate or bust.'[2] Nobody would have contested the fundamental importance of maintaining flexibility, and conceding a large measure of local independence to the men who ran the factories and sold the products. Yet, undeniably, the pendulum had to some extent swung away from the full faith in *laissez-faire*. The organization charts for 1949 and 1965 reflected the measure of change and the latest shows how the trends have continued.[3]

First of all the advisory departments in the centre had increased and multiplied. Divisions concerned with technology had grown along with the development of research institutions which were themselves now the size of large factories.[4] The growth of departments concerned with marketing and advertising reflected the growing sophistication of this whole area of what had once depended on the hunch of individual salesmen. There was a

---

[1] *The Organization of Unilever.* Address to the Institute of Public Administration, 1949 (revised 1955, p. 11).
[2] In a discussion with Kenneth Harris. *The Observer*, 6 and 13 January 1963.
[3] See Figures 1, 2 and 3.   [4] See Chapter 4.

growing and irresistible tendency to uniformity in matters of wages, pensions, welfare services and the like, demanding more and more co-ordination. Laws affecting the entire activities of manufacturers and defining company responsibilities, including taxation, were becoming ever more complex. The march of technology, especially towards automation, demanded centralized expertise. The selection and promotion of staff was a science in itself.

Other departments especially reflected the new role of the social sciences rather than of the physical sciences. Unilever was employing many more economists and statisticians in 1965 than in 1949. Their task was to help the manufacturer and the salesman to explore the market by studying particularly changes in income, social habits and class structure; to investigate the supply and use of resources, the flow and use of money, the changes in overseas transactions, and the fluctuations in raw material markets. Already they had modified conventional accounting systems by substituting relevant current costs for the old convention of money prices and by introducing new methods of assessing investment projects. This was the sort of change that could be compared to the change in navigation from steering by hunch to steering by radar. Together with the physical scientists, they were responsible for developing the use of computers and scientific programming systems in order to help the executive to choose the right objective from a number of alternatives.

Another new service was supplied by the department which came to be called Information Division. Unilever had been rather slow to admit the need for a specialized public relations department. Indeed, Lord Heyworth disliked the title and it was never brought into use in the company. 'Public relations', he said, were the responsibility of every employee of Unilever, from the Chairman down to the office boy. Nevertheless, he recognized that a large company had large public responsibilities. These might be misunderstood and there was no reason why it should not, from time to time, give its version of the facts to the public, put the record straight, or even prevent it from being put crooked. Information Division, therefore, came into existence in London and a similar organization in Rotterdam. Their job was to keep the press and what was (perhaps optimistically) believed to be 'informed opinion' correctly and objectively informed of what Unilever and its companies were doing. Their function was defined: 'to protect,

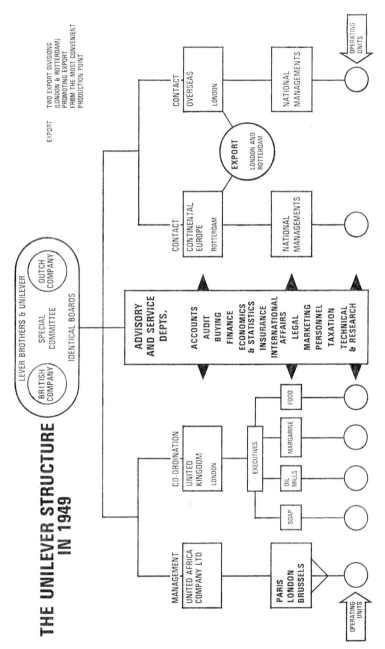

THE UNILEVER STRUCTURE IN 1949

LEVER BROTHERS & UNILEVER

BRITISH COMPANY · SPECIAL COMMITTEE · DUTCH COMPANY

IDENTICAL BOARDS

MANAGEMENT
UNITED AFRICA COMPANY LTD

PARIS
LONDON
BRUSSELS

OPERATING UNITS

CO-ORDINATION
UNITED KINGDOM
LONDON

EXECUTIVES

SOAP · OIL MILLS · MARGARINE · FOOD

ADVISORY AND SERVICE DEPTS.

ACCOUNTS
AUDIT
BUYING
FINANCE
ECONOMICS & STATISTICS
INSURANCE
INTERNATIONAL AFFAIRS
LEGAL
MARKETING
PERSONNEL
TAXATION
TECHNICAL & RESEARCH

CONTACT
CONTINENTAL EUROPE
ROTTERDAM

NATIONAL MANAGEMENTS

EXPORT
LONDON AND ROTTERDAM

CONTACT
OVERSEAS
LONDON

NATIONAL MANAGEMENTS

OPERATING UNITS

EXPORT TWO EXPORT DIVISIONS (LONDON & ROTTERDAM) PROMOTING EXPORT FROM THE MOST CONVENIENT PRODUCTION POINT

Figure I

THE UNILEVER STRUCTURE IN 1965

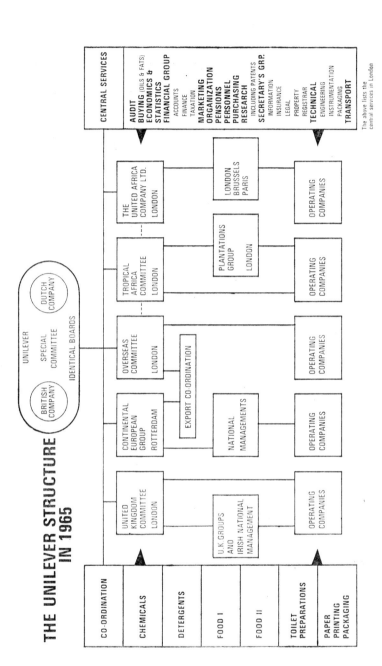

Figure 2

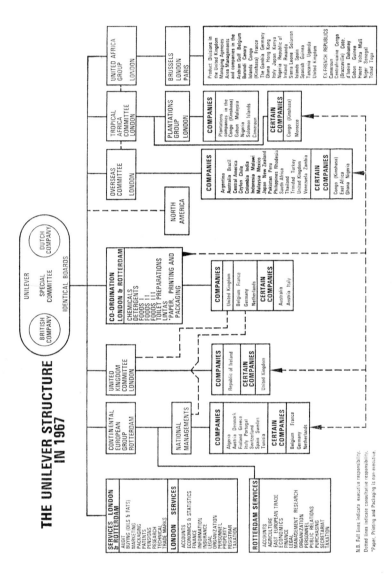

THE UNILEVER STRUCTURE IN 1967

Figure 3

maintain and develop the good name of Unilever inside and outside the business by all legitimate means.'

The other major change revealed by the organization charts[1] was the appearance of individuals or committees responsible for co-ordinating the nature of Unilever products throughout the world's markets. And behind this lay once more the need to adjust an organization which had developed centripetally to the changing forces of world competition. For everywhere, both in the fully developed and the developing economies, Unilever was feeling the impact, in the 1950s and 1960s, of high-pressure American competition. Its biggest competitor in detergents, Procter and Gamble, originally developed centrifugally in the great domestic market of the United States, had first penetrated Europe in the 1930s. It was now fully launched as a major competitor, not only in North America, but in Europe. This, of course, was not a phenomenon limited to those markets with which Unilever was concerned. The great wave of American investment in Europe affected everything from razor blades to bulldozers, from Coca-Cola to jet airliners. But the impact of its drive and efficiency was nowhere felt more sharply than in the detergent market. It thrust the results of new research and technology deep into the markets of Europe, Asia and Africa, capitalizing on a few brand names which modern advertising and communication could make as familiar in Bangkok as they were in Cincinnati or New York. To meet such competition it became urgently necessary to survey the traditionally varied products of the Unilever organization, to prune, trim and streamline, if necessary ruthlessly, so as to cut out all those lines that were inessential, reduce costs, and concentrate on the high quality of the products and the methods used to market and advertise them.

One inference at least could be drawn from these developments. However its new functions might be viewed, Unilever could not now adequately be described as merely 'a holding company'. Indeed, for most of those concerned with the day-to-day running of the companies, the original financial functions of the parent companies were important mainly as the basis of all the other service and advisory functions provided by headquarters.

The need for all this was undeniable. So were the risks. Unquestionably the race for the technological lead, the growing

[1] See Figures 1, 2 and 3.

battle for markets, the disturbance of once comparatively tranquil markets and established habits—all these demanded that local manufacturing or selling companies should have access to the best technical advice of every kind that could be provided. The risk was that advice might become mandatory, that the old flexibility and preference for persuasion and discussion would give way to orders and blueprints. It began to look to some (especially in the operating companies) as though Unilever might begin to resemble a great Department of State (say the Admiralty) pivoting on a permanent bureaucracy of experts and a central planning staff handing out orders rather than advice. Some executives indeed held that this *was* happening, and that it was not merely inevitable, but right. A few even deplored the lack of written definitions of duties and blueprints as a legacy of the bygone age of *laissez-faire*. This state of affairs (such critics argued) was reminiscent of the hand-to-mouth days when many a businessman either could not or would not read or write more than the absolute minimum. A less improvisatory and more bureaucratic order would cut out much waste and confusion. Local diversity was to such critics a thing of the past, killed by the spread of uniform ideas and habits through television and international advertising. Henceforth products would rule rather than geographical areas. If Unilever was to keep abreast of their competitors the policy makers at the centre must not merely guide: they must command.

Few amongst Unilever's top management wanted to push centralizing doctrine to extremes. But most recognized that economic and technological trends demanded that the centre of gravity be shifted towards the centre. In one respect political trends reinforced the argument. The emergence of great supranational areas like the Common Market suggested that local differences of taste and habit were likely to diminish. Equally, however, even those who recognized the force of such pressures also recognized the risks. Progress of Professor Parkinson's law had to be checked. A large and prosperous company was too attractive a honeypot not to attract a certain number of dispensable visitors to the feast. Historians have more than once observed that any age of spectacular innovation inevitably breeds a race of operators amongst whom it is not easy to distinguish the geniuses from the charlatans. Hence the constant need for vigilance as well as openmindedness. There was also the ever-present threat to any large organization that it might fall into that condition depicted in the large American company by the friendly critic:

> Along these lines from toe to crown
> Ideas flow up and vetoes down.

They would, however, have also recognized that the centre of gravity must not be shifted entirely. Many Unilever companies in all parts of the world had begun as *local* enterprises. The natural and intimate knowledge of local affairs contained in these companies was still valuable. Even increasingly similar markets could still contain awkward local idiosyncrasies, and these were especially important in some of the new areas of production into which Unilever had moved, especially foods. A sausage was one thing to an Englishman. It was a very different thing—indeed many different things—to a German or an Italian. *Petits pois* might suit the French. They were not popular with the English, whose love of the large minted pea outraged most Continental tastes. European connoisseurs were sharply divided on the respective merits of hard or soft ice-cream. The Latin American countries preferred stronger scents but liked their fats more neutrally flavoured. Tastes, the individualist might console himself, were still varied and peculiar. So were responses to different types of advertisement.

Beyond such subtle psychological problems, and of more immediate urgency to the local manager, were those parochial, political and social issues which increasingly absorbed much of the time and ingenuity of local managements. As government everywhere intruded more frequently and more forcibly upon private enterprise, so the local managers' tasks became more complex and more delicate. From Helsinki to Cape Town, and from North America to Indonesia, the local manager found himself daily handling issues that were fundamentally political rather than commercial. A large international business had always to be ready to meet charges that it was monopolistic or alien, or that its policies were in some way contrary to local welfare, as it was interpreted by one or another local interest. Everywhere conditions of labour, negotiations with unions, problems of import and currency controls and the like, complicated the task of management to a degree not previously known. This increasing range of complex and delicate problems demanded that the manager's intellectual muscles should be well flexed. Methodical professional training in the technical articles of his trade was indispensable. Management was now a highly professional affair. This did not mean that old-fashioned human qualities were less important. The most indispensable of all the manager's equipment remained the physical and mental stamina to face unpredictably awkward and exacting situations; and the wit to act with speed and resource. Without stamina and wit neither intellect nor training was much good. The tasks of local managements might be changing; they were not becoming less crucial.

Nor would many experienced campaigners have been sanguine that these duties and relationships could usefully be enshrined in blueprints or charts. To enshrine was, by definition, to embalm, and the trouble with written definitions of responsibility was always that they might suggest the maximum a man had to do, rather than the minimum. In an imperfect world there were always those for whom they would become the signal for another demarcation dispute, rather than a green light for action.

The truth was that the fundamental issue had often been put in too crude a form. In real life it was not simply a problem of confronting local independence with centralized authority. It was far more complex than that. It was a matter of deciding which kind of problem demanded the kind of knowledge which could best be accumulated in an expert central repository, and which demanded that close and immediate knowledge of local affairs which only the man on the spot could provide. Even more, of determining who should take which decisions. This division could only be stated in very broad terms. Technological information, for example, could not be assumed to be in any way a monopoly of a central bureaucracy of scientists. It might be a relatively small factory which suddenly threw up a startling discovery of great economic importance to the entire Unilever organization; for example, an engineer at the Kleve margarine factory in Western Germany developed a method which increased the wrapping of margarine packets from 90 to 140 a minute. In a score of ways such local assets could prove still to have great value. They might later be seen to have even greater value if the pace of innovation were to slacken, if the intrusive force of North American investment were to tail away, local tastes to reassert themselves. In short, prudence suggested that (as usual) the real problem was to strike the right kind of balance.

The balance had in fact been changing since the late 1950s. The new trend in organization, reflecting all the external pressures of competition and internal need for better communication, was broadly described as 'co-ordination'. January 1959 saw the establishment at Rotterdam of the first 'Product Committee' for Continental Europe. It was followed by others. Three years later, 'Co-ordinators' were set up to ensure uniform policy on international brands for edible fats, foods, detergents and toilet preparations for the United Kingdom and overseas markets. Yet there were those who felt that none of this went far enough. Even in 1962 Harold Hartog (who was later to become Chairman of Unilever N.V.) was pointing out that the traditional organization of Unilever based on geographical regions worked against the specialized, professional accomplishment that was necessary to meet the rivalry of great competitors in the modern world. The best talent in Unilever went into national management posts, and these were essentially un-specialized in terms of *products*. The best men (he thought) ought to be charged with operations related to a single group of products over as large an area as possible. They would not then become merely Jacks-of-all-Trades.

Such arguments did not go unchallenged in a debate that lasted another four years. But the preliminary essays in 'product co-ordination' had unquestionably brought benefits and finally, in February 1966, Unilever took the plunge. The regional organization, it was stressed, was not to disappear entirely or at once, but the direction of change was from 'regional' towards 'industrial product' organization. The national managements would have a continuing, vital, if reduced role to play. The basic decision was to appoint co-ordinators for six product groups: a Food Group I of which edible fats was the largest; Food Group II including meats, frozen foods, prepared foods, fish, etc.;[1] Detergents; Toilet Preparations; Chemicals; Paper, Printing and Packaging. The aim was to place on the co-ordinator the responsibility for formulating policies that would stimulate expansion in his group of products anywhere in the world where opportunity offered.

This exercise in reorganization was probably the most fundamental ever undertaken in Unilever. Yet it was only the climax of a long series of adjustments over the years designed to improve communications within an historically decentralized organization in the interests of competitive efficiency. One much earlier device

[1] A Food Group III was to be set up, at a later day, for Meats.

(which was incorporated in the new co-ordination scheme) was the 'Contact Director'.

Good communications had always been the nub of Unilever's problem. During the immediately post-war years when many of the operating companies had to be reconstructed from practically nothing, contacts between headquarters and those responsible for reconstruction were urgently needed. The responsibility was assigned to particular directors of the parent companies. These directors, known as contact directors, formed the link between the national managements and the Special Committee. They were to relieve the Special Committee of what might be called medium-level policy decisions, in the same way that the national managements were to relieve the contact directors of detailed responsibility. They were there to encourage rather than criticize. 'Mr Rijkens' said a minute in 1949, 'felt that this point should be emphasized; he had during his recent tour felt the tendency for matters to be put to London for decision was too strong, and he felt the local managements should be encouraged to take their own decisions even at the risk of making mistakes.'

As time passed, experts, other than members of the Board, joined the contact directors' organization. Gradually the arrangements were changed until five committees had replaced the original four, each charged with special responsibility for a particular area—the United Kingdom, the European Continent, the rest of the Overseas Markets, Tropical Africa, while The United Africa Company retained responsibility for its rapidly changing business. Members of these committees were, in turn, assigned a particular area within the total. Thus more continuity and greater specialized knowledge were introduced into these liaison arrangements than had been possible in the days when a single contact director had presumed to take the whole of the United States, Canada, the West Indies and South America 'under his wing'. Like the national managements, the contact directors remained essential to the organization. Flexibility remained the essence of the system. Only those concerned could know how tight or how loose the reins should be kept in any particular case, and the importance of getting this answer right pointed back to the need for judgment as well as specialized knowledge amongst those charged with these heavy responsibilities.

One thing was plain beyond any doubt. Journalists might enlarge on the dangers of the organization man. Other journalists, management experts, and forward-looking Ministers of the Crown might continue to pay tribute to the idea that it was men who determined the fortunes of great industries as of other institutions. Yet it had become clear that industry had now entered a stage at which even the best men could only be effective if they provided themselves with the right context of organization. And just as managers could only manage within a properly organized system, so this system in turn could only be effective if it was properly located in relation to the society and economy of which it formed a part. The Unilever group consisted of industries which had always been intimately connected with the processes of social change in the outside world. Their creators had been able to act as enlightened employers partly because their labour costs had been low; partly because they had been intelligent enough to see that their own personal interests coincided with those of their employees and with the rising welfare of the working and lower middle classes who formed the majority of their customers. These socially progressive pioneers, politically and socially liberal and enlightened, had handed down to their managerial successors a rather special *ethos*. A concern which numbered its customers by the million was constantly kept aware that human feelings and preferences were crucial, and this awareness gave it its special character. It was necessarily sensitive—a lay observer might sometimes think hypersensitive—to the changing climate of public taste and opinion.

Yet even the Victorian ancestors of Unilever had enjoyed a much larger measure of freedom to run their businesses as they thought fit, regardless (if need be) of what the world thought, than was enjoyed by their successors. The continued success of a business like Unilever had come to depend not least upon its awareness of contemporary economic, social and political movements. It was equally important that the world should know that Unilever was not merely the name (little understood and sometimes mispronounced) of a faceless monolith; but of a large and varied group of *people* engaged in tasks economically and socially important to other people. From the 1920s the Unilever managements had increasingly become involved in various forms of public service believed to be of concern to their business. Now it became more and more the practice for them to undertake such outside responsibilities. Most of the directors, and many others, thus became associated with government and other institutions, commissions and enquiries mostly—but not exclusively—of an economic or social character.[1]

These secondments gave the outside world a chance to see the kind of men who were responsible for Unilever policies. For Unilever, they opened fresh windows on the contemporary world. It had always been a principle in Unilever to draw its leadership to the maximum possible extent from its own ranks. Between 1945 and 1965 all those who were appointed to the Boards of Unilever Limited or Unilever N.V. came from inside the business. Now and again the need might arise for some specialized knowledge that could not be provided in this way, but increasingly Unilever was felt to have failed itself if it was unable to provide its own leadership from its own resources. It certainly ought not to be necessary to rely, as industry had often relied in the past, upon the services of retired politicians, soldiers or sailors, however dedicated or distinguished. This in turn reinforced the need that the experience available to potential leaders from within Unilever should not be limited to experience of Unilever itself. Business conditions in the mid-twentieth century demanded that it should extend also to the affairs of the world in which Unilever had to operate.

[1] In the United Kingdom, for example, with the Prices and Incomes Board set up in 1964; the London Graduate School of Business Studies; the Royal Institute for International Affairs; the West African Export Council; the British Railways Board; the British Association; the Northern Ireland Development Council. In the Netherlands, the Netherlands Bank; the Rotterdam School of Economics; the International Chamber of Commerce; the Federation of Netherlands Employers' Associations; Utrecht University; the Eindhoven College of Technology, etc.

CHAPTER 3

MEN

T HE most articulate of all Unilever's ancestors, William Lever, used to declare that the source of wealth was not merely labour, nor even capital and labour; it was 'a three-legged stool'—capital, labour and management. Sometimes management was 'part of the activities of Capital and at other times must be included with Labour'. Capital was accumulated by the joint activities of management and labour. 'Good Management always accumulates Capital.' Good management provided the guidance without which both capital and labour must be sterile. Good management was to capital and labour what the organist was to the organ—'someone to play and touch the notes.'[1]

The theme was to become a commonplace of the history of industrial capitalism and not merely of Unilever. Nevertheless, repetition has not diminished its truth. Businesses, like all other institutions, are the creation of men. Men make wealth just as they make history. To select, to train, to appreciate and to utilize men was the fundamental problem Unilever had to face in these years, and it became a more and more specialized task as the business grew and as social and psychological sciences were developed to assist in the assessment and use of human ability.

Firms have become larger—Unilever not least—partly because they have sought a larger measure of economic stability. With time, the business company has become an institution with long-term objects and policies. Yet there were countervailing risks. 'Institutionalization' could mean bureaucracy, a loss of personal contact between management and labour. There was always the risk that the demand for personal security amongst the managers themselves might blunt the edge of efficiency and enterprise. Management might grow soft and stodgy. If, therefore, the quest for economic stability was not to be self-defeating, management had to find ways and means of keeping itself alert to every technological and commercial opportunity in the new conditions of competition, alert

[1] See Viscount Leverhulme, *The Six Hour Day*, 1918.

also to every aspect of its relationship with those upon whose skill and morale the prosperity of the business turned. The dangers were not inevitable. Management now had greater scientific resources of knowledge and better communications than ever before if only it would use them. But the smooth and humane working of a business demanded that management should use its new resources with all the intellectual ability and human understanding it could muster.

First, the size of the problem. In 1938 Unilever employed 127,000 people: by 1965, 294,000 people. Of these more than half were employed in Europe, about 80,000 in Africa and the rest in the United States and a large number of overseas territories. By 1965 about 10 per cent of the total were managers of all kinds, from directors to junior or supervisory grades. Even if Unilever had been living through less revolutionary times, the problems thrown up by such vast and varied manpower would have been formidable. But a number of factors gave the manpower problem in the postwar period an aspect of urgency which it had never worn before, both as regards management and labour.

The nature of the manager's function had undergone tremendous changes in these years and these demanded new and exigent training. On the one hand, more specialized knowledge was demanded of certain types of manager—the techniques of advertising and marketing were becoming as scientific in method as current manufacturing technology, which itself called for specialists in research laboratory and factory. Yet while the tendency was for the world markets to align themselves on a basis of internationally-known products[1] in a way that demanded more of these specialized skills, the importance of the national markets remained at least as great as ever. Whether he was appointed to a post in Europe or the Americas or to one of the developing African or Asian nations, the top manager who did not intimately understand the institutions of the society in which he worked could be disastrous. The manager therefore had to be selected and trained not only for specialized business performance, but also to conduct continuous local diplomacy with government departments, trade unions and representatives of local institutions like women's organizations, chambers of commerce, farmers' associations and the like. The time was long past when his business was merely to make and sell soap and margarine with a suitable degree of

[1] See Chapter 2.

aggression. He was now required to be at once more specialized and yet more general in his outlook than ever.

All over the world local nationals were being moved in to managerial posts once manned by Europeans. The need for aptitude at negotiation and diplomacy was felt accordingly not only in Unilever's relations with the outside world, but also in the inter-company and international relationships within the Unilever organization itself. Even in the 1890s William Lever had his problems with his associated companies in Europe. Some local managers made no secret of their dislike of what they regarded as domination from Port Sunlight. As the operations in overseas countries extended and as these countries in turn grew in stature, so the need grew for Unilever to work as a 'commonwealth' rather than as an 'empire' centred on London or Rotterdam, or as an army taking orders from its generals in those capitals.

The recognition of these local aspirations was suggested not merely by justice or common sense or convenience. Sometimes it was a legal requirement that all commercial operations in a country should be managed by nationals of that country. This was an extreme case, but less xenophobic, more rationally defensible rules elsewhere made complete centralization out of the question even if it had been desirable. It was therefore vital not only that managers of all these different nationalities and races should understand their own technical business problems, but that they should understand one another. This meant continuous effort to build up a mood of tolerance and understanding by consultation and communication.

The pattern of functions within the total manpower force of management and labour was changing perceptibly, and in places rapidly. Throughout the entire working population of Europe and the world, the trend was towards smaller numbers of unskilled and semi-skilled workers and greater numbers of skilled workers. As industry became more mechanized and automation increasingly took hold, the demand for maintenance engineers and highly qualified technicians increased. The number of the machine-minders declined. Weekly wages gave way to monthly salaries. Factory labour became treated more like office staff. Security of employment, pensions and fringe benefits characterized a labour force where the differences between office staff and factory staff were becoming obliterated.

These trends were plain within the pattern of Unilever's

working force. Over the ten years between 1955 and 1965 there was an increase of total manpower of over 10 per cent. Within this total, however, the number of managers increased by nearly 50 per cent, reflecting the increasingly sophisticated markets and complex technology with which the Company had to deal. Unilever's pension contributions and other payments for retirement and death benefits rose from £1·8 million in 1945 to £25·6 million in 1965. The assets of the pension and provident fund increased in the same period from £20 million to £233 million.

Yet it could not be taken for granted that fundamental changes in the structure of industry would be introduced without problems. On the contrary, new plant automation and the like might mean dismissal or removal or upheaval for men and women who had worked in a factory all their lives. The effects upon them and their families and lives must be anticipated by management and any damage avoided or at any rate mitigated to the utmost extent possible. Changing technology demanded alert and sympathetic handling of the crises it sometimes precipitated. The more capital that was locked up in plant and equipment, the more disastrous were stoppages created by conflicts with the smaller number of men who operated the plant. How was a modern company to recruit and train men who increasingly had to combine two very different types of ability—the expertise of the specialist together with the potential ability to undertake general duties of management—display good judgment of situations and people, and co-ordinate the efforts of the specialists as well? In the old days companies were in general managed by executives recruited almost exclusively through personal contacts. Although the system worked better than modern opinion might suppose, it became increasingly evident that it suffered from two disadvantages. The wastage rate from failures was high, and it could not provide a flow of men of the right quality in sufficient numbers to meet the demands of a modern company. In the 1920s, therefore, Lever Brothers in the United Kingdom began to tap university sources of graduate trainees, especially through the Cambridge University Appointments Board, of which D'Arcy Cooper was for many years an advisory member.

From 1928 to 1939 graduate trainees from the British universities were coming in at the rate of about eight a year. They were chosen on interview alone. There was little pretence of scientific methods of selection. What developed thereafter was an intensive campaign with all the help that the combined forces of common sense, the social sciences and psychological sciences could muster, to reduce the margin of error in selection and make better prediction of a man's promise. Similar systems of planned selection came into operation in all the countries where Unilever operated, with two principal selection centres in London and in Rotterdam. In the United Kingdom alone the intake rose steadily until it was running at about a hundred a year. On the Continent as a whole probably another hundred or more graduates were recruited each year. Similar recruitment in proportion to size went on for the other overseas markets.

Unilever kept in touch with universities and other similar institutes of higher education in a variety of ways. In some European countries, the sole channel of recruitment was newspaper advertising. In others, direct contact was maintained with professors and academic heads of departments, and this was especially valuable where scientific specialists were concerned. There were other indirect contacts, for example through university appointments boards and through the dissemination of books and pamphlets outlining the prospects open to graduates in Unilever management.

Whatever methods were used, the testing of potential recruits was done on a broadly similar basis. In the United Kingdom, as on the Continent, a panel of some hundred selectors was chosen from amongst the top managers of the company. The selection procedure began with simple psychological tests (the 'matrices' method). Interview with a psychologist followed. The entry forms filled in by the candidate were then studied by the selectors. Then a group of selectors interviewed a group of candidates. In the first discussion the candidates themselves arranged a topic for discussion. This was followed by the discussion of a problem set by the selectors—normally a business problem—with the candidates acting as a 'board of directors', trying to solve the problems. Finally, each candidate was interviewed by two selectors. About one-third of the total candidates survived these ordeals successfully. Roughly four-fifths of these survivors accepted the invitation to join the company, and of these another four-fifths survived the course after three years.

This system, which represented the first stages of the scheme known as Unilever Companies Management Development Scheme, dated from 1952. It was introduced and was later modified, in accordance with scientific advice from the Tavistock Institute of Human Relations. Experience helped to eliminate some of its early weaknesses. But nobody pretended it was a foolproof system. The contribution of the psychologists and psychiatrists was advisory. The psychological experts helped to interview; they sat with the selection board. Under the British system their opinion was given before the board as a whole made up its mind. Under the Dutch system, their views were not heard until the rest of the board had made a provisional decision. The object throughout was to refine a process which everybody recognized could not be infallible. But in so far as experience, common sense and scientific method could be combined to reduce the risks of error, the selection process seemed to offer a fair and reasonable avenue of progress.

In Continental Europe, the selection system had in time to accommodate itself to the prevailing customs of local systems of higher education. In Holland, for example, final examinations are not conducted *en masse* as they are in the United Kingdom. Traditionally, graduates leave Dutch universities and colleges of technology at all times of the year. In Holland, therefore, and in most Continental countries group selection boards gave way to interviews of individual candidates by an *ad hoc* body consisting of two senior managers working in co-operation with an expert selection officer.

The new concentration on graduate entry did not mean that it was regarded as an exclusive source of talent, nor that university men contained by nature the ingredients of successful management. 'We try to see' said the Chairmen in 1956, 'that in our business there is always a ladder by which a man with the right qualities can climb to the next stage. If we succeed in this, there will always be found at every level of our management men whose only university has been what William Lever used to call the University of Hard Knocks.'[1] Alongside the graduate selection channel, therefore, was another channel of recruitment direct from school, and yet another for men of promise coming up inside the business from the factory floor. There had also to be separate recruitment of specialists vitally necessary to the business. But, broadly speaking, the world experience of Unilever pointed inevitably to the university graduate as the most likely source of management talent for the future. Obviously only a proportion of

[1] From 'The Managers', a speech delivered on 24 May 1956.

graduates could be recruited as starters in the race, and of these some would be eliminated long before the finish. But these were men who had enjoyed the unique opportunity to spend three or more years being put through more or less rigorous exercises in scientific thinking. (The phrase is used in the broad sense of systematic handling of knowledge, whether in the humanities or the sciences.) It was reasonable to assume that their intellectual fibre was generally toughened by the process and that their moral fibre was at any rate comparable with the non-graduate.

None of this represented any real break with the past. The new graduate recruits to professional management found themselves grafted on to an older managerial stock, just as the first generation of professional managers—Heyworth, Rijkens, de Blank, Davis and many others—had been grafted on to the generation of owner-managers.[1] Nor did the old names—the Van den Berghs, Jurgens, Hartogs—disappear. But now they were there no longer by right of ownership but of managerial ability. Unilever was fortunate in its continuity of management. Which type of university training was best designed to produce the potential manager remained a matter of hot debate within Unilever, as outside. While some favoured more technical, economic courses, or specific business-college training, there were still many who held that a normal honours course, whether it was in the natural sciences, or in classics, or history, was the best set of hurdles for the potential business leader. Some Unilever executives were still inclined to suspect that the arts graduate absorbed ideas more readily and was more generally adaptable than the science graduate. Possibly (they went on to suggest) the science graduate went into industry rather too sure that he was there to teach rather than to learn. This claim to premature experience might be a hindrance rather than a help. (Another school of sceptics believed that the explanation might lie, not with scientific youth, but simply with youth.)

The pioneers of graduate recruitment like D'Arcy Cooper were initiating a change which after 1945 acquired in Britain and elsewhere the momentum of a social revolution. Before the war, the average university graduate was drawn towards public service, the Church, or the professions; hardly at all towards the business world. In a matter of twenty years this was wholly changed, and by the 1950s it was the older professions which were finding it

[1] See *The History of Unilever*, vols I and II.

difficult to compete against the attractions of business careers. The change was not entirely smooth. The discovery of the graduate by industrial leaders was perhaps a little too sudden, a little too uncritical. The graduate was sometimes expected to perform miracles. When he failed to do so, disillusionment set in on both sides. Graduates coming into industry after several years of intellectual freedom sometimes found the contrast between their new but often modest responsibilities and their previous dreams of power hard to endure. The problem was, as always, a matter of mutual understanding. Much of it was eliminated by more contact and greater experience. Each side developed a more practical assessment of what it might expect from the other. One line of practical progress was the refinement of the training system itself, and its co-ordination with a better-planned system of promotion and placing.

While the new Unilever trainees were put through various courses designed to enlarge their understanding of the business in general, they were fairly swiftly sent into what is known as 'on-the-job training'. The idea of business management courses run by outside institutions was welcomed generally in Unilever, but there was undeniably a feeling that the Unilever manager must receive his basic specialized training in Unilever itself. Those who survived to acquire knowledge and achieve success comprised a group of several hundred men. Their careers were the special concern of a committee which watched their progress and placing. Upon this élite the success of the business depended. Their development was therefore a matter of vital concern to the top management. Good managers were the most scarce and therefore the most precious of all the resources owned by Unilever. 'The limits of effective expansion' A. W. J. Caron, a director of Unilever, wrote in 1964, 'are likely to be set very largely by the extent to which an adequate number of capable managers with the appropriate experience can be developed to meet the changing needs of the concern.'[1]

It was to avoid any unnecessary wastage of these precious talents that the 'management of managers' became a top priority in the forward planning of Unilever. Each operating company had to submit a five-year plan forecasting the state of its business and the management organization to fit its predicted needs. These forward plans were then co-ordinated in London and in Rotterdam

[1] 'Management and Economic Growth: A Unilever View.' *Progress*, I (1964).

with the evaluations of the managers themselves arrived at by the
bodies assessing managerial policy. In this way the assessment and
prediction of human abilities was built into the planned progress
of the entire Unilever business, being co-ordinated at all points
with the scientific development of invention, technology, production and markets.

What were the risks? That in all these proliferations of selection
procedures and committee judgments, Unilever would, consciously
or otherwise, find itself devising a type of manager who suited the
criteria of professional selectors rather than the facts of life?
Would the final product that emerged from these compromises,
these searchings for paragons of tact, academic ability or sharp-
wittedness, be real individuals? Or would they be the chameleons
who adjust their colour best to the light shining through them?
Would they be, in an American phrase, 'organization men'?
And would they be *more* organization men the longer they went
on in a business increasingly ruled by committee methods?

Certainly such risks existed. Certainly the risks were recognized.
Throughout Unilever there was a lively apprehension that the
large business might always turn into an amiable dinosaur. Hence
the constant emphasis on an organization that would combine the
economic benefits of size with decentralization and individual
initiative, speed of decision and the ability to meet ever sharper
competition. In practice (so far as an outside observer can judge)
the selection and training system worked well, judged by results.
Of course, every society has its own kind of conformism. Dark
suitings signify conformism in business; the equally calculated
absence of dark suitings symbolizes the conformism of academic
life. The tendency to regard the non-conformist as an exhibitionist
is not merely a characteristic of the business world. Anyone who
wore a bowler hat, a dark suit and a neatly rolled umbrella per-
sistently in a university would suffer the same fate as the
businessman who turns up to his office wearing tweeds and a
brightly-coloured tie.

Such criteria of social behaviour seem to be becoming more
exigent in modern society rather than less. The pressures tending
to produce a conventional type of business manager came as much
from outside the business as from inside. It was the expectation
of those outside the business—the Civil Service, the unions, and
the rest—that the spokesman for the company would be balanced,
reasonable, tactful, and so on. This reinforced the trend towards

conventionality. No doubt in the process some rough diamonds of quality got excluded. But if experience and success rubbed the sharp edges off some men, they emphasized the individuality of others.

By and large, Unilever managers tended to be self-critical, genially irreverent about the company 'image'. They were not only ready to accept the likelihood that Unilever could be improved. The assumption that it could and must be improved became a permanent frame of mind amongst them. In all these respects Unilever came well out of a comparison with the public services, the armed services, or academic institutions.

One of the factors which helped to keep managers alert and responsive to the changing needs of the times was competition and a high degree of mobility. One of the advantages of size in a concern like Unilever was the cross-fertilization of ideas and experience which became possible by the exchange of managers between different businesses and the different countries. 'Differences in national character' Mr Caron has written, 'usually enhance the quality of a management team and internationalization provides a number of senior managers who have obtained a broad concept of our world-wide business.'[1] Such circulars as the following appeared regularly on the desks of the Unilever management:

Mr A.B.C.——, Chairman of Lever Brothers & Associates Limited, will be retiring at his own request at the end of this year. He will be succeeded as Chairman by Mr D.E.F.——, at present Marketing Director of Lever Brothers & Associates Limited.

Mr F——'s successor as Marketing Director will be Mr G.H.I. ——, a director of Lever Brothers Limited, Canada.

Mr J.K.L.——, Managing Director of Lever S.A., Belgium, will re-join the Board of Lever Brothers Limited, Canada, as a Vice-President of the company.

Mr L—— will be succeeded in Brussels by Mr M.N.O.——, at present Managing Director of Thibaud Gibbs & Cie, S.A. Belgium.

The successor to Mr O—— will be Mr P.Q.R.——, Marketing Manager, A/B Vinolia, Sweden.

Unquestionably this intermingling was a vital element in keeping management alert and efficient. Did it sometimes go too far? One body of opinion held that Unilever moved its managers, particularly the young ones, too often or too early; that in the

[1] *Progress*, I (1964).

attempt to keep men lively, it could have the effect of making them restless, depriving them of the deeper knowledge of the business in favour of superficiality. In practice, nearly 20 per cent of managers in the middle and senior grades were serving outside their own native country in the early 1960s.

In earlier times the relationship of management with a labour force which in those days contained a very large element of un-skilled or semi-skilled labour was highly personal. Employers like Lever and the Van den Berghs still managed to know a consider-able number of their employees personally. Their temperament and the current climate of thought and feeling still favoured a personal relationship between employer and men.

The idea of the enlightened capitalist died hard. It had been built into the structure of several of the Unilever companies as a matter of history from the time when model villages were con-structed by those firms. Not only Port Sunlight, but van Marken's village at Delft and Price's village at Bromborough, were all evidence of a characteristic attitude towards labour relations. So was Lever's profit-sharing scheme which he called co-partnership. Yet all were from the beginning open to certain criticisms. Inevitably there was an element of paternalism in the 'model village' scheme. The villagers had to obey rules which some of them naturally interpreted as interfering with their personal liberty, a reversion to a kind of industrial feudalism. The co-partnership system, it was said, was really merely a gift out of the private pocket of the sole ordinary shareholder, who was also the employer.

Splendid as the intentions of such schemes were, they could not but smack of charity or at any rate patronage. There was, moreover, the question of the right to strike. Was such a right prejudiced by the insistence of the co-partnership system on 'loyalty' amongst the members? For these and other practical reasons the removal of labour relations on to a more impersonal plane was in some ways a change welcomed with relief by manage-ment. Yet though the problems altered, they became no easier.

None of the problems facing the new generation of management was more delicate than that of its relations with labour. Nor did anything else reveal so clearly the need for local knowledge and local freedom to deal with a problem that never took quite the same shape in any two places. Everywhere, as management became increasingly divorced from ownership, it found itself faced with growing demands from governments, the public and especially from employees for a bigger 'right of say' in industrial affairs. The aspiration was universal; the emphasis differed from place to place. Older ideas of industrial democracy and direct control that derived from Marxism, Syndicalism and Fabianism jostled with individual and collective rights of a liberal kind guaranteed by statute (as in England) and with new manifestations like 'co-determination' in Germany, workers' councils in Yugoslavia or systems of 'accountability' as in Scandinavia.

Unilever industries thus found themselves facing widely different economic and social systems in different countries. Flexibility in this area of management was not merely desirable, it was vital. History, politics and social circumstances combined to fashion a unique context for each country. In Britain, the background to labour relations was a long history of recognized trade unionism and the right to strike. The cornerstone was the system of voluntary collective bargaining by which employers and unions negotiated towards agreement. The post-war trend here was one of increasing union membership; one in two manual workers and one in five non-manual workers were union members. Unilever's labour relations were, almost everywhere, governed by agreements reached through negotiation with the unions or through statutory joint industrial councils representing both sides of industry.

The apparent contrast with two other major countries where Unilever had its largest markets could hardly have been more striking. In the Netherlands, trade union membership was generally low—about 35 per cent. During the years of reconstruction after the war, opinion came to accept draconic measures of government intervention in the general interest. Workers could not quit their jobs nor employers sack their workers without official permission. Government and the Foundation of Labour, representing the Trade Unions and Employers' Associations, combined to operate a wages policy within a central economic plan prepared by the government planning bureau. Wage increases were deliberately linked with productivity. In spite of various attempts to relax control, it seemed as if government intervention was increasing rather than slackening down to 1963. Much as the system was disliked by many employers, the general atmosphere was pretty rational, in spite of full employment and a general shortage of labour.

In West German industry, once a hotbed of conflicting social ideologies, the old quarrels were laid to rest in the post-war years of reconstruction and later of prosperity. Union membership fell, and with it union militancy. German workers were more concerned with increasing incomes than with class conflict. Labour aspirations found their outlet rather in more representation in industrial management—the so-called 'co-determination' system. Compared with the Dutch system, the German relied far less on direct government intervention, reflecting in this respect the new-found faith in economic freedom that characterized the new Germany.

Twenty years, then, of contrasts. But as the second post-war decade closed there were signs that these different systems of labour relations might be moving closer together. In the Netherlands it began to look at last as if the voluntary element in an incomes policy might become greater, government dictation less. In Britain, on the other hand, the Labour Minister of State for Economic Affairs ended 1965 by speaking of the 'jungle' of trade union negotiations and threatening the need for compulsory wage regulations. Britain, in short, seemed to be moving nearer to the post-war Dutch pattern of central planning, including incomes and wages controls.[1] In Germany, too, there were signs that the doctrines of economic freedom might no longer be adequate to cope with growing economic difficulties.

Thus labour relations were not only different in each country; they were everywhere in a state of flux. Hence the need for continuous and alert attention, especially in an age when the transition to new technologies meant fewer workers and higher skills with all the possibilities of labour dislocation this might mean. Only thus could disastrously expensive labour troubles be avoided. Two developments were important here: the emergence of a special category of manager charged specially with labour relations, and the special attention given to the training of labour supervisors (once called 'foremen').

The personnel manager's responsibilities ran right through the whole gamut of industrial relations—manning, working conditions, morale, efficiency—and the importance of his task grew steadily. In many respects, his job was to fulfil, with more specialized training, those responsibilities towards labour which had in earlier days fallen to the boss himself. In Britain, therefore, where the traditions of company independence were strong, local Chairmen of Unilever companies often appointed their personnel managers

[1] The official 'freeze' of wages and prices became law on 6 October 1966.

themselves. In Continental Europe, where organization was rather more centralized, personnel managers tended to be recruited, trained and appointed by the national managements. Whichever system was in force, nobody doubted that here was a science of human relations of crucial importance to the health of the business.

This reorganization of labour management went along with greater efforts to provide wider training for those promoted to supervisory jobs amongst the labour force itself. The narrowing of the gap between white collar workers and manual workers was itself evidence that a new kind of factory worker was emerging. The day of the cloth cap was passing. There were even prophets who foresaw the ultimate disappearance of distinctions between management and labour. Already the new technicians were men who daily handled specialized problems of great complexity and carried heavy responsibilities towards both their employers and fellow workers. For them, therefore, just as for the new generation of managers, Unilever organized a regular and continuous series of training courses. Some were designed to equip them with the specialized information directly needed for their work. Others were designed to help them to see their responsibilities in a context wider than that of their own factory.

If a slate remarkably clean of strikes and labour troubles was anything to go by, these efforts were worthwhile. Large schemes of technological innovations, reorganization and redeployment in post-war decades were carried through quietly, without fuss and on the whole without serious labour difficulties. One impressive instance was the closing of John Knight's Silvertown soap works in the East End of London, under the scheme of 1959. Under this scheme soap production was to be transferred from Silvertown to the North of England, and the site itself was to go over to the manufacture of glues and adhesives. Some 500 workers were involved and the problem of redundancy was serious. From the beginning the operation was carefully planned by the Chairman and Personnel Manager, in conjunction with the employees and the unions (mainly the Union of Shop, Distributive and Allied Workers). Instead of the original nine-months period, the transition was given two to three years. Everybody concerned was kept fully informed. Every employee was interviewed by the Personnel Manager and given an opportunity to discuss the changes and particularly his personal problems. The unions were kept in the picture. The Ministry of Labour was informed in advance. Joint

Workers' councils were made a forum of news about progress. The local house magazine doubled its frequency. Every method that could be employed to reduce redundancy was tried. Those nearing retirement were retired early with compensation and full pension rights. Younger men were re-employed in the glues and adhesive business. A joint statement by the company and the union was issued promising six months' notice to all full-time employees declared redundant, explaining the principles on which redundancy was to be dealt with, and giving an assurance that every effort would be made to re-employ workers in other Unilever companies. Those who had to be laid off were part-time workers, all of them married women, and most found new work in the highly industrialized area round Silvertown without much difficulty. Only one employee left because he was dissatisfied with the alternative work offered to him.

The Silvertown experience showed that, even in an area where 'company loyalty' was often low, a well-established system of joint consultation could reduce and almost eliminate the problems of industrial reorganization. The system itself had the effect of putting management 'under the microscope and making them account for what they are doing'.[1]

The British system of voluntary negotiation might often seem a façade that disguised mere chaos. The Silvertown scheme was only one of many which showed that the system could work, and work well, if the basic problems were tackled with method and humanity.

Another instance where an obstinate problem was methodically tackled by rational methods was the modernization of the great Hartog meat factory at Oss in North Brabant. Oss had always been known for a spirit of robust independence. It was the scene of one of the few strikes to blot Unilever's post-war copybook. How would it take proposals of work-study experts for modernizing a strongly traditional factory process? The answer was that it accepted a large measure of mechanization on the packaging side of the factory, and although labour difficulties over such matters as work-study reports and bonus schemes were not entirely eliminated the system of consultation between management and labour was greatly improved so as to alleviate difficulties substantially. The main margarine factory in Holland at the Nassau Quay,

[1] Mr W. J. Deverall, Chairman of John Knight Limited, in a personal interview on 30 September 1963.

Rotterdam, offered wider scope for mechanization and modernization. The new bulk-production methods nevertheless made it vital
to have effective consultation between management and labour
so that problems of redundancy and retraining could be handled
without major troubles. Here, then, a Personnel Department
including trained sociologists, medical staff and administrators
helped management to keep the transitional process under surveillance. Proposed changes were explained, discussed, understood
and accepted. No factory management can ever afford the luxury
of supposing that it has permanently solved its problems, but
unquestionably experience and research combined in these
years to improve enormously the system of consultation between management and labour and reduce the risk of serious
stoppages.

The part increasingly played by medical science in various
forms was significant. Industrial medicine was in fact a form of
preventive medicine. It started from the conviction, first enshrined
in Britain in the Factory Acts, that in certain hazardous industrial
occupations it was the duty of industry to avoid and prevent
damage to health. This was now extended, through largely
voluntary enquiries, into the whole process by which people at
work reacted, normally and abnormally, to industrial conditions.
The minimal aim was to reduce absence from work; the maximum
aim to achieve the highest possible standard of health and
happiness amongst work people. This was sought through a
systematic organization for examining workers medically, for
ensuring conditions of hygiene and reasonable tranquillity, for
combating illnesses and accidents, and for co-operating with
public health organizations, including preventive medicine departments in universities and social medicine institutes.

Company doctors and nurses played a vital part by recording
and analysing the ills and injuries of an industrial life and by
helping management and men to understand the importance of
health measures. The position of the medical officer was not an
easy one. He had to preserve a position of trust both towards
management and staff, and conscientiously observe the professional secrecy which his profession imposed on him. He had to be
independent and sympathetic. Throughout the world-wide Unilever organization some sixty-five full-time doctors, another 100
part-time doctors and at least 200 nurses provided medical care for
staff of all grades. Their work steadily became an indispensable

element in Unilever's plans for improving social welfare and industrial relations.

Beyond the problems of the active working life lay the provisions for pensions. Characteristically, William Lever saw the problem as early as 1905. He expressed it and his proposed solution in terms blunt, clear and personal. His intention was, he said, to pay over to trustees £5,000 a year to be applied for providing old age, widow and orphan pensions for employees of the Lever companies throughout the world. 'There is no unpleasant taint' he went on, 'of pauperizing philanthropy in this—those who do their duty to the Firm will remain with the Firm if they cannot do better for themselves elsewhere. Those who do not do their duty to the Firm will never retain their position long enough to entitle them to a pension . . . if an employee has remained long enough with the Firm to qualify for a pension, he has done his duty and has earned his pension.' From that day the Lever pension fund began.

Van den Bergh's tackled the problem rather later, in 1920, both in Holland and England. With good advice they provided an unusually wide scope of benefits, based on a contributory scheme, which helped to give the whole system its proper aspect as a matter of legal right, not of charity. When the Margarine Union was formed, therefore, in 1927, the Van den Bergh scheme was chosen for the new combined business. And when two years later Lever's joined the Margarine Union in Unilever, the Van den Bergh scheme was again chosen as the model. From 1920 until his retirement in 1942, Albert Van den Bergh had no prouder boast than to claim to have fathered this scheme, which slowly became the model for Unilever companies throughout the world.

By 1957 there were altogether fifty-four separate trust funds set up to cover the needs of retirement and death. They covered over 100,000 employees and 16,000 pensioners in twenty-six different countries, and their assets came to over £100 million. By 1965 the equivalent figures had risen to nearly 128,000 employees, nearly 24,000 pensioners, and the total investment of the funds had gone up to £236 million, spread over a wide variety of investments, including industrial shares and debentures, mortgages and property and government investments.

The principles on which the pensions schemes worked could not stand still in two decades which saw concepts of welfare revolutionized in one society after another, while successive doses of inflation eroded the value of money. By the middle 1950s Unilever found itself having to supplement existing pensions, based on contributions from employer and employee, in order to maintain them at a satisfactory level. Yet each individual adjustment created a more complicated system. Nobody could predict what his pension would be and the system was getting more and more costly to operate. The growing importance of state pensions further complicated the issue. In 1962, therefore, a new and simplified system was introduced. First applied in the United Kingdom and the Netherlands, it had spread to a number of Unilever companies in Continental Europe by 1965. By 1966 its effect was to ensure that all employees on reaching retirement age with normal service would receive a pension which (including the state pension) would represent 70 per cent on the first £1,500 of the last year of pay, and 60 per cent on the excess over that figure.

There was a further change of great significance. Hitherto works staff had had different pension arrangements from office staff. This difference was now abolished. The social gap between those who worked in offices and those who worked in factories was itself rapidly narrowing. The same principles were now applied to both. Within four years a substantial majority of all staff had entered the new scheme. Thus in a single scheme were comprehended plans further to ensure the employees' sense of security and to recognize those changing social concepts of a new industrial order which might be summed up as the passing of the age of the cloth cap. The cost to Unilever of running the new scheme amounted in 1965 to over £25·8 million.

The concept of the Welfare State spread rapidly in the post-war world. So far from being a burden to industry, it was in general welcomed by managements that were increasingly and everywhere divorced from ownership. Nor in general did shareholders show vocal or effective opposition to the apparent deduction of these costs from their own share of the profits cake. The expanding productivity of industry proved well able to take care of the extra finance required, and most efficient industries saw the operation as a well-worthwhile form of investment in better industrial relations. Knowledge and practice in the sphere of welfare spread rapidly, so that in this respect, as in so many others, the Western world at any rate achieved a considerable degree of uniformity. This again meant that, as a factor in competitive costs, the provision of pensions was something which most industries in most industrialized communities had to shoulder. In this, as in all spheres of industrial relations, the problem for a business like Unilever was to put to the best advantage its international resources and experience, to keep itself informed of developments so as not to be taken by surprise, and to keep clear and efficient the lines of communication between management, unions and governments so that the human relations within industry were not only managed with efficiency but with sympathy and humanity.

CHAPTER 4

RESEARCH AND TECHNOLOGY

A TABLET of soap or a packet of washing powder in 1965 might still look much the same as it did in 1939. In reality it might well be a quite different product. The tablet might no longer be made of soap, the washing powder might well be no longer a soap powder. Both might be manufactured from materials that were virtually unknown a quarter of a century ago, by processes of which manufacturers were then equally ignorant. This revolution, springing from chemical knowledge, had transformed an industry which was previously relatively lightly affected by science or research.

In 1945 the oils and fats industries could look back on a reasonably tranquil history, little disturbed by inconvenient invention. Upheavals there had been, but not for many years. The discovery of the hydrogenation process, which had enabled the manufacturers to turn oils into hard fats, had certainly shaken the industry just before the First World War.[1] The possibility of incorporating vitamins had opened up new claims for margarine from the 1920s.[2] But even these were largely the result of scientific discovery outside the industry rather than of internal research. Unilever's pre-eminence in this period had rested on the arts of the market-place rather than the sciences of the laboratory, and in this respect it was sharply distinguished from the most progressive firms in the chemical industry, whose progress and profit alike rested upon a systematic pursuit of elaborate, costly and continuous programmes of scientific research and development. The post-war decades were to see these two types of industrial organization come closer together as both came to realize that research and marketing were the Siamese-twin components of success. But even in 1945 this truth was only just beginning to dawn.

Many Unilever factories possessed works laboratories, but they were small, few of the staff had university training and their work was mainly routine work of the analytical kind. Port Sunlight had

---

[1] See *The History of Unilever*, vol. I, chapter IX.   [2] Ibid., chapter XIX.

a laboratory of this kind which might well claim to be the 'mother' of the other Unilever research establishments in Britain, for it could trace its history back to the 1920s, but even here the cost and impact of research was very modest before the late 1940s. The Dutch margarine industry had employed two laboratories to deal with general problems since the mid-1920s, but it was not until the 1940s that their work became more specialized—Zwijndrecht dealing with health problems, Rotterdam with the microbiology of margarine. The staff thus collected formed the nucleus of the later laboratory at Vlaardingen in 1954.

By 1965 this picture had altered. Unilever had no less than eleven major research establishments throughout the world, as well as smaller establishments in West Africa, the Congo, and the Solomon Islands, together with numerous laboratories and pilot plants for developing new processes. Between the 1940s and the 1960s the various research establishments assumed specialized functions, subject only to a measure of duplication and overlapping between the different laboratories. This overlap was partly the unavoidable accident of research progress, but increasingly a result of deliberate policy. For as communications between the different laboratories and scientists improved to a point of high efficiency, it became more likely that duplication would be something deliberately encouraged in the interests of progress, rather than a mere accident. In scientific enquiry as elsewhere two heads may be better than one. Moreover, different national backgrounds and aptitudes might suggest different ways of approaching the same problem, thereby increasing the chances of success.

Port Sunlight in Cheshire became particularly concerned with research on detergents, chemicals and timber (this last in connection with the United Africa Company's timber interests in Africa).[1] Colworth House (Bedfordshire), established as a research centre in 1947, was concerned with the scientific problems of food preservation, animal nutrition and with associated problems of bacteria and medical safety arising from toothpastes, shampoos, etc. Unilever's growing investment in foods created a wide variety of horticultural experiments into vegetable plants, their cultivation, harvesting, vulnerability to diseases and so on. The scientific basis of Colworth's work was therefore biological and even zoological as well as chemical. The specialized research required for toilet preparations was carried on at a new laboratory at

[1] See Chapter 9, pages 218–20.

Isleworth in Middlesex. In 1963 a fourth British laboratory was established at Welwyn. This was to house a team investigating problems of texture and flavour in oils and fats, especially lipo-proteins[1], and problems related to ice-cream, which had to be moved from Port Sunlight to make room for the expansion of detergents research.

In Continental Europe the largest establishment was set up at Vlaardingen, near Rotterdam, in 1954, to undertake all types of research from the most fundamental to the immediately practical on edible oils and fats as well as detergents. By 1962 it was fully operative, but still expanding and developing. The youngest off-shoot was the laboratory at Duiven which carried out agricultural and food research.[2] In Germany, the laboratory at Hamburg was principally concerned with the research problems of paper and plastics[3] and with problems of edible and technical oils and cheese. A smaller laboratory at St. Denis, near Paris, handled research into toilet preparations with a special eye to French tastes and fashions. In the United States the research in connection with all Lever Brothers Company products, whether detergents, edible oils and fats, foods or toilet preparations was concentrated in a new and modern laboratory at Edgewater, New Jersey, established in 1952. The particular problems connected with the products of Thomas J. Lipton, in particular tea, salad dressings and soups, were investigated in a special laboratory not far away in Hoboken, New Jersey, and later at Englewood Cliffs.

Altogether in 1964 Unilever was employing a total research staff of 4,035, of whom 772 were scientific graduates of the calibre to undertake individual or group research. The total cost was £8,425,000, five times that of 1952, when the amount spent was £1,676,000. By the end of 1965 this had reached over £10 million. This greatly enlarged budget took no account of the growing number of development units attached to operating companies, whose work on adapting and testing new or modified processes was of vital importance. The total cost of research and development remained small if compared with, say, advertising costs. But then there was no particular reason why the two costs should be

[1] A lipo-protein is a combination of a lipid (or fat) and a protein.

[2] See pages 201–3.

[3] See infra, pages 207–10, for the development of the German paper and printing group.

compared. Research had to grow, relevantly and organically. Merely to inflate it would have been absurd. The really important change was a quite new attitude to research and technology through the business, symbolized *inter alia* by the decision in 1961 to appoint as a member of the Special Committee of three a research scientist, Dr E. G. Woodroofe. In 1965 another scientist, Mr J. G. Collingwood, joined the Board. Such appointments emphasized the need to accelerate the progress of scientific ideas in Unilever, and to speed up the growth of research as a dynamic force making for greater competitive enterprise.

In 1959 Dr Woodroofe was able to point out that although research effort had lagged down to 1956, it was by 1959 running at a satisfactorily higher rate where edible fats were concerned. For detergents progress had been slower, while research on toilet preparations and foods had gone ahead faster than the expansion of sales. In this way the intensity of research on edible fats and foods was about equal to the intensity of research on detergents. These were fairly long-lived products. Toilet preparations needed twice as much research as other products because of their short life. The problems of fitting this new dynamic factor into the business were already beginning to emerge. Some were the problems of management, notably to preserve amongst the scientists in industry a sense of purpose and a spirit of lively enquiry. There was inevitably some conflict here between the aspiration of the scientist to enjoy the freedom of enquiry that he enjoyed in the academic world and the need of the company to achieve results. The scientist was apt to resent the commercial expert breathing down his neck and demanding results on time. Equally, the commercial man was still apt to be sceptical of the scientist's belief in totally new products. Such a product might be ingenious, but would it sell? The young scientist grew old. Perhaps he ran out of creative ideas. What was to happen to him then? He might be totally unfitted to administrative responsibilities. Conversely, there was the risk that the scientist who was able in a practical way would be drawn away too early into the toils of administration, attracted perhaps by the higher rewards that such responsibilities were apt to carry by comparison with backroom jobs.

Some of these problems were partially solved by the process of growth in the research departments themselves and by better communications between them. As departments grew in size the

UNILEVER RESEARCH LABORATORIES 1965

● Main laboratory for the product group concerned

PRODUCT GROUPS	CONTINENTAL EUROPE				UNITED KINGDOM				U.S.A.		INDIA
	VLAARDINGEN	DUIVEN	HAMBURG	ST.DENIS	PORT SUNLIGHT	COLWORTH	WELWYN	ISLEWORTH	EDGEWATER	ENGLEWOOD CLIFFS	BOMBAY
margarine and other edible fats	●		○				○		○		○
other foods		○				●				○	○
detergents	○				●				○		○
toilet preparations			○	○				●	○		○
chemical products	○		○	○	○						
packaging			○								
others					○	○				○	
STAFF	985	163	310	80	885	1050	342	263	458	108	87

Figure 4

process of mutual interest and competition inevitably provided a continuing stimulus and this could be increased by cross-fertilization of ideas between establishments by means of regular conferences. The first of these was held at Leicester University in the 1950s. A growing staff of scientists thus multiplied their contacts with universities and technical and scientific institutes. They were encouraged to publish their findings and participate in the life of the scientific community. The industrial scientist was likely to find himself less lonely and more an established and secure part of industry. On the other hand, the problem of age became more serious as time went on. Rapid expansion inevitably reduced the average age of scientists working in an industry. But in time the average age necessarily rose and with it the problems of staff organization and the problems of retaining creative freshness of mind.

Beyond the internal problems of scientific organization lay the broader problems of the relationship between the scientist and the commercial and production side of the industry. It was pointed out in 1959 in reply to some searching questions from the Special Committee that well over half of the research endeavour of Unilever went on what was called 'protective research', that is research that was designed to maintain existing products in a competitive position. Another quarter went on 'service' work, mainly designed to assess the performance of competing products, and giving advice to various users and consumers. 10 to 15 per cent could be said to be concentrated on genuinely novel developments which would bring new and additional business to Unilever. This (said the then Head of Research Division, Dr Woodroofe) was, for a company of Unilever's size, 'woefully inadequate, but it is sad that I have to assure you that we in research are under no pressure from marketing to increase this part of our work'.

Another five years of experience of the relationship between commerce and science showed that the problem was not a simple one, and that while time had improved the ratio of new products being carried into production, the problem itself was to remain obstinate. Remain obstinate because there is perhaps no more fundamental business problem than the relation between the scientist and the market. The organization of research proved indeed to be related to conceptions of business methods which varied widely from one country to another. In the United States the customer was generally and justifiably regarded by the producer as fickle—easily interested by a new product and possessing less of that propensity called 'brand loyalty' than his or her European counterpart. One product therefore gave way quickly to its successor, although the successor might appear different only in some marginal aspect from the original. In Europe a good product took a lot of killing, so that a name like Lux or Lifebuoy would be about twice as old as Unilever itself.

Closely connected with this difference between markets was a different emphasis in research. Lever Brothers Company in the United States spent well above the Unilever average on research. Any accurate comparison with other countries would, of course, have to recognize that research in the United States was more costly than elsewhere. Nevertheless, when their Edgewater research establishment was inaugurated it was in at least one respect a model for other Unilever research organizations, for nowhere could the co-ordination of marketing and research be seen to work so efficiently as it did here. Many factors combined to bring scientist and salesman in the United States more closely together than anywhere else in the world. The social prestige of industry and a widespread regard for scientific knowledge were not competitive in the United States; they were complementary. Nor was a good scientist ashamed of placing his talents fully at the disposal of his commercial colleague. Research, in short, was devoted here to objectives agreed upon by both the researcher and the salesman. It was the latter who for the most part defined the target, and the former whose business it was to see that the target was reached. Exceptions there might be. An Edgewater scientist might in the course of some commercially orientated project stumble on something unforeseen which was nevertheless commercially viable. Thus, its research on detergents suggested to public authorities that Edgewater was well placed to investigate medical problems of the skin. Hence research contracts on matters of common concern to medical science and industry. But generally these were exceptional cases. The bulk of research at Edgewater was strictly directed to commercial ends.

So, in the long run, of course, was most industrial research, but in Europe management was more disposed (as an American executive put it) 'to leave its research investment in the bank longer than American management'. In short, research in Europe tended to contain a larger element of long-term research of a fundamental character and was therefore slower to yield immediate profit than its American counterpart. In this way a pattern of the division of research labour seemed to be emerging. The close market–laboratory link of the United States system often proved of great value to the European businesses, while fundamental investigations carried out at Vlaardingen and elsewhere were equally valuable to the North American business.

At Vlaardingen different programmes and different philosophies ruled. The primary emphasis was on research into edible fats, and a main preoccupation of Vlaardingen has been with the composition and quality of margarine. On the composition largely depend the costs of production. Raw materials have always been the main determinant of margarine price. A large part, therefore, of the Vlaardingen programme was concerned to investigate processes by which raw materials, which were formerly unsuitable because they developed bad tastes or qualities after being hardened, could be made into margarine of first-rate quality. The financial and competitive implications of this kind of investigation do not need to be laboured. Soyabean oil was at one time unpopular with the manufacturer, but improved refining techniques changed this. Ultimately they revolutionized the whole situation as regards raw materials for margarine, resulted in vast savings, changed the patterns of world trade in raw materials and set in train a whole succession of technological innovations in Unilever.

Closely associated with such research was a series of enquiries into the quality of margarine, which had to be not only cheap and keepable and spread well on bread, but also possess a good flavour and high nutritional value. Vlaardingen gave special attention to processes for isolating 'off flavours', the smallest traces of which could affect the taste of large quantities of margarine. These defects were apt to form during the hardening of liquid oils into solid fats. They were isolated by newly developed methods which provided the analyst with measuring techniques of great accuracy. Only one milligram of one of the components of butter flavour was present in one ton of butter. Unilever scientists were swift to seize on new techniques first developed by medical research. The processes of gas chromatography—to locate—and spectroscopy—to identify—these tiny particles were used. The isolation of the components of butter flavour and the development of ways of making them meant that hardening and refining techniques had to be improved before these components could be incorporated into margarines. If the added butter flavours were to be really

effective the margarine maker needed oils of very special quality.
The problems of human health were also much in the minds of the
scientists who were constantly trying to modify refining and
hardening processes in order to preserve the maximum amount of
so-called fatty acids which are essential to certain biological
functions. So that the solution of one problem suggested another.
The endless processes of research continue. But they have already
revolutionized margarine production both as regards raw materials
and flavours. In earlier days the problem was to try to imitate
butter; now it was to establish a product with its own claims on the
consumer's attention.

In their scientific approach, Colworth House and Port Sunlight
might be said to occupy an intermediate position between Edgewater and Vlaardingen. Scientists, like other people, display
certain national characteristics. Scientists in Holland and Germany
seemed to be specially apt at devising analytical techniques within
a known field and working out correct answers. The American
scientist was adept at getting the laboratory method into operation
in the plant. The British scientist was often at his best in experimental techniques where an imaginative flair had high value. These
traits were not, of course, exclusive or necessarily dominant all the
time, but they seemed to represent and partially explain some
major trends in the different establishments.

Such traits, identifiable in other fields, were linked with the
demands for specific answers that differed from one industry to
another. The margarine industry developed, quite spontaneously,
research into fundamental aspects of microbiology that were
essential to its competitive position *vis-à-vis* butter. The soap
industry was concerned with such problems as colour, scent,
lathering and the change in the nature of fabrics to be washed.
Different problems suggested different methods of approach.
Here, a steady systematic pursuit, there an imaginative flair.

Pretty well all the research done at Colworth had a fairly
definable commercial end, but it covered the whole spectrum of
enquiry, from basic to applied and development work. Many
ideas for new products evolved here. The limitation on their
appearance in the shops was the technical and marketing ability
of the selling companies, which found it difficult to keep up with
too many products. The dehydrated pea (and subsequently
dehydrated bean), for example, was the result of ten years' research
and development work at Colworth. These investigations had to

include a search for the right kind of fresh products, finally selecting only four out of twenty-one varieties tested. A new process which not only dried the pea but pricked each one in order to perfect rehydration had to be tested thoroughly by means of a pilot plant. Finally the production and marketing of the pea was handed over to a manufacturing company (Batchelor's), who installed a £2 million plant for commercial production, designed to run continuously during the height of the pea season. Thus was launched Surprise Peas, an entirely novel process and product with a current turnover by 1965 of £3 million.[1]

Port Sunlight demonstrated the same mixture of short-term and long-term research. Although lying originally in the fields of soap and detergents, its work came to be defined more broadly as 'surface physics and chemistry'. Increasingly this led the Port Sunlight scientists into fields other than soap and detergents, notably into chemicals. Research was divided into four areas— a basic research area, without specific targets; product development, for new products and the improvement of existing products; process development, for new processes and the improvement of processes; and product appraisal, to survey social conditions and the preference of consumers, so that these could be translated into terms of products. Computers were used in many of these aspects of research, but particularly in the process known as Programme Evaluation and Review Technique—an unwieldy phrase for a simple idea; briefly the planning not only of research projects but of research, development and marketing projects so that operations were carried out in the most logical and economical fashion. Here again was a method that began in wartime (to assist the U.S. Navy to plan such operations as landings) and was now transferred to the economic problems of society in peacetime.

In all the laboratories it became evident that research was a seminal process, suggesting and creating new ideas which often carried their inventors a long way from where they began. At Port Sunlight a polymer resin was developed which proved valuable to the clothing trade as an adhesive for the interlining of garments. Other adhesives were passing on to the building trade for constructing prefabricated timber buildings. An emulsifier emerged, suitable for paint manufacture. Many of these new inventions and developments were patented and passed on to other industries. Others were retained for manufacture by Unilever companies.

[1] See Chapter 7, pages 174–5.

They illustrated the way in which research work could itself create the conditions for new economic diversification.

The debate on the nature of research within Unilever continued lively. The combatants ranged from those who—like many scientists—believed that research was likely to be the major producer of dynamic change and progress, to those who still saw the research scientist as the handmaiden of the market place. The debate must inevitably work itself out in terms of practical achievements. Undoubtedly the problems of organization and decision posed by research constituted an increasing challenge to the top management of a company like Unilever. Were there enough new products? Were new products getting through to the market at the right pace? Were the arrangements for securing and patenting new products adequate?—this last was almost a novel problem for a group of companies which in the days before the war had relatively little belief in, or need for, patents. Were the research establishments themselves organized by the best people in the best way? Were they approaching the problems of research in the ways most likely to yield fruitful and profitable results? Was research a bottomless well of invention or merely a bottomless pit of expense? How should money, resources and perhaps most important of all, men, be allocated in this colossal gamble called research?

Nobody expected that complete answers were likely to be produced to these questions, but a few points became plain. First of all, while scientists of very ordinary talents could serve a valuable purpose as members of a well-organized team, nothing less than the very best scientific brains should be entrusted with the shaping and execution of scientific research policy and organization. Secondly, the need was increasingly recognized for the arrangement and grouping of scientific problems into 'areas of study'. Individual and unrelated subjects of research led nowhere. 'There is nothing vague about research objectives', said Ir H. B. Peteri, Head of Research, Continental Europe, in 1964. 'If the objectives cannot be described clearly the chance of success is remote. No success comes by chance.' The new arrangements for research therefore aimed at ensuring that specific enquiry took place within a broad area of investigation which kept all those individuals concerned in it alive not merely to their own problems but to the related problems of fellow workers. The diagram opposite illustrates this kind of organization as it was worked out at Port Sunlight. Progress in research organization depended upon experience, and experience necessarily contained a considerable element of the empirical. Organizations had to be kept flexible and individuals kept lively. The fundamental problem of how closely research ought to be geared to marketing admitted of no simple or single answer. It was determined in each area according to the nature of markets and indeed sometimes of personalities. There was no precise answer to the question, how profitable has this or that particular piece of research proved? Here and there the results were perfectly obvious. It could be shown that a new flavour to a particular margarine was worth £x millions. But the economies and profits from research were not necessarily wholly revealed in new *products*. They might equally be manifested in cost-economies arising from new potentialities in raw materials. In other respects the whole movement of new thinking in Unilever has been towards reducing the areas of uncertainty and the increased use of mathematical techniques and even economic concepts where previously hunch ruled alone. Whatever the difficulties of achieving precise

TYPES OF SOAPS AND NON-SOAPY DETERGENTS FOR:

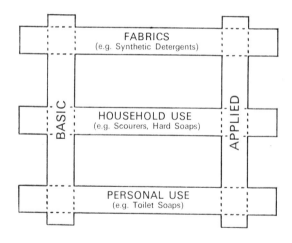

Each product group contains men from a variety of scientific disciplines. There are also the two groups doing general basic and applied research. There is constant interflow of ideas horizontally and vertically and men can be transferred from one to the other.

Figure 5

answers to the fundamental questions about research, nobody really doubted that research was taking its place along with marketing as one of the major dynamos of the oils and fats industries and the various other diversified industries that had become associated with them in the Unilever complex. At the least negatively, everyone knew that the research departments were indispensable for the maintenance of Unilever's position, and most people accepted that to maintain a position inevitably meant going forward to improve on it. However differently the relationship of research to the other activities of the business might be envisaged, nobody doubted that research had become a vital part of the competitive equipment of Unilever in the battle of trade.

Technology is defined by the Oxford Dictionary as 'the scientific study of the practical or industrial arts'. It constitutes one of the major forces deployed by modern industry, the other being the nucleus of commercial skills that come under the name 'marketing'. The distance separating technology from research into the principles that govern the character of scientific phenomena varies enormously from one industry to another. Within Unilever the two were closely associated. In the United States research (as we have said) was almost exclusively directed towards immediately practical objectives. In England and the Netherlands, Port Sunlight and Vlaardingen both carried their enquiries fairly deeply into fundamental aspects of science vitally important to the industries they serve. It must always be a matter of judgment how far an industry would benefit from a greater or lesser degree of latitude in its laboratories. But nowhere in Unilever were the two aspects divorced. In any case, much new knowledge was generated beyond the fringe of basic research; it proved a common experience of Unilever scientists and technologists that important problems arose between the research laboratory, the pilot plant when a new invention was tested and the full production plant. The technologist was ceasing to be merely a rich relation of the poor research scientist: he was himself becoming an important source of knowledge.

In the post-war years, when demand was running at a level unprecedented in history, when labour was everywhere scarce and when wartime experience had demonstrated so many spectacular applications of science, technology assumed a new and increased importance. Industry entered a new phase of activity to which only perhaps the first industrial revolution could be compared, so dramatic was the impact on the growth and distribution of social wealth. Unilever, as has been shown in this and preceding volumes, had inherited from the past a relatively simple technology. Its progress historically had been due more to commercial than to technological ingenuity, but now Unilever joined the great commercial and scientific industries in placing a new emphasis upon technological change and innovation. The voice of science and technology was strengthened at the top. By 1965 the Board of Directors included six scientists. (A Vice-Chairman of Unilever Limited and third member of the Special Committee triumvirate was Dr E. G. Woodroofe.[1] Mr R. G. Jurgens, a Vice-Chairman of Unilever N.V., and Dr E. Smit, both graduates of the University of Amsterdam, were contact directors, and Mr J. G. Collingwood, a graduate of University College, London, was Head of Research Division. The Director of Technical Division was Mr A. F. H. Blaauw and he and Mr G. D. A. Klijnstra, another director, were both graduates of the Delft Technical University.)

Essentially, the expansion of the Unilever industries depended upon those technologies immediately related to the manufacturing process; but these were in turn enveloped in an outer cocoon of technologies such as engineering and transport. For example, Unilever depended upon the transport of raw materials from all parts of the world to factories located in forty different countries. Copra from the Philippines had to be carried 9,000 miles to Western Europe, palm oil nearly as far from Indonesia, ground nuts 5,000 miles from West Africa, and wood pulp 1,000 miles from Sweden. Efficiency of transport, the Chairmen said in 1955, was 'as important to Unilever as efficiency of manufacture'. If production was to be economical, smooth flow was essential. This could only be achieved if raw materials flowed in and manufactures flowed out at an even rate. Yet demand varied from week to week. Hence an investment in transport and handling equipment to achieve the flow inwards, plus a buffer system of warehouses and depots to achieve the flow outwards, valued in 1955 at £18 million, or about 15 per cent of Unilever's total investment in manufacturing and distribution facilities. Rapid services of the latest kinds of insulated vehicles were essential to the distribution of margarine, where delays and exposure to varied temperatures could be fatal. Hence also the introduction of such revolutionary methods as the fork-lift truck and the pallet,

[1] See supra, page 25.

which helped to move and store goods more efficiently and cheaply. Such innovations were vital if the economies of large-scale manufacturing were not to be lost. Most of them came from outside Unilever, though here and there Unilever made useful adaptations designed to meet its own needs.

The same was true of such devices for automatic control as computers. By the 1960s Unilever was using computers on a considerable scale throughout its world business. Here again Unilever was very largely drawing upon external experience. The computer, a distinguished physicist has said, 'can do for thought what the steam engine did for muscle'.[1] The steam engine did not do anything that could not be done by men, horses or windmills, but it did it more cheaply and on a larger scale. The job of the computer was to relieve men of tasks they could do for themselves but only at the expense of vast amounts of money or of scarce labour. The computer could carry out any mental task that could be precisely defined. It was therefore an indispensable part of any system of automatic control of production or distribution of goods, capable of saving both manual and clerical labour on an heroic scale. Again here was an outside invention which Unilever proceeded to adapt to its own needs. These 'outer' technologies, however, could be distinguished from those 'inner' technologies of manufacturing where the Unilever contribution was of a different order. The largest field here remained the general technology of oils and fats.

Throughout the entire spectrum that began with the expelling and extracting of raw materials and ended with completed products, the manufacturing processes of Unilever oils and fats section went through an important series of improvements in the post-war years. Oil is obtained from oil seeds either by squeezing them or dissolving them. Both processes have undergone important changes in recent times. The 'solvent extraction' process was developed for the latter. In the former, the so-called high pressure 'expellers' replaced the old hydraulic presses. In many ways efficient, the old hydraulic process meant hard, dirty and uncongenial work for the men who operated it, and considerations of welfare played a large part in the development of the expeller. This was rather like a vast mincing machine, in which the prepared

---

[1] 'The Language of Machines' by Professor Sir Edward Bullard in *Endeavour*, vol. XXIII, no. 90, September 1964. This is the best short description of the computer's function available.

seed was forced along the barrel by a rotating screw. Expellers had been used on the Continent for some years. The first one came into operation in the Unilever Oil Milling Group in the United Kingdom in 1942. By the 1950s the old hydraulic presses had nearly all gone. The oil mill became cleaner, brighter and tidier. The capital cost was high, but labour was saved, processing costs dropped and the product improved; instead of emerging in 10-lb. slabs, it emerged in fragments ready to be filled into bags or moved in bulk. It kept down the cost of foodstuffs to the farmer and therefore ultimately to the consumer. It hastened, on the other hand, the decline of the oil mill in Western Europe, for it was gradually adopted by the countries producing oil-bearing seeds (mostly extra-European) who saw it as a means of raising the value of their own economies.

The next stage of the process was the treatment of crude oil, which had to be refined, neutralized, bleached and deodorized. At each of these stages there had been losses, not only of oil but of by-products. Technological advances since the war have substantially cut down these losses, at the same time developing new by-products which are of great value in food manufacture. Where the neutralization process was employed continuously on the same type of raw materials, new centrifugal machinery could be used which occupied a much smaller space, operated continuously under automatic control, and led to better oil yields. Nor were new technological methods always the exclusive product of the central research institutions. One radical advance in oil refining promising substantial savings of costs, for example, came out of the relatively small Kunerol factory in Vienna. It was largely the work of the local Unilever scientist disposing of only slender resources, and it illustrated vividly the benefits to be derived from co-operation between the central research services and the operating companies.

The hardening of liquid oils had become possible with the Normann invention of 1910. It involved the use of a catalyst and recent work in the Unilever laboratories focused on making the catalyst more selective. Special methods for producing hydrogen improved the hardening process. Closely connected with this were enquiries into the nature of the texture of margarine. These made it clear that the plasticity of a fat depended upon the chemical combinations of glycerine and fatty acids. By the use of alkaline catalysts these chemical combinations were rearranged so as to make it possible to use oils and fats which in earlier times would have been unusable. Scarce and costly fats could therefore be supplemented by commoner and cheaper fats. The variety of 'starting materials' thus became almost unlimited. Yet there were scores of practical problems of plant and process to be conquered before *basic* knowledge could be deployed to revolutionize the manufacturing process. The methods of preparing the margarine emulsion, cooling it, giving it a uniform texture and packing, were gradually moulded into a continuous and totally enclosed system of production which could manufacture margarine from a widening range of such raw materials as might be available, with predictable and uniform characteristics. In Continental markets the new processes were particularly valuable, for here a growing proportion of consumers liked an unsalted margarine. To keep such a margarine fresh in the shop had always been a problem. Now under the new conditions of manufacture which excluded air and slowed down the process of deterioration it could be produced and marketed without difficulty. Factories were remodelled. The trend, already strong, towards supplying ever larger areas from ever larger factories received another strong boost.

Thus while the scientists were busy identifying the chemical elements of 'flavour', manufacturing technology was being adapted for a new phase in the age-long competition with butter. Levels of salt flavouring were steadily reduced, desirable butter flavours were produced by synthesis, together with others based on the 'trace' components which had been found responsible for the characteristic 'butter flavour'. This in turn opened up a new area of enquiry which was important to the entire complex of Unilever food industries. Flavour came to be recognized not merely as an emotive force but as something which was firmly bedded in a matrix of chemical structure. Here was a technology closely connected with the technology of perfumery but far more complex. One of its many aspects was the detection and analysis of so-called 'off flavours'. Closely connected with this problem of 'off flavours' was the development of packaging which preserved the new and improved flavours. Such were the technological preliminaries necessary before the housewife could be invited to say whether she could tell margarine from butter.

This growing body of technological knowledge meant that Unilever could enter other manufacturing operations not only to supply its own needs but for other industrial users. The chocolate confectionery and biscuit industries, for example, needed a fat which, while normally hard, would melt rapidly in the mouth. In the past such fats had been produced by allowing natural fats to solidify slowly. They were then pressed in woollen bags to expel the liquid fraction. The new process called 'solvent fractionation', developed simultaneously in the United Kingdom and on the Continent, enabled Unilever scientists by 1956 to set up experimental plants at Port Sunlight and Vlaardingen to produce such a fat from other vegetable oils. From this there emerged large plants operating a continuous process at a cost of £1·6 million in Britain and Holland. This modern plant, almost entirely automatic, was controlled by a foreman and two operators. It replaced the old 'press house' which had employed one foreman and thirty operatives. It produced three times as much and to more refined specification than had even been possible before.

Simultaneously Price's plant at Bromborough, previously largely a manufacturer of candles and glycerine, developed a new series of products.[1] The first stimulus to the new phase was the war, which cut off supplies of products from Germany essential to the manufacturers of greases and lubricants. Then in 1951 came innovations in the isolation of fatty acids which gave rise to a whole range of oleo-chemicals necessary for a variety of manufacturing industries—textiles, leather, cosmetics, lubricants, plastics, polishes, stencils, pharmaceuticals, and so on. The development of these fatty-acid products became increasingly important[2] as the amount of fatty acids produced by the margarine industry increased, while the proportion formerly absorbed by soap-making dropped with the coming of synthetic detergents.

The synthetic detergent dated back to the pre-war years. It had long been recognized that in areas of hard water natural soap was a relatively inefficient product. This had stimulated attempts to find a synthetic compound which would not form insoluble deposits in the shape of a scum when used in hard water, as natural soap did. Pre-war experiments were not very successful. In any case they were interrupted by the war. Immediately after the war further development in the United States produced a very different and much superior synthetic product as good as soap in soft water and much better in hard water. It could be produced in bulk by a continuous process, spray-dried in large towers.

[1] See Chapter 7, pages 176–82 and Chapter 8, pages 196–7 for the development of Unilever's chemical interests.

[2] See below page 179. The decline of natural soap-making proved less rapid in practice than had at one time been predicted. See Fig. 13.

Yet here Unilever, and even Lever Brothers Company in the United States, proved uncompetitive. Shortages of materials and men in Europe and too slow a realization that the new technology was as essential a part of the competitive apparatus as marketing methods, left them a long way behind their competitors in the United States and elsewhere. The haul to catch up was a long one, but by 1950 Lever Brothers Company had brought into production their first spray-drying plant. Three others followed, in St. Louis, in Hammond, Indiana, and at Lever Brothers Ltd. in Canada. Elsewhere Unilever was still hampered by the shortage of essential raw materials, by financial restrictions, and the problems of restoring war-damaged plant. European experiments were unsuccessful. The life of Wisk, a powder launched in September 1948, was short and dismal. Only from 1952 onwards were the new non-soapy detergent powders successfully launched in Europe—first in Britain, France and Holland, then more widely in Europe, and finally throughout the entire Unilever organization.

The main active ingredient for the new product came from the petro-chemical industry and was processed in Unilever's own factories. For the first time Unilever found itself unavoidably involved in a world of chemical technology, presenting an entire range of new problems unknown to the former technology of oils and fats. These problems rapidly proliferated, for each particular market proved to demand its own kind of non-soapy detergent. New washing machines used in Europe demanded detergent products with immediate and low lathering properties. Africa, Asia and South America, where housewives washed with cold and often soft water, needed high lathering formulae. The highly sophisticated markets of the United States had more specialized demands. One new product was a tablet which was designed to dissolve rapidly in lukewarm water. Its success was limited, for its cost was very high. Another was a concentrated liquid detergent which was supposed to replace the so-called heavy-duty detergent.[1] Yet another was for use in cold water and was successful. An important market proved to be for a liquid dishwashing detergent to clean crockery, glassware and cutlery. This market was first explored in North America, later in Europe and the Commonwealth.

Thus, after a long period of initial difficulties, synthetic detergents gradually invaded and conquered many of the markets for

[1] See below, page 232.

soap-based products. There were still less affluent markets where soap held its own for economic reasons. Britain was slower to respond than the United States. There virtually only one last main stronghold remained—the toilet soap market. Here it proved difficult to achieve the right properties at reasonable cost in a synthetic formula. The ring round the bathtub seemed for long to defeat all the wiles of science. In America, Lever Brothers' Dove, a fully synthetic toilet soap, had a considerable success. But again it was costly—too costly perhaps for less affluent markets.

Though superior to any soap in many ways, synthetic detergents presented one very serious problem: they formed great masses of foam in sewage systems and rivers. In the late 1950s it became apparent that this problem of effluent disposal was a serious one, especially where river water was being used for domestic water supplies. Unilever, like the other detergent producers, had to concentrate considerable effort to overcome this problem. New processes were designed and by 1965 at least three countries—the United States, the United Kingdom and Germany—were using more 'bio-degradable' detergents, that is detergents which were easily broken down biologically in sewers and rivers, and did not interfere with the working of the public sewage system.

The age of synthetic detergents brought other problems. As early as 1953 the Chairmen pointed out that the rapid increase in margarine production had led to an increasing supply of fatty acids at a time when soap-making was contracting. These inedible residues had made an excellent element in natural soap-making. Now there was a superabundance of refinery fatty acids in Europe. Market prices were falling. Hence the need to find new outlets for fatty acids. The other obvious consequence was to accelerate the search for economies and improvements in natural soap-making. In 1945 soap was still made by the same method used in Port Sunlight at the time of its foundation. Soap pans were large and expensive. Manufacture in batches called for sudden demands for steam which were highly uneconomic. If a continuous process, reliably controlled, could be devised, more consistent qualities would be possible, together with large savings in labour and steam. Crosfield's at Warrington, who made Persil soap powder, were the first to develop new methods for the washing of glycerine from soap. The horizontal pans were replaced by continuous vertical trays embodied in a tower. The costs still remained high.

Meanwhile two other Unilever companies, at Port Sunlight

G

and in Norway, were working independently on the same problem. They developed a technique known as the divided pan unit and this in turn was refined by the Unilever Australian company into a highly manageable system. Crosfield's had meantime developed a system of washing 15 tons of soap per hour and extracting a very high percentage of glycerine in the process. Thus patient enquiry, empirical experiment and a growing knowledge of the physico-chemical principles involved steadily transformed the soap industry into a compact, continuous, fully-enclosed manufacturing process, based on scientific controls. The quality of the soap manufactured came under constant scientific scrutiny. It was no longer dependent as it had been for centuries on the skill of the individual soap boiler. Plant was made in stainless steel and the product was whiter and cleaner. Thus the natural soap-makers managed to hang on to a diminishing market with lower costs, more flexible raw-material formulae and better profits.

Meanwhile Unilever was putting its eggs into several new baskets. Each contained potential profits and actual problems. Amongst these forms of diversification the largest was food—prepared and preserved. Foods were preserved in three ways: by canning, by freezing and by drying. From an earlier age Unilever had inherited an interest in the canning process. Quick-freezing and drying were known before the war in principle. (Accelerated freeze-drying was first used to preserve blood plasma for transfusion. Drying sprang out of the production of dried vegetables for the armed services during the war.) After the war Unilever acquired a firm in the United States which produced dried soups in packets.[1] One was the famous Chicken Noodle soup which still forms the bulk of the dried soup business in nearly all the fifteen countries where Unilever markets this kind of product. Dried soups were followed by dried meals—curries, pastas and the like, providing a quick meal with the minimum of trouble.

There were several different kinds of drying. Some products lent themselves to one system, others to other systems. The right choice involved intricate test work to find out which type of preserving system most enhanced colour and flavour. In the freeze-drying process the product was first frozen and then placed in a vacuum. The ice in the tissues evaporated directly into water vapour and the tissues kept their shape and size with minimum

[1] See Chapter 10, page 235.

damage to their chemical structure. They could be rehydrated quickly so that the housewife only needed a matter of minutes to prepare a meal. The various Unilever research units in the United States, Continental Europe and at Aberdeen and Colworth House (Bedfordshire) in the United Kingdom put Unilever into the pioneer class with this type of product.

Surprise Peas were another major success when they were launched by Batchelor's in Britain,[1] and a similar product was introduced by Hindustan Lever at their factory in Ghaziabad.[2] Dried foods had the advantage that they found a ready market among housewives who did not own a refrigerator. Thus, preservation by drying represented enormous possibilities of food conservation and massive advantages to farmer and consumer. In the age of the 'population explosion', food saved was as good as food grown.

In another food-manufacturing enterprise, that of Wall's ice-cream, the main problem was to streamline production on a large scale. Wall's were anxious to find out how far they could apply automatic techniques of production in an industry where seasonal labour was scarce and where there appeared to be a rising future demand for a standard product. So far ice-cream had been made on a 'batch' basis. The methods employed left much to be desired in accuracy and consistency. Here again, if the process could be made continuous and controlled there were large savings on costs and great improvements in quality might be expected. To these objectives the Wall's team, in conjunction with Unilever Technical Division, addressed itself in the 1950s. The target was to have a new plant at Gloucester in full automatic production for the 1960 season. In spite of obstacles the date was kept. The new system worked well; a similar method was applied also at the Langnese factory built to supply the southern half of Unilever's ice-cream market in Germany. Substantial savings in cost (especially in heat extraction and labour) were achieved, though at Gloucester the idea of simple standard products had to give way to a rather more complex pattern of products, which limited the possibilities of automatic control. Both factories nevertheless proved remarkable experiments in continuous automatic production.

The pressures which accelerated the search for technological improvements in these years were many and varied. They included (as in the case of margarine) the need to produce an improved product, to reduce the cost of an existing product (as in the case of

[1] See above, page 73.   [2] See Chapter 10, page 240.

soap) or to launch an entirely new product (as in the case of
synthetic washing powders). Throughout the whole gamut of
Unilever production it was vital to reduce costs and save the most
scarce and dear commodity of all: labour. Sometimes welfare
entered into the policy of change. Employers and employees both
welcomed new processes that ended the need for disagreeable and
unhygienic manual tasks.

All in all, the new technology made the arguments for large-
scale production irresistible, even where in the past the size of a
market and the need for transport over large areas had in earlier
days suggested a multiple system of factories. 'We find' said the
Chairmen in 1955, 'that provided adequate transport facilities
exist, the economies we can reap from large-scale production tend
to be greater than any saving we may achieve on transport. Thus we
tend to concentrate production in single units.' Canada was a
classic case of a market that seemed geographically so large and
underpopulated that to serve it Lever had built up a chain of
works stretching right across the country—one in St. Stephen,
three in Toronto, one in Winnipeg, one in Calgary, one in Vancouver and one in Victoria.[1] Over the years these had become
reduced to four. Now they were concentrated into a single
national factory and Vancouver obtained its margarine from
Toronto, nearly 3,000 miles away. Everywhere new or remodelled
factories designed for larger and larger production bore out the
truth of the Chairmen's argument. It worked in another direction
too. The capital costs associated with the new plant, automatic
control, continuous processing, and the like, were very high—so
high that they were only justified if they were worked on a sufficiently intensive scale. The fixed capital costs therefore became in
themselves a reason for more concentrated production.

The significance of the new technological advance did not stop
there. Each advance in scientific knowledge underlined the
essentially *chemical* character of the detergent industry, and the
combination of chemical and biological elements that entered into
the food industries. The point has already been made that the
impact of the new synthetic processes of manufacturing detergents
removed or diminished a principal market for the fatty-acid by-
products of the edible-fat industry.[2] It thereby stimulated the
search for alternative markets, and in turn emphasized the need
for more chemical knowledge.

[1] See also page 247.   [2] See page 83.

Thus in various ways the technology of oils and fats and of the various foods in which Unilever was concerned became a generating force. The emergence of a coherent body of technological knowledge was an increasingly important influence on those responsible for co-ordinating policy on new investment in Unilever. The finger pointed in fact very clearly towards those doors marked 'chemicals' and 'foods'.

By 1965 nobody could doubt that Unilever had passed through a new phase of management thinking. Technology had become built into Unilever's industries, not merely as a useful ancillary to progress, but as a dynamic, creative force. Yet this did not mean that the older importance of commercial skills, so long characteristic of Unilever, was in any way diminished. On the contrary, if the two post-war decades had a lesson to teach it was that technology which was not married to market opportunity might be an extravagant waste of time and money. Most of the technology surveyed here was closely related to the known tastes, preferences and pockets of consumers. But any failure in the liaison could prove very expensive. The cost of launching a new product, now all the higher in an age of genuine mass production, was so great that every step that could be taken to reduce the element of luck had to be taken.

A single example showed that in business as in surgery the operator might achieve a technical success: the patient might still not recover. Unilever had long been interested in the toothpaste market, and was therefore concerned with problems of dental decay. In the middle 1950s Unilever scientists investigating dental caries in children confirmed the traditional belief that an apple eaten immediately after a meal reduced dental decay. Could the process be reproduced synthetically? The final result of much testing and research was a tablet (marketed under the name Dentabs) which stimulated saliva and washed away food debris without damaging the teeth. Clinical trials amongst children verified the hypothesis that such a cleansing agent used after eating could reduce dental decay. Dentabs were test-marketed in 1960. Market research showed that they had made a considerable impact and won a considerable measure of approval. Alas, only one thing was wrong. Dentabs did not sell. The habit of teeth brushing (which after all Unilever had itself helped to build up over the years by very heavy advertising expenditure) was too firmly rooted to be shaken by a new product which was fairly expensive to buy and was not in any case intended to replace the toothbrush entirely. As a commercial venture they were a failure and the failure seemed to lie in an inadequate appreciation of the marketing factors arising from a new technology. The incident underscored the moral: that the marriage of research to commercial awareness must be permanent, continuous and indissoluble.

In the 1960s a technique which had originally been developed for the Polaris project in America came into prominence as a means of achieving this integration. In a situation where the launching of even a relatively simple product involved complex decisions, continuous teamwork and mutual understanding between many different departments from development to sales, network analysis provided a logical and authoritative framework for their various activities. The basic consideration was that whether you were doing something as simple as making a cup of tea or as complicated as constructing a new plant to make an oleo-chemical product there was a logical and a less logical order in which you could carry out the operation. Money, time and resources of all kinds would be saved by following the logical order. Network analysis, in short, merely meant planning the order of events before the project was undertaken rather than waiting for muddles to show up in practice.

Applied to a new product, network analysis was designed to show up all the activities involved in the project and their interdependence. These were set out in a diagram which represented the order in which the different parts of the plan should be executed and the logical sequence of these events. The direction of the arrows indicated the logical flow of work. A typical project might involve one of the Unilever research laboratories which would be concerned with formulating the product, preparing it experimentally for tests, testing the processing methods, the 'storage life' of the product and the best type of packaging. Next would come the development department of a factory which would work with the research laboratory in experimental processing and the design and planning of pilot and full plant. The raw material department would be involved with the specification of ingredients. Packaging experts would investigate more closely the right type and size of pack. The brands department would define the market objective and the strategy for marketing the product. They would also select the test market area and the amount of the product required together with the sales department. Together with the advertising agency they would select the brand name. Many other activities would have to be worked in at the same time, for example the legal requirements for printed declarations on the package.

The essence of network analysis was logic applied to industrial planning. It was not a *nostrum* that solved all the different problems nor was it a substitute for thought, but properly used (and by 1965 something like two-thirds of Unilever firms were making use of the technique) it could help to clarify the complex relations between specialist departments created by the ever-growing division of function in modern business organization. In short, this was a logical way of trying to put together again the Humpty Dumpty that had once been the old simple business partnership between the man who made the product and the man who sold it.

CHAPTER 5

MARKETS

IT has become currently fashionable since 1945 to speak as if science, technology and technological innovation were the sole determinant of economic and business progress. This is a less than half true judgment, and a dangerous one. Undirected or misdirected scientific enquiry can be as wasteful in industry as elsewhere. For many things that are scientifically interesting, novel, and remarkable are unsaleable or, at any rate, uneconomic. At all stages the prime task of the well-managed business ever since the Industrial Revolution, and maybe before, has been to keep the scientific or technological aspect of its affairs as closely integrated as possible with commercial opportunity. The Chairman of the Unilever Company responsible for the manufacture and marketing of detergents in the U.K. put it thus: 'I wonder if we are not in danger of breaking our hearts trying to sell what we can make rather than trying to make what we can sell.'[1] The thought was worth pondering in relation not merely to Unilever but to the British economy as a whole.

It is this kind of division of function which had been handed down to the infinitely more complex business organizations of the present day. But the principle remains precisely the same. Articles have to be manufactured; they have to be sold. The second part of the process is not less important than the former, with which it must always be most closely associated. As Alfred Marshall, the Cambridge economist, once wrote: 'The marketing man is continually forecasting future developments of demand, endeavouring to turn to account the rising force of new methods of production to supply something which can be produced in large quantities at a low cost and so force its way into general consumption.'[2] The qualities of mind and character which created first the British and later many other industrial economies were focused as much on the marketing as on the production problems of business, though

[1] Address by Mr E. Brough to the Market Research Society on 15 June 1967.
[2] *Industry and Trade*. A. Marshall, Macmillan, 1932, page 47.

they have for some curious reason never been examined or valued as much as the associated technological virtues.

In the twentieth-century company, the personal hunch of a Bentley or a Matthew Boulton or a William Lever or a Sam Van den Bergh has given way to a more bureaucratic and complex organization. Here, attempted scientific analysis and a proliferating division of functions has replaced individual intuition and experience. The aim is greater precision of measurement and production. Whether this is generally achieved is still open to question. The developing organization of the past twenty years which is described below can record more impressive achievements. It must also confess to some resounding flops. But comparison with the past is impossible because the evidence for such comparisons is largely non-existent. Even if it were available, this kind of historical test, however interesting, is of little real value. The immediate problem is one of the conditions of the 1960s. Whether we like it or not, the methods a modern business employs cannot be those of the 1780s or even the 1880s. The increasing complexity of production and marketing and the vast expansion of markets as well as the rising expense of innovations, means that the division of labour must increasingly be a controlling principle of business. Marketing, then, must comprise or utilize an increasing range of specialized activities and skills—market research, product development, advertising, transport, distribution, printing, packaging, labelling, merchandising, selling. The co-ordination of all these specialized activities into a meaningful strategy designed to attract and satisfy the consumer and ensure maximum long-term profits to the business, must be a constant preoccupation of the topmost management.

'The old concept of selling,' wrote A. W. J. Caron,[1] 'the idea that "the consumer can be persuaded to buy almost anything"— has given way to the contemporary concept of marketing—"let us find out what the consumer really wants". Industry is now employing economists, sociologists, statisticians and psychologists to analyse and predict consumer demand, and only after such a demand has been tested in the market is it finally decided to tie up capital in building factories and in transport and distribution of the product. In this atmosphere of intelligently searching for, creating and then supplying demand over-expansion is less likely to become a general feature of the economy.'

[1] *Progress*, I (1964).

Of all the activities which came to comprise the general activity of marketing, market research was the most novel, in the sense that it not only intruded upon all the other aspects of marketing, but aimed most overtly at increased precision through scientific method. An element of market research has always existed in an empirical way in most industries manufacturing for a mass market. William Lever knew his market of housewives from his early experience as a Lancashire grocer. A great part of his correspondence with his subordinates was devoted to exhorting them to see how best they could achieve 'hypnotic effects' with special advertising. 'The whole object' was to 'build a halo round the article.' A continual stream of lectures on the social habits of the consumers was directed at his salesmen. It was from this social knowledge of the market and, hardly less, of the structure of the industry and the grocery trade, that success came. Even so, it was Lever who made the classic admission that one half of all advertising expenditure was wasted, but the trouble was (as he added) no one knew which half. Scientific methods of enquiry were designed to reduce, if not eliminate, precisely this uncertainty.

The task of the market researcher was to help the men who made and advertised products by providing them with information about the probable impact of any particular commodity upon a particular market. His prime business was therefore to try to predict what consumers would like and prefer, and this meant not only scrutinizing the product or the proposed product but also the social structure and the psychology of the consumers themselves. Sometimes it would be a marketing company or an advertiser who wanted to know what the reaction to a product or an advertisement was likely to be. At other times it was the researcher or producer who wanted to know whether his new idea could be translated into a profitable real commodity.

The need for such research was felt in Unilever in the early 1930s, before there were any outside market research agencies. In the early days market research was merely one part of the activities of a private advertising agency called Lintas (Levers International Advertising Service), which had developed out of the smaller agency set up by Lever Brothers in 1929 to run their advertising campaigns. By 1948 the demand for these services led to the formation of a special division in London, separate from Lintas. This continued to be the main centre of Unilever market research in the United Kingdom until 1962, when the growing work of this section was transferred to a special research bureau co-ordinating all market research activities. Outside the United Kingdom, market research units existed in most of the larger countries. Elsewhere market research was provided from outside agencies.

The normal work of a market research department fell into two broad categories. In the 'field surveys' expert investigators collected evidence from consumers on their responses to products both new and old. They included not only the housewives who bought the largest volume of Unilever products for the home, but also the farmers, doctors, dentists, dieticians and representatives of other industries, all of whom were concerned with Unilever foods, animal and human, toothpaste and chemicals and technical products. Other departments carried out the work of processing and interpreting data collected from the field surveys.

Given the wide spectrum of differing social conditions within which a business like Unilever had to operate, there must be a wide variety of enquiries each appropriate to the society which it investigated. To obtain a reliable picture of future prospects Unilever had not only encouraged its own research departments to undertake enquiries for other industries but also employed outside market research advisers whose experience covered a larger area than that of its own products. The United States, where consumers were generally more responsive to novelty and change than those of the Old World, assumed a natural lead in the science of marketing.[1] Here it was easier to sell a product for the first time than anywhere else in the world. But this meant that 'loyalty' to older products was less strong. It was harder to hold the existing market. All this was the mark of a society where immigration, geographical movement, social mobility and a moving frontier were historical facts. It was here that the possibilities and limitations of market research emerged most clearly; for example, some products, like scents, depend on an irrational choice by the buyer that defies further analysis; others, like household cleaning materials, are more susceptible to systematic enquiry, analysis and interpretation.

Many of these post-war developments in marketing derived in the United States from techniques introduced in the first place during the war. The American armed services made greater use than any others of the social as well as the physical sciences. With the peace many a scientific sword was beaten into a psychological

[1] See Chapter 10, pp. 231–2 et seq.

plough-share. Mathematical techniques for measuring morale turned into techniques for measuring advertising efficiency. As the costs of research, inventions, development, production and advertising all grew, the North American market was compelled to cast about for means of reducing the enormous capital at risk when a new product was introduced to the consumer. The outlay for advertising or promoting a new brand of toothpaste, margarine or detergent in its first year might run anywhere from $6 million to $30 million. With capital of this magnitude at stake, methods for reducing risk proliferated, especially during the past two decades.

Many ideas for new products failed to survive the rigorous testing to which they were submitted: to be precise about 9 out of 10. Different companies in Unilever developed a number of specialized techniques to help them reach decisions in marketing. The so-called Pa$$ Technique aimed to put the idea of a new product to the consumer *before development* to see what the putative reaction would be before too much capital outlay became involved. Another device was the O.A.T.S. (On Air Testing Service), designed to find from the subsequent behaviour of customers whether a specific television advertisement did or did not change opinion about a product. The so-called 'dynamic difference' analysis tried to assess the effect which different types and levels of advertising expenditure produced on the share of the market held by the investing company.[1] All these devices were designed to reduce ultimately the necessity for the so-called 'test marketing' to the inescapable minimum. For test marketing (the launching of a specific product in a specific experimental area), though a valuable device for reducing risk, was itself costly. It also increased the time taken to get such products from the laboratory into the market. If this time and cost could be reduced, the competitive power of the business might be increased and the risk of other competitors taking advantage of a new idea correspondingly diminished.

For the most part, the highly sophisticated markets of the world, enjoying high standards of living, mass education and a high level of material ambition amongst the population, were characterized in these years by refinements in the kind of products Unilever sold, rather than by revolutionary innovations. Colour, shape, smell,

---

[1] This particular 'model' has received strong support from empirical tests of historical data carried out in a large number of markets.

taste, price—all these were attributes to be exploited by the marketing experts to give the business an advantage over competitors. Inevitably the refinements seemed to be becoming increasingly marginal. Here and there a new invention might still produce a total novelty such as the synthetic detergent or the detergent which pitted its merit of making no suds against the older merit of making much suds or the detergent that could be used in cold water, and so on. The marketing expert might even have to envisage such possibilities as disposable clothing which would abolish or reduce the need for detergents, and suggest diversification into the manufacture of such textiles. In foods and chemicals, possible new products deriving from biological and biochemical knowledge were infinite—but remote. At the opposite end of the spectrum another possibility seemed to be ultimate stabilization-through-boredom—boredom with the values which at present control everyday purchases of such things as detergents, toothpastes, after-shave lotions and so on. But this again remained a remote future. Tests suggested, for example, that customers were often unaware of anything less than really major price differences between one product and another. The classic theory that customers go where the goods are cheapest was becoming less reliable in an affluent, impressionable society. The perennial object was to exploit the consumer's desire for satisfaction in a world where now every competitor worth the name was doing exactly the same thing. This resulted in a mass of minor product refinements, limited only by the restrictions of taste or of law.

The enormous volume of data and the increasing complexity of the whole marketing operation demanded ever more refined methods of reducing risks and predicting future market trends and opportunities. Hence the use of marketing models based on mathematical techniques, increasingly with the aid of computers.

In the less developed markets, where tastes were simpler and pockets less full, the pace was a trifle less hot. Yet even here the manufacturer lived in a shrinking world. The impetus given to industrial competition through business efficiency and advertising and perhaps through a new set of material values was being felt. William Lever's own advertising ideas even in the 1880s and 1890s were powerfully influenced by what he learned on his journeys in the United States. These influences were now penetrating not only Europe but Africa too. Two American developments had an immediate effect upon Unilever's methods of presenting, naming and advertising its products. American industries like Procter and Gamble or Colgate-Palmolive, operating from a powerful home base, were spreading over other continents old and new. Their highly centralized character was in strong contrast to that of Unilever, the aggregate of a very large number of businesses which had grown together through a long process of competition and ultimate combination spread over nearly a century. A major Unilever task has been at various times in history to reduce and co-ordinate the very large number of individual products with different names sold through the individual companies which make up the whole called Unilever. It was by conducting such an enquiry with conspicuous success that Geoffrey Heyworth first made his reputation in the 1930s.

From the 1950s a somewhat similar situation recurred. In order to compete effectively upon international markets with a few products of high excellence known to millions by a single brand name, Unilever had to undertake some more energetic streamlining. The process was far from simple: something sold in a local market by an individual firm within Unilever might still have great value. A brand might be supported by local patriotism and recollection of older and easier times. One of the tasks of the 'co-ordinators' appointed in 1962 was to deal with this proliferation of local brands. It was a task of persuasion rather than compulsion. Nor was the traffic in persuasion entirely from centre to periphery. If the tide seemed to have turned against the doctrine[1] that the best way to manage Unilever was simply to leave the operating companies to get on with their job by themselves; if a larger measure of centralized control seemed to be suggested by this world trend of competition; yet still the need for local knowledge and initiative remained.

What changed was the form which this initiative took. As the world became—sadly—more uniform in its tastes and habits, Unilever had to make sure that its products were not only labelled as far as possible with the same names everywhere, but that they represented the same qualities. The opportunities for doing this, as well as the limitations on doing it, must nevertheless be assessed by the local manager. Only he could say whether a particular product was likely to be successful in his particular area; or whether politics, social taboos, xenophobia or taxation of this or that commodity made it a bad bet. Even in Europe the

[1] See *The History of Unilever*, vol. II, page 380.

conservatism, rational as well as customary, of, for example, the French consumer had to be taken into account. So had the greater responsiveness of Swedish society to American patterns of living. Nevertheless, just as regional brands gave way to national brands in the first half of the twentieth century, national brands seemed to be losing ground to international brands in the second half.

Such considerations as these had led to the establishment in 1960 of the International Package Design Committee. Its purpose was to provide as broad a basis as possible for the development and adoption of truly international pack designs.

The second development was likewise of American provenance. We have shown elsewhere[1] how the growth of great chains of retail stores, supermarkets and self-service shops formed part of the economic context in which Unilever as a producer and marketer must operate. In the Common Market countries and in the United Kingdom by 1962, plus or minus two-thirds of soaps and detergents and of margarine and fats were sold through such large stores. This fact has faced Unilever with both problems and opportunities. In one respect this retail development could be seen as part of the growth of an affluent society designed to enlarge the sale of household necessaries, comforts and luxuries, to an ever-growing army of consumers.

The problem raised by the swift growth of the supermarket and similar large stores was a fundamental one of competition and economic power. A large supermarket chain might well be in a position to compete for profits by having its own brand of detergent or margarine manufactured under its own label. It might well think it could use its bargaining position to ask a large manufacturer to make such a quota specially for this purpose. Should the manufacturer accede? or should he refuse? or should he counter by reducing the amount of profit he expects from selling his own brand? or should he in turn riposte by buying his own way into the new retail arrangements? In the event Unilever did not repeat the earlier policy of the 1920s of expanding its retail outlets for its own products. On the other hand, two of Unilever's existing food retailing companies in the United Kingdom and Germany themselves entered the supermarket world. In 1964 Mac Fisheries, after experimenting with their own type of supermarket, bought up the Premier supermarket chain. But the object of this was to widen the range of a business hitherto largely limited to a single

[1] See Chapter 1, page 19–21.

commodity—fish. A piquant problem was whether these Unilever supermarkets should themselves sell their private label brands (for example, peas) in competition with (say) Birds Eye? The answer was yes.

The growth of the supermarket and self-service store powerfully influenced methods of presenting commodities to the public. While direct advertising grew—from manufacturer to consumer through media, old and new, through newspapers, posters, radio and television—self-service gave a new importance to packs and labels, display and distribution. Much of the success a product might achieve in a self-service store depended upon its being packed in a container that was the right shape for the shelf and which itself presented a striking and attractive front to the customer. It had to be convenient for the retailer to handle and present. It had to catch the eye of the passing customer. The 'middle processes of distribution' seemed to offer good opportunities for investment as well as being a fundamental element in competition.

This in turn explained the entry of Unilever into a number of diversified manufacturing activities—paper, cardboard, plastics, adhesives, printing. While a great volume of toilet preparations was still sold in traditional fashion to small chemists' shops, an increasing proportion of detergent sales went to larger retailers. In the United Kingdom the separate sales forces of Lever Brothers, of Crosfield's and of Hudson and Knight's, which had existed since the 1920s, were amalgamated in 1960 into a single force. Nearly half the force was abolished; the remaining half found that their functions had been radically changed. Much more of their work was concerned with helping retailers to arrange displays and promotions, and the economies of scale involved meant that it was only economic for the manufacturer to deal directly with fairly large customers.

The so-called 'promotion' was as old as the trade itself—a device to launch a new product or increase sales of an existing one. It might take many forms—free samples, door-to-door demonstrations, talks to women's organizations, discounts to the trader so that he might offer cut prices, special displays, gifts in the pack, coupons with monetary value, competitions, and so on. In no market could a manufacturer any longer rely on the 'loyalty' of the user. Customers won over by competitors' 'promotions' had to be won back by another 'promotion'. The growth of self-service shops meant that Unilever had to look again more closely at the whole idea of promotions, to bring in marketing experts to advise on their market implications. Virtually eliminated in the 1950s, they came back in greater force in a context where the importance of catching the self-service customer's eye became paramount. Promotions were of many kinds and degree of sophistication. Some were still reminiscent of the naïveté of the Victorian period. A salesman dressed as a maharajah might still be seen asking housewives whether they had any Lever products and taking those who had to a caravan topped with minarets to choose a prize. At the other end of the scale was the return to plain dealing which tried to eliminate offers of free artificial flowers, clothes pegs, toothbrushes and the like, and to replace these by an offer of more volume of detergent for the same price.[1] This achieved some success, though less than rationally minded social improvers could have wished.

All in all, by 1960 about two-fifths of Unilever's total advertising expenditure went on 'promotions'. The other three-fifths went on those other forms of advertising which went straight to the consumer, often in his domestic pensive moments, and were not physically associated with the consumer as a shopper or with the retail supplier.

All told, in a recent year 'marketing' cost Unilever over £400 million in world markets for foods, detergents, toilet preparations and edible fats alone. This expenditure included not merely advertising and so-called 'promotions', but all those activities necessary to bring to the consumers the products of their choice—marketing and selling costs, transport, storage, and the profit margins allowed to the traders who sold the goods. Since the very early days the devising of advertisements has been one of the fundamental bases on which Unilever sales rested. William Lever's own genius was as a salesman and the same was in great measure true of the Van den Berghs, the Jurgens and the Schichts. It could be taken for granted that the products, whether detergents or edible fats, were of excellent quality; what marked them out from scores of competitors was the skill with which they were marketed and especially the ingenuity with which they were advertised.

Before 1914 advertising had meant posters, newspapers, magazines, displays and promotions. By 1939 radio and cinema advertising had been added. The 1950s and 1960s saw these all

[1] See pages 102–3.

(except promotions) dwarfed by the new medium of television advertising. To employ these multiplying channels of advertising expenditure to the best advantage, a number of specialist agencies and service departments emerged. When it was founded, Lintas[1] met a need in the United Kingdom because outside advertising agencies were not fully developed. A similar situation existed in the Netherlands; there, and in twenty-six other countries where skilled advertising agencies were not available, Lintas agencies were also founded. As well as its own agency, Unilever used independent agencies and this tendency increased with the proliferation of brands and the complication of new media.

In each country an agency, usually the local Lintas branch, was selected to buy the so-called 'media' for Unilever advertising, such as space in newspapers and magazines, and time on commercial television screens. The increasingly international character of markets has not yet suggested that it is time to extend this centralization of national buying to international centralized buying. Most press, radio and television appeal remained fairly parochial, though some television advertising overlapped national boundaries where a common language straddled the frontiers. Until the day comes when it is truly international in appeal, the establishment of centralized control seems likely to be limited to national boundaries.[2]

Another link in the chain binding the factory to the consumer was transport and warehousing. As early as 1918 William Lever founded S.P.D. Limited (Speedy Prompt Delivery) to ease the distribution of Lever Brothers' products from Port Sunlight. Before 1939 S.P.D. operated sixteen depots. After the war, forty of those acquired during wartime were retained and thirty-eight new depots were planned and built in various parts of the country. Here the most economic methods of handling and transporting were employed to achieve savings in operational labour costs put at some 50 per cent. Here again, however, time did not stand still, and the shrinking numbers of retail outlets served by Unilever's manufacturing plants caused the plans for this side of Unilever activities to be re-thought. The re-thinking was still in progress in 1965.

[1] See page 92.

[2] The rapid invasion, particularly of Europe, by international companies has since 1965 led to more use of international advertising appeals. Agencies have set up international liaison departments to satisfy the new demands; Lintas International was formed for the purpose in 1967.

At the centre of the marketing process was advertisement, the most direct link between the manufacturer and his final customer. From the beginning, the Unilever industries owed much of their competitive success to the skill and persistence with which they advertised their products. Yet the place of advertisement in the success story must be seen in perspective. Advertising was successful only because it was bonded into the total 'marketing' process. The other ingredients have always included close study of the consumer and the consumer's needs (or at any rate an intuitive knowledge of what they are), an appropriate set of relationships with distributors and retailers, whoever they might be, careful attention to such matters as packaging and labelling, and adroit handling of the price factor; last and most important—a product that was not only excellent but appropriate to the market it served. This last was a factor sometimes taken for granted. It should not be; the Unilever experience was that no amount of money expended in advertising would sell a product which was below standard or inappropriate to the market to which it was directed.

The advertiser's ways and means changed dramatically after 1945. The largest and most controversial of the media through which he sought to influence his audience was television. Used on a vast scale in the Americas, its incidence in Europe and elsewhere remained variable. It became available in Britain in 1955. Coming as it did on the heels of a number of new Unilever products, notably soapless detergents, improved margarines and frozen foods, it was inevitable that Unilever should feature as a major spender on this new medium. Between 1957 and 1965 the estimated Unilever expenditure on television advertising throughout the world rose from £9·6 million to £41 million. Although press and commercial radio advertising budgets fell as a result, the total effect of television was enormously to increase the opportunities for advertising initiative. It also gave rise to another round of anxiety in the detergent industries about total advertising costs in relation to turnover and profits, while the repeated slogans of the advertisers raised critical doubts in many sections of society, not excluding the manufacturers of the articles themselves. What might be acceptable and even entertaining in a newspaper advertisement or even on a hoarding might seem intrusive and undesirable when inserted into entertainment programmes in the home. 'The advertising of detergents [wrote two recent observers] has attracted more criticism than that of any other product, except, perhaps, more recently, cigarettes. Particularly since television brought the night-ly repetition of "white lies" into millions of homes, objections have been raised in Parliament and elsewhere about the cost and content of the "advertisements".'[1] The same authors added that the root of the objection was the 'lack of apparent differentials in the presenta-tion and advertising of the products competing in this market. To the housewife the detergent manufacturers seem all to be shouting the same odds, and in unnecessarily loud voices.'[2]

The problem of how to reduce advertising budgets without losing selling momentum remained nevertheless the prize dilemma of the detergent industry. Fundamentally, the reason why it obstinately eluded all attempts at solution lay in the psychology of the customers and in the competitive character of the trade. Those attractions of advertising, especially in its cruder form, which caused wailing and gnashing of teeth amongst the critics, continued to evoke an apparently cordial response from the average housewife. It remained as true as it was in 1939 or even 1889 that 'in the soap industry it does not merely pay to advertise, it is death not to advertise.'[3]

To reach durable agreements with other manufacturers in the trade was totally impracticable. Just as in the 1890s, when members of the British Soap Makers' Association similarly tried to reach agreements to restrict competition, the reward for the breakaway was too big, too tempting. Where the manager's duty by contract was to ensure the long-term welfare of the shareholders' capital, it was impossible to expect him to sit back in virtue while the break-away newcomer collared the lot.

Nevertheless the voices of the critics did not go unheeded. Unilever turned its advertising in a new direction when it came to launch a new pack of its detergent Surf called 'Square Deal Surf'. Instead of pushing this product with special advertising claims or periodic price cuts, or gifts, or coupons, the manufacturers simply advertised the packet as containing 18 per cent more detergent than was offered by other brands at the same price. The experiment was tried out in East Anglia in 1961, and was successfully extended to first the London area and then the whole country in 1962. Some critics thought that it would have been more sensible to have

---

[1] Ralph Harris and Arthur Seldon, *Advertising in Action*, for the Institute of Economic Affairs, 1962, page 148.
[2] Ibid., page 152.   [3] *The History of Unilever*, vol. II, page 356.

reduced the price rather than increase the size of the packet, but the experienced advertisers disagreed. As Lord Heyworth and Mr Tempel had pointed out a few years earlier, permanent price reductions had not proved to be the alternative to 'promotions'. The amount of money (they thought) saved by dropping promotions was too small to make any significant reduction in price. As it was, here was a type of promotion which was greeted with interest 'by students of advertising, other manufacturers, agencies and media-owners',[1] but the complexity of the advertiser's problem was well illustrated by this particular experimental appeal to rationality. For Square Deal Surf achieved only a small share of the market.

The substance of the advertiser's task remained unchanged in spite of the changing character of the media used. Yet the task itself was not uniform. It might be to launch a new product or to maintain an existing product, or even to refurbish therapeutically an old or lapsed product. Those who clamoured for more techno-logical innovations and less salesmanship failed to appreciate a fundamental fact of commercial life. Many consumers had to be *persuaded* to change over from a familiar to an unfamiliar product. Hence more technology, more innovation, entailed more marketing skill, more advertising. The two were complementary, not mutually exclusive.

In the early days of soapless detergents it was necessary to build up a vast market if the new products were to compete with soap; it could only be done by mass advertising. The initial outlay ran into many million pounds. During the ensuing battle between manufacturers in the years 1948 to 1956 many small makers were eliminated. This was not, however, the result of advertising alone. Many of the products eliminated were poor in themselves and were manufactured by firms without the knowledge of the other aspects of marketing and distribution which were possessed by the large makers (Unilever, Procter and Gamble, Colgate and Henkel) who emerged with practically the entire market. Nor was the end of the story one of monopoly or monopoly prices. Compared with a rise of 200 per cent in average prices since 1938, the 60 per cent increase in detergent powders suggested that a recent analyst of the soap industry was correct in his judgment on this period: 'Overall the general picture which emerges is one of effective or "workable" competition in the soap and detergents industry. At least during the period reviewed, there have been reasonable

[1] Harris and Seldon, op. cit., page 153.

profits, expanded output, a progressive technology, improved products, and prices in reasonable relation to the cost of production.'[1]

Another novel branch of manufacture which made dramatic use of the new medium was the frozen-food industry. It was calculated that in the early 1960s nearly one-third of the married women in the United Kingdom had a job outside their home. No comparable figures exist for Continental Europe, but there, between 28 and 44 per cent of the total female population of working age had paid jobs. The numbers of married women at work were substantial, but evidently fewer than in Britain.

The special appeal of the so-called 'convenience' food was that it saved the working housewife time in the kitchen in return for a larger outlay on the product. By 1959 these new foods had come to account for nearly one-fifth of total household food expenditure for Britain, and the proportion was rising. One of the leading manufacturers, Birds Eye Foods Limited, became a wholly-owned subsidiary of Unilever in 1957, after fifteen years during which the ownership had been shared with General Foods Corporation.[2] At the end of 1961 Birds Eye still held about two-thirds of the growing market for these new frozen foods. From 1951 onwards Birds Eye had conducted a planned campaign of advertisement to educate retailers and housewives in the possibilities of the new frozen foods. Once the retailers had installed the refrigerators, the housewives had to be interested in the possibilities of frozen foods generally. Next came the advertisement of Birds Eye products specifically, and then presentation of the merits of individual products packed by Birds Eye. The cost of this advertising rose from £30,000 per annum to £1·5 million per annum between 1951 and 1961, more than 75 per cent of the budget going on television after 1955. The result: an increase of sales from £1 million to £37·5 million. 'Television advertising' it has been said, 'has clearly played a large part in the opening up of this market. It seems doubtful whether any alternative forms of promotion could have achieved this result as quickly or efficiently.'[3]

Advertising of soapless detergents and frozen foods in the early days came into the category of 'introductory advertising', a

[1] H. R. Edwards, *Competition and Monopoly in the British Soap Industry*, Clarendon Press, Oxford, 1962, page 254.

[2] For details of Birds Eye see Chapter 7, pages 171–3, *et seq*.

[3] Harris and Seldon, op. cit., page 271.

necessarily costly phase of innovation which must be seen as in the nature of a capital or investment expenditure. The money was invested in the creation of a connection in the market, this being the outlet for the product of large-scale manufacture. It had to be achieved as quickly as possible so that the manufacturer might achieve a steady volume of sales at the highest level and with a few dominant brands. Only in this way could the large plant installations at all stages of production be utilized. In the words of Lord Heyworth and Dr Paul Rijkens:

> Introductory advertising, the cost of which is undoubtedly heavy, has to be regarded as a kind of capital investment which will have a potential effect on manufacturing costs in the long run because the blenders and suppliers of ingredients can plan with greater certainty the required outputs.[1]

A great deal of advertising expenditure, however, came under other headings. When margarine in the United Kingdom was showing a tendency in the mid-1950s to lose ground to butter and to drop its share of the total edible fat market to 40 per cent from the 50 per cent of ten years before, Van den Bergh's introduced a new higher quality margarine, Blue Band, to try and attract customers away from butter. This was not a new product in the sense that frozen peas were, though it had features which could be emphasized as in some way novel; for example, it spread more easily than butter at low temperatures after coming out of a refrigerator. This was part of a campaign which was extended to a number of brands of margarine, and again it was assessed as reasonably satisfactory. Down to 1961 the rate of decline in total margarine sales had been arrested. The improved quality and wider variety of makes had established a stronger position than would have been possible otherwise in keen competition with butter.[2]

Other advertising campaigns were lavished on such old favourites as Lux (founded in 1907) and Lifebuoy (founded in 1899). Persil, half a century old by 1961, still managed to hold one-third of the market for washing powders sold in the United Kingdom, though it remained a soap powder and not a synthetic powder. The theme of its advertising had remained constant: 'Persil washes whiter'. Here again technical improvements had

---

[1] From *Synthetic Detergents*, speech to the shareholders, June 1953.
[2] Harris and Seldon, op. cit., pages 272–4.

certainly been introduced—to disperse scum, remove stains and give brighter whites and better suds, but Persil, like Blue Band margarine, was an improved product, not a brand new one.

Whether the advertising process was applied to new or existing products, its costs varied from somewhere between 5 to 11 per cent of total receipts from the sale of the products advertised.[1] In absolute figures the millions so spent seem enormously high. Yet it is worth remembering that they were proportionately less high than in the early days of William Lever's intrusion upon the British soap industry. During the first twenty years of Lever Brothers Limited the expenditure on advertising ran at a rate of some $12\frac{1}{2}$ per cent of the total revenue from sales.[2] All the same, the vastly increased expenditure in hard cash caused the manufacturer to scrutinize very carefully the end and purpose of his advertising and even more carefully the efficiency of the methods used. Advertising was essentially part of the marketing of a product and marketing has been described as 'The planning and execution of all aspects of and activities with a product, so as to exert optimum influence on the consumer to result in maximum consumption at the optimum price, therefore producing the maximum long-term profit.'[3] Whereas many external critics have suggested that this process necessarily involves 'exploiting' the consumer, this was not a view shared by the producer even in the privacy of his own advertising conference. On the contrary, if there was one dictum more repeated than any other by the marketing experts it was that it was the consumer's needs and interests which determine the characteristics and behaviour of a product. Only if the marketing expert studied the consumer and briefed correctly everybody from technologist to manufacturer, could a product be successfully advertised.

The businessman's object is to achieve the maximum long-term profit. This meant establishing the right price so as to produce the maximum sales. Given this, he could then go on to fix the amount of advertising which the product could bear. Thus, theoretically, advertising costs should never get out of hand. Yet it was no secret that there were times after 1945, and more especially after 1955, when rising advertising costs were a matter of anxiety to the Unilever management. Hence the emphasis on methods of testing

---

[1] Figures from H. R. Edwards, op. cit., page 249.
[2] Ibid., page 155.
[3] J. P. Stubbs, in talk to United Africa Company, October 1960.

the efficiency of the various forms of mass advertising upon which these hundreds of millions of pounds were spent. Nobody disputed that advertising was an indispensable part of modern marketing. Many would agree that it was most effective 'when used by a firm sailing with the wind, that is, when the general conditions of demand are favourable'.[1] The combination of product and advertisement might vary from good advertisement for a good product down to bad advertisement for a bad product, with the corresponding gain or loss.

Advertisement could overcome the apathy or objection of consumers and retailers to new products. It was not easy to go beyond such generalization confidently in assessing advertising efficiency. But there were important advances in measuring the response of consumers, particularly to television advertising. Research established that people who 'remember' advertisements do not necessarily act on their remembrances. And those who act on their remembrances are not necessarily able to recall later what they were. The most effective advertisements seemed often to be those which convinced a consumer that the product was of interest and service to him. The viewer had to be left 'fully and agreeably aware of the product's services'.[2] Such conclusions might seem little more than truisms, but they had the effect of inducing Unilever to test advertising copy and techniques on representative samples of consumers before taking the plunge with the mass audience. The essence of all these advertising tests was to discover the qualities in a product that most appealed to the consumer so that the advertisement could be framed in its most effective form; but if after all the advances of modern advertising, critical doubts still remained in the reader's mind, he could ponder a final comment from the Unilever advertising research experts: 'One effect of commodity advertising in a busy competitive market is to make the ordinary housewife more critical and shrewd in her shopping—and consequently more reliant on precise and accurate communication from the advertiser.'[3]

[1] Harris and Seldon, *Advertising and the Public*, 1962, pages 157–8.
[2] Alex Mitchell, 'T.V. Commercials made to Measure', *Progress*, November 1961.
[3] Ibid.

CHAPTER 6

CAPITAL AND FINANCE

FEW words carry more overtones than 'capital' and 'capitalism'. Between them they have been credited with most of the benefits and most of the faults of life in the modern world. In what sense is it correct to include 'capital' as one of the dynamics of business? There is one sense, and a very obvious one, in which capital is the ultimate dynamic. For it is the investment of capital that determines the physical shape and size of the business. Without capital investment the business cannot grow. In another sense, however, it is also dynamic. The invested capital of the modern public company represents certainly the best, and maybe up to date the only, yardstick for measuring what we call 'business efficiency', and which, but for the rigours of company law and the strict conventions of the accounting profession, embodying the experience of at least a century, would otherwise remain a concept as impalpable as it is virtuous.

The modern public company rests upon a contract between those who provide the capital and the corporate body whose business it is to make the decisions, employ the money borrowed from the shareholders, and carry out the undertakings, explicit or implicit, to give the shareholders their due return, whatever this may be, according to the rules. Unilever is such a public company. Yet it has not always been so. Most of the operating companies making or selling products which made up Unilever in 1965 began in a different way—in the way described by William Lever in 1903: 'In the old days a manufactory would be an individual concern. Next . . . a partnership, and that was a state of affairs which continued until quite recently. Then it grew beyond the capital available by two or three joining together as a partnership, and limited companies became necessary with appeals to be made to thousands of investors, in order that still larger capital might be got together.'[1]

[1] See *The History of Unilever*, vol. I, page 72. William Lever addressing a Men's Meeting at Port Sunlight, 11 January 1903.

At the time he was speaking, public limited liability companies were relatively new. His own partnership only became a public company in 1894. Van den Bergh's were incorporated in the following year when they too had to go to the public investor to acquire the money they needed for expansion. The history of the twentieth century was a history of a series of combines. Again to quote William Lever: 'Now we have reached a further stage again, when a number of limited companies require to be grouped together in what we call a combine, the object being concentration of capital and the concentration of effort. . . .'[1]

The transition from private partnership to public company was not made in one bound. In the companies which are now subsumed by the parent companies of Unilever and in many of those which are subsidiary undertakings, the former partners first of all appealed to the public for investment in the preference capital only, or sometimes in loan capital or debentures. The bargain was understood to be something in this wise: debenture holders and preference shareholders invested their capital and were granted a place at the top of the queue for the fixed return on their investment. So long as the business remained solvent they were assured of their due. It was Lever's conviction that there their concern with the company ended. Policy, management and risk were all the business of the ordinary shareholder, who only began to benefit when the obligations to the debenture holders and the preference shareholders had been fully discharged. It made possible not only his private fortune but also made for consistency of policy if the entire holding of the equity capital remained in the hands of one man, and that himself.

Likewise, a great deal of the equity capital of a number of other businesses that came into the group in the twentieth century was held amongst members of the original partners' families; none, however, to the same extent as in the Lever business. This led to serious problems when the final combine of 1928–9 was being discussed. For it meant, as the Dutch negotiators who came to examine the gearing of Lever Brothers' capital found, that the enormous increases in capital acquired in previous years had taken the form largely of additions to the preference shares carrying

[1] Ibid., page 72.

fixed dividends. The ordinary share capital remained a small proportion. Lever had in fact limited the capital which bore the brunt of the risk to the amount he could create and purchase from his own pocket. In 1929 the capital was represented by some £54 million of preference shares and £2·5 million of ordinary shares.

The changes since 1929 in the capital structure of Unilever can be briefly set out. The total capital employed by the two parent companies, Limited and N.V., amounted in 1945 to £186 million. Out of this, preference shares accounted for £72 million. Ordinary shares accounted for £28 million, reserves for £40 million.[1] In 1965 the total capital employed had risen by nearly 350 per cent to £827 million. £82 million of this was represented by preference capital, £99 million by ordinary capital, while no less than £469 million represented profits retained in the business and other kinds of reserves.

These vast increases in the total capital employed in Unilever had not been accompanied by any substantial increase in preferential capital. The biggest change in the structure was the growth of equity capital and of reserves. The increase in equity resulted from a rights issue (which gave existing shareholders the right to buy new shares in proportion to their holdings), the conversion of notes into ordinary shares, and scrip issues, which gave existing shareholders new shares free in certain proportions to their holdings. In this way £79 million of reserves was converted into equity capital of both parent companies. Twenty years of gigantic growth had been largely self-financed. The capital requirements of this period of expansion had been found out of profits, together with very large sums in the shape of depreciation provisions needed to maintain the value of the substance of the business. Appeals to the financial market-place had accordingly been limited to issues by Unilever Limited of £10 million debenture stock in 1950, a rights issue of £3·4 millions and an issue of £14 million debenture stock in 1951 and another of £14 million debenture stock in 1965. (The 1950 issue was the first time Unilever Limited had raised money publicly since 1935.) Unilever N.V. made an issue of Fl. 40 million four per cent Preference Capital in 1947, followed by an issue of Fl. 75 million convertible notes in 1949 (converted into Fl. 30 million ordinary shares in 1954 and 1955), a rights issue of

---

[1] The rest of the aggregate capital was represented by such items as Loan Capital and Outside Shareholders interests in subsidiaries.

Fl. 43 million in 1951 and a note issue of Fl. 300 million in 1965–6.[1]

In 1959 the Chairmen of both Unilever parent companies could nevertheless claim that 'The emerging pattern is one of a wider circle of people having money in the business.' The international spread of Unilever's share ownership was stimulated by the listing of N.V's ordinary shares on the world stock markets. The process began with Paris in 1955. Other European Bourses followed and in 1961 the New York Stock Exchange agreed to list both N.V. and Limited ordinary shares as investments likely to impress and attract United States investors. In 1959 about 35 per cent of the ordinary capital of Unilever N.V. was held outside the Netherlands. And, increasingly, local arrangements were being made for the expansion of Unilever enterprises, quite apart from the parent capital. In the 1950s Unilever showed itself ready to enter into local financial partnerships for founding or expanding enterprises. These partnerships took many forms. In Turkey it might be an agreement with the Iş Bank; in Pakistan, Kenya and Burma partnership with the local government or government agency. There was no doctrine about this. The financial arrangements had to be proved sound and they had to preserve to Unilever the right of controlling expenditure and making management appointments. If these had not been preserved, Unilever would have become merely an investment trust.

Who were the owners of Unilever's capital? So far as Unilever N.V. is concerned it was very difficult to say, for a large part of the capital of Unilever N.V. was represented by 'bearer scrip' and the number of shareholders was unknown. For Unilever Limited better estimates could be made. The number of shareholders hovered round 190,000. In 1950 the average shareholder in Unilever Limited held just over £360. By 1965 this figure had risen to £523.

An analysis of the holding of ordinary shares in Limited in 1961 showed that 42 per cent of the capital was held by some 46,000 individuals. The rest was held by institutions—insurance companies, investment trusts, pension funds, banks, charities, and the like. Amongst individual shareholders, the largest number held

---

[1] In 1953 the book value of the net assets was increased by £18·5 million as a result of re-valuation of fixed assets, and was decreased by £60·9 million as a result of writing off intangible assets. The above figures should be adjusted accordingly.

somewhere between £100 and £250. The second largest group held from £1 to £100, and from there the size of each group decreased as the size of holdings increased, so that the number of those who held over £50,000 worth was only four. By far the largest shareholder was the Leverhulme Trust.[1]

By 1964 there had been some changes in the structure of share-ownership in Unilever Limited. The number of individual shareholders had risen to nearly 58,000, but this larger number held a smaller percentage of the capital—only 36 per cent as compared with 42 per cent three years earlier. The biggest increase was amongst those who held between £1 and £100, and the average holding was tending to become smaller. One change in an age of increasing egalitarianism was worth recording: the number of individuals who held more than £50,000 increased from four to five.

What did Unilever do with the capital it acquired from shareholders or from retaining profits which would otherwise go back

[1] The position of the Leverhulme Trust was explained to the shareholders in the Annual Report in 1961 in the following words: 'The Will directed that persons appointed as trustees should always if possible be Directors of the Company. . . . The trustees were directed not to sell the shares, and today the Trust owns £6,338,118 nominal of ordinary shares in LIMITED. This is about 19% of the total issued ordinary capital and about 7% of the voting capital.

Under the Will the Trustees were directed to apply 20% of the annual income, which later through the failure of another bequest became 25%, to certain charities, and to the provision of scholarships for purposes of research and education. Under this head the Trustees today contribute about £225,000 annually to Universities and other research centres and to Leverhulme Research Awards.

The trustees were also directed by the Will to pay a proportion of the Trust's income, ultimately fixed at 62½%, to the Directors of Lever Brothers Limited and the Chairmen of its associated companies.

With the merger of Lever Brothers Limited and the Margarine Union Group in 1930 it became inappropriate for the holders of offices in the Lever Group to receive benefits under the Will to which the holders of corresponding offices in the Margarine Union Group were not entitled. Accordingly a subsidiary of Unilever purchased the existing rights of the persons then entitled to a share in the income, and today all persons appointed to any such offices renounce their rights in favour of a subsidiary of LIMITED. The result is that 62½% of the Trust income, amounting to about 12% of the aggregate ordinary dividends paid by LIMITED goes to one of its subsidiaries. The net amount received in 1961 was £606,000. This is equivalent, before deduction of income tax, to £989,000, which is included as part of income from trade investments in the consolidated profit and loss account.

In view of the remoteness of the termination of the Trust the ultimate distribution of its capital will almost certainly require direction by the Courts but, so far as can be foreseen, no part of the capital will go to LIMITED or any of its subsidiaries.'

to the shareholders as dividends? It is not easy here to compare figures over long periods of inflation when methods of accounting have also been changed and modernized. What we can say is that according to the 1945 accounts £120 million out of £186 million total capital was represented by fixed assets—buildings, plant, equipment—or investments in subsidiary companies. The remaining £66 million represented working capital, that is the total value of current assets such as stocks, debts, bank balances, *minus* such liabilities as debts owed, bank overdrafts, tax contingencies. The value of stocks was put at some £37 million, 20 per cent of the total capital employed. In 1949, when conditions were becoming rather more normal, Unilever employed a total capital of £273 million, of which £154 million was represented by fixed assets and investments, and £119 million represented by net current assets. Stocks were valued at £122 million, or 45 per cent of total capital employed. By 1965, when the total capital employed had risen to £827 million, £490 million was represented by fixed assets, etc., while £336 million was represented by net current assets. Stocks made up £332 million, or 40 per cent of total capital.

Thus, the relative importance of working capital and fixed assets fluctuated. But the trend was clear. The importance of fixed assets rose until they represented well over half the total capital. This tendency, for more money to be put into buildings and plant and less to be tied up in stocks, seemed likely to represent a consistent movement in industries steadily becoming more mechanized, continuous and automatic in their operations. Many factors worked in the same direction. Whale oil, which had to be bought at a single moment for use in production during the whole year, became less important; raw materials for detergents came in a constant flow from the oil refineries; the merchandise business in Africa lost much of its importance and some of the food industries required smaller stocks; above all, the policy of shortening the stock position was vigorously pursued. Other chapters have shown how research and technology were combining to make raw materials more flexible. There was, therefore, less need for Unilever to be dependent on any particular market or to build up vast reserves of materials as an insurance against rising prices. This was for a hundred years the dominant factor which had governed the profit of the oils and fats industries; its potency was now less, though of course raw material prices remained vital to the health of the business. In various ways, however, they were coming under the control of science, while science came more under the control of Unilever.[1]

This very degree of control, however, cost money. It meant investment of a different kind—investment in buildings, plant and knowledge. It is fair to say, therefore, that one investment risk was replaced by another investment risk. The raw materials markets in earlier days involved hazards over which Unilever or its predecessors could have, in the nature of things, little control. It could only be hoped that the skill of raw material buyers would help (as it certainly frequently did) to cushion the business against large rises or falls in market prices. The new risks were of a different kind. While economists might be able to help to iron out the risks of raw materials buying,[2] better crop forecasts being available, most economists agreed that when it came to capital investment or new products, 'hunch' still counted.[3] It was, however, hunch modified and supported by systematic knowledge and enquiry.

A look at the major projects completed in 1963 gives some idea of the magnitude of decisions where fixed assets were concerned. They included an ozonization plant at Gouda;[4] a cold store for quick-frozen foods and ice-cream in Germany; offices and research laboratories for Lipton's at Englewood Cliffs, New Jersey, and a tea plant in New Jersey; a plant for tea, soups and sauces in Bramalea, Ontario, Canada; a detergent factory in Ghana; departmental stores in Ibadan and Port Harcourt. Another £59 million was approved for work in progress—for increasing and modernizing production facilities of all kinds £13 million; new or improved shops £1 million; two refrigerated fishing vessels in Germany £1·5 million; a power station on Merseyside £1·25 million; a hydrogenation plant at Zwijndrecht £1·5 million; office buildings £2·25 million; research laboratories £4 million; welfare and housing for employees £800,000; a tobacco factory in Nigeria and a rubber plantation £1·25 million; motor vehicles £4·74 million.

Ventures of this size demanded a machinery of assessment and decision such as no previous decade needed. It had to be more scientifically precise, to represent the consensus of the most expert and responsible opinion in the business, filtered through all the

---

[1] Chapter 4, pages 78–80.   [2] See Chapter 2, page 36.

[3] See the paper on 'Economics in Business', by R. Brech, read to the British Association, September 1958.

[4] See Part II, Chapter 8.

necessary channels until it reached the top. Yet it had to work rapidly. For speed still remained essential to business decision. The bigger the prize, the greater the loss if the decision was too late. The need for certainty had always to be balanced against the need for speed. The problem was that decisions invariably had to be taken against a background of rapidly changing tastes and habits and an equally rapidly changing apparatus of technology.

The results, as presented in modern accounts, have been said to be as good a yardstick of failure or success as anything. What emerged from the results as presented in the Unilever Accounts since the Second World War? Between 1949 and 1965 the turnover of Unilever throughout the world rose from £800 million in 1949 to £2,326 million in 1965. If internal sales between companies inside the Unilever concern were excluded, the resultant figures ('Third party sales') rose in the same period from £490 million to £1,822 million. Less than ever was Unilever a *soi-disant* vertical combine. The firms which composed it were more than ever dependent on outside supplies of materials. In this period of seventeen years third party sales rose, as a percentage of total turnover, from 61 per cent to 78 per cent of the total turnover. Total third party sales increased by over three and a half times.

What return did all this investment of capital produce? Here it is best to restrict our calculations to the period from 1954 to 1964, where the statistics were on a fairly consistent basis. Between 1954 and 1964 the net profits rose from £31·9 million to £62·7 million. The return on capital employed in this period may be seen from the following graph:

RETURN ON CAPITAL EMPLOYED

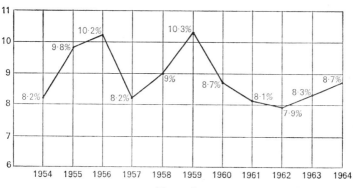

Figure 6

Many factors combined to affect the return on capital employed. The fall in that return in 1957 was largely due to a deterioration in world economic conditions from which Unilever suffered along with many other enterprises. From 1959 to 1962 there was another longer and rather steadier decline which only began to be reversed in 1963. Here, some important internal factors were at work. Some of the biggest were those factors to which much of this study has been devoted, especially the allocation of a large volume of capital to establishing research and development facilities and to diversifying the whole business so as to give it a broader base than its original preoccupation with oils and fats.

These ventures into previously unfamiliar territory were undertaken as a means of diversification, a spreading of risk, a broadening of base. For the most part, the new commercial and industrial ventures depended on the operation of the same economic and social forces as the old products. When management was taking the decision to invest or not to invest, it asked the same questions that it had asked in the past. Was the population going up? Was the standard of living rising? What was the state of competition? Were materials, labour and transport available? Was the government stable? What was its attitude to foreign investors? Above all, would the venture yield a satisfactory profit? And so on. The products, that is to say, were mainly consumer products for the mass market, whether in Europe or America, or in Asia or Africa. But they demanded more scientific knowledge—chemical, biological, technological. To hold its position in a growing world economy, Unilever needed to expand in real terms by three or four per cent a year, and this expansion could not be provided simply by relying on existing products. But research and development were expensive. They represented long-term, not short-term investments, and their fruit was slow to grow and to ripen. To launch into new products, as Unilever did in the 1950s and 1960s, was to face a crop of teething troubles. Obviously there had to be some outright failures; but even the successes were far from bringing in large immediate profit. Most of the food ventures made relatively small profits during the first years of their existence. Even on a longer view, experience in the United States and elsewhere suggested that even established food businesses did not find it easy to make high profits.

Generous criteria of public expenditure loosely ascribed to Lord Keynes and illustrated by Professor Parkinson can have no permanent place in the world of private competitive industry. Unilever's business was carried on in a market place in which there were numerically fewer competitors than there used to be; but this did not mean that the edge of competition was any less sharp than before. In some ways it was sharper than ever. Neither welfare economics nor Parkinson's Law had any place in Unilever's system of management, though the severity with which proposals were scrutinized inevitably varied in some degree with circumstances. The falling yield on capital after 1959 resulted in a demand by the Chairmen that management should review costs (especially those costs known as 'indirect expenses'—mainly those costs which cannot be attributed to any one product, for example management salaries, certain marketing expenses, buying departments, service departments). Advertising budgets in particular were to be subjected to very special scrutiny. There was increasing awareness of the need to find an efficient means of measuring the effectiveness of advertising so that it did not become a kind of independent and self-motivating activity. The index of the yield on capital drew attention to the need for greater efficiency and lower costs.

Owing to central control of finance there had been a tendency for managements to be less developed in their financial approach to problems than would be the case in independent businesses, and to improve this state of affairs the Special Committee in December 1952 set up a Finance Committee under the chairmanship of the future Chairman of Unilever Limited, George Cole.

'To make people sparing in the use of capital and conscious of the cost of providing it . . . to strengthen the appreciation by management of the ratio between profits and capital employed . . ., to provide throughout the organization on a realistic basis a method of comparing the profitability of the various commercial activities.' Such were some of the aims of the Finance Committee which reported in June 1953. Its first observation was that this report '[offers] no cut and dried remedy satisfying our terms of reference'. The increased 'finance consciousness' which it aimed at could only come from constant discussion at all levels within the operating companies and between those companies and head office.

The report of this Committee was another step along a road towards budgetary control, which probably started from D'Arcy

Cooper and the reconstruction he carried through in the 1920s after the debacle of the Niger Company.[1] The new Committee reported at a time when decentralization was much in the air. Some critics alleged that insufficient authority was delegated to the operating units under the existing procedure for estimating capital needs. The procedure recommended by the Committee and ultimately adopted was an important step in the process of turning the debate on centralized *versus* decentralized authority into a sensible and balanced reality, for it sought to leave the utmost commercial initiative to the man in the field while ensuring that ultimate financial control remained at the centre. Only in this way could finance act as the measure of efficiency and profit which was one of its proper purposes. Henceforth, each operating company annually was to assess the minimum capital, both fixed and working, which would be required to operate its business efficiently and earn the estimated profits. Each operating unit was to compare its real performance with its estimates every three months. The system was not to act as a straitjacket nor were failures to forecast accurately to be unduly penalized. The purpose was to assess the needs and sources of capital so that enough money would always be available to finance the plans of the whole concern and make possible the management of short-term finance.

One vital point which the Committee emphasized was the distinction between expenditure for working capital (raw materials, packing materials, and so on) and the far more fundamental and long-term decisions to incur capital expenditure on plant and buildings. Here, once money was allocated, it would be locked up for a very long time. In any such proposal, therefore, Technical Division at headquarters was to act as the assessor. They were to advise whether the proposal merited the approval of the Board or not. Again, one can see here the steady transformation of the holding company into an advisory and controlling organization.[2]

Closely connected also with the capital–profit relationship and the growth of fixed capital was the problem of the depreciation of fixed tangible assets. How to allow for the wear and tear and ultimately the replacement of buildings and plant, bearing in

[1] See *The History of Unilever*, vol. I, pages 270–1.

[2] It may be remarked in passing that in the Netherlands, where the National Plan has been developed to a very high order of precision, Unilever N.V. have made a practice of comparing growth rates in the firm with growth rates in the gross national product.

mind that under current methods of financing the company this vast item, if not sufficiently allowed for in calculating the cost of the products, must be found out of profits? The size of the problem may be judged from the fact that in the decade from 1949 to 1959 depreciation was assessed at £182 million. From then on the annual appropriation continued to rise until it steadied at £41 million in 1964 and £45 million in 1965. A fundamental problem throughout the whole of the post-war period, though varying in intensity from phase to phase, was how to maintain the *real* capital of Unilever in a time of monetary inflation. The matter had been dealt with in several stages. In 1947 the shareholders were told that the normal provision for depreciation, mainly based on the pre-war cost of fixed assets, was not enough. Prices had risen everywhere and additional reserves for replacement of assets had to be made. Again, in 1953 they were told that, since the process of inflation seemed to have been halted and assets revalued at current economic value, the special replacement reserve intro-duced in 1947 had been discontinued. On the other hand there would be no deviation from the principle that depreciation had to be based on current prices and that if a major degree of inflation returned reserves would have to be re-created for this purpose.

A committee was set up to reconsider the matter in 1957 when inflation threatened once again. It was under the chairmanship of P. A. Macrory, the secretary of Unilever Limited, and it began its report with a quotation: 'Depreciation is probably the most discussed and most disputatious topic in all accounting.' The report bore out the truth of the maxim. In deciding what system should be followed it was important to keep a sense of proportion. In absolute terms the figure for depreciation was important, but compared with the much higher costs of materials, labour and marketing it was not enough to justify an unending quest for theoretical perfection. Fixed assets should be divided into a small number of broad categories, with average rates for each category. Depreciation should be adjusted to take account of the changes in the value of money—to be expressed in 'today's £s' by appro-priate price indices. For product costing purposes the latter proposal was adopted throughout the organization; in the published accounts in 1964 that part of the profits to be retained was set aside as a replacement reserve.

It was a measure of the change of outlook since 1957 and 1952

UNILEVER - EMPLOYMENT OF CAPITAL YEARS 1949 - 1965

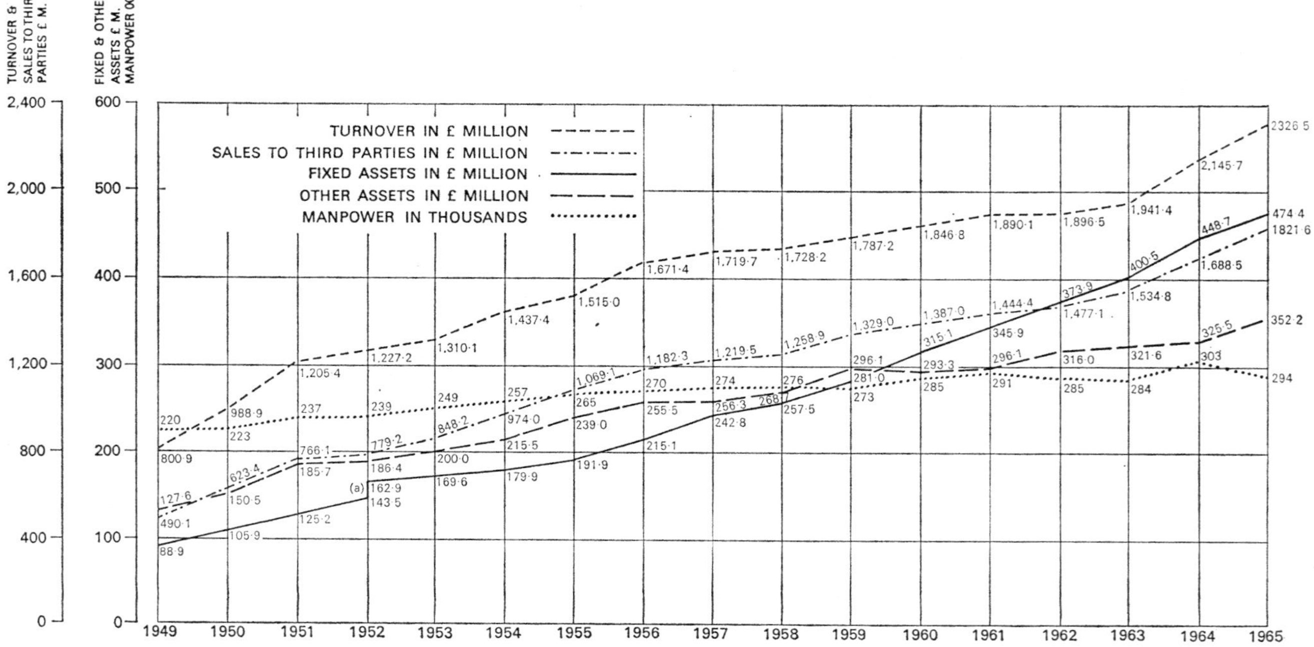
TURNOVER & SALES TO THIRD PARTIES £ M.
FIXED & OTHER ASSETS £ M. MANPOWER 000's
TURNOVER IN £ MILLION
SALES TO THIRD PARTIES IN £ MILLION
FIXED ASSETS IN £ MILLION
OTHER ASSETS IN £ MILLION
MANPOWER IN THOUSANDS
2,400
2,000
1,600
1,200
800
400
0
600
500
400
300
200
100
0
1949
1950
1951
1952
1953
1954
1955
1956
1957
1958
1959
1960
1961
1962
1963
1964
1965

(a) In 1953, following revaluations of fixed assets in the United Kingdom and the Netherlands, as at 1st January 1953, current rates of exchange were adopted for the conversion of foreign currency values of fixed assets.

Figure 7

that a body of opinion now developed in Unilever (as elsewhere in the country) for which the urgent problem was less that of educating managers in economy of capital than of educating them to see the possibilities of economy through *more* capital investment. This school of thought would hold that while the possibilities of capital investment in new processes and new machinery which reduced costs, especially labour costs, were appreciated by top manangement, the real potentialities of such investment were less appreciated farther down the line amongst local managements. Here the economies of new investment were sometimes obscured by inadequate understanding of factors such as tax allowances. Investment tended to look more expensive than it really was.

Again, new methods which cut down the need for labour might upset carefully nurtured labour relations built up over many years. It was not unnatural that local management should sometimes be reluctant to see the work of a lifetime destroyed by some new automaton. Yet there was in reality no contradiction between the attitude of the Finance and Depreciation Committees and the new school of thought. All were agreed that the *efficient* use of capital was indispensable to the progress of the business. But, as usual, the real problem of reconciling innovation and human relationship was tossed back to the ultimate victim: the manager on the spot.

How did all this look to the shareholders? It will be remembered that Unilever Limited and Unilever N.V. were holding companies, linked by a series of agreements, of which the principal was the Equalization Agreement,[1] and that for all practical purposes Unilever was managed as if there were only one parent company. The object of the agreement was to secure that the benefits accruing to the ordinary shareholders of Limited and N.V. 'shall as nearly as possible be the same as if each unit formed part of the ordinary capital of one and the same company'.

The dividends declared by Unilever from 1949 to 1965 were as follows (after allowing for the rate of exchange between the pound sterling and the guilder, these dividends were equivalent within the meaning of the Equalization Agreement):[2]

---

[1] See *The History of Unilever*, vol. II, pages 307, 314, 375.

[2] See *The History of Unilever* vol. I, pages xvii–xviii, and vol. II, pages 307 and 314.

	Limited %	*N.V.* %
1949	10	8·9
1950	$13\frac{1}{2}$	12
1951	$13\frac{1}{2}$	12
1952	$13\frac{1}{2}$	12
1953	$15\frac{3}{4}$	14
1954	$15\frac{3}{4}$	14
1955	$15\frac{3}{4}$	14
1956	$17\frac{1}{2}$	$15\frac{1}{2}$
1957	$17\frac{1}{2}$	$15\frac{1}{2}$
1958	21	$18\frac{1}{2}$
1959	22·71	20
1960	24·54	21
1961	24·79	21
1962	26·13	22
1963	22·50	18·9
1964	25	20·9
1965	25	21·1

The net dividends expressed as a percentage of the profit accruing to ordinary capital were as follows:

	Combined	*Limited*	*N.V.*
1949	14	8	21
1950	19	11	27
1951	19	10	35
1952	21	11	37
1953	19	10	36
1954	21	11	35
1955	18	12	24
1956	19	12	27
1957	22	14	31
1958	23	18	26
1959	24	15	35
1960	30	19	44
1961	31	23	37
1962	33	26	38
1963	35	28	40
1964	33	23	41
1965	32	21	42

Unilever's reputation as 'a growth company' brings us back to those methods of capital finance that have been adopted in Unilever as in most large companies since the Second World War. Between 1949 and 1959 approximately £30 million a year was added to the capital employed in the business, of which by far the greater part was provided out of retained profits. Some part of this was then issued to the holders of existing ordinary capital on the basis of one new share for every 'x' shares held. The benefits of this policy to ordinary shareholders between 1953 and 1963 were as follows:

	N.V. Fl.	Limited £
On an ordinary capital holding in 1953 of:	1,000	100
the 1953 dividend was:	140	15·75
The equivalent capital in 1963 after adjusting for scrip issues:	2,600	260
the 1963 dividend thereon:	468	55·61
an increase of:	234%	253%
Taking into account the reduced purchasing power of Fl. and £, the 1953 dividend expressed in 1963 money values:	185	20·95
i.e. an increase of the 1963 dividend over 1953 of:	153%	165%

In the first instance, after the war, this system of self-financing was inescapable. The government Capital Issues Committee on the one hand and high taxation on distributed profits on the other made it difficult, if not impossible, to raise capital on the market in England. In the Netherlands official permission was required to raise capital on the market and for some years dividends were statutorily limited. When each Chairman addressed his shareholders at the Annual General Meeting in 1960 he defended the continuance of this method of internal capitalization stoutly. The directors considered, he said, that they looked after the shareholders best if they financed themselves mostly from earned profits. He believed that most shareholders in Unilever were concerned with long-term rather than short-term profits. He doubted whether anybody was aggrieved by the system. The alternative—to go to the money market—would have manifest disadvantages. Unilever would be hard put to it to find the amount of capital it needed. Again, it might want money at an awkward moment—during a credit squeeze or a deflation. Unilever would then have to pay the market rate at a time when the rate did not suit them. With strong resources of their own they could choose the moment that suited them as they had done when they went to the market for debentures in 1950.

The argument against the system he paraphrased as follows: 'Some people say we ought to rely far more heavily on the market for capital, and pay out more of our profits to the shareholders. That way, they say, we should have to look even more carefully at the return offered by new projects, because we should have to balance it against the cost of raising the money. At the same time we should be giving the ordinary shareholders a more rapidly rising income, which is what they expect.' His final comment was that he did not want to imply that Unilever would 'never want to look for money outside our own business'—only that the system had worked well and seemed likely to be necessary for some time if the long-term interests of Unilever were to be protected.

Later on, the voices of the critics became rather more articulate. One of them put the matter as follows: by a curious paradox, the more conscientious a director, the smaller will be the dividend which he will recommend for the shareholders. For his paramount duty will be thought of not as to *them*, but as to the corporate body called the *company*.[1] In this view, the compulsory retention of corporate earnings was economically undesirable and morally reprehensible. The system of retaining profits as cheap capital meant that much of it tends to be invested in projects giving a low return. Diversification became a craze for its own sake. The free market for risk capital was narrowed. Corporations were able to go into new ventures without having to justify themselves through prospectuses as they used to do in the old days. Share values did not go up in proportion to funds retained and thus enable shareholders to recoup the ploughed-back profits through capital gains. Only a minute part of retained profits reappeared in the value of

[1] Alex Rubner. *The Ensnared Shareholder*, Macmillan, 1964. See also *The Director*, September 1964: 'What Slice of the Profits should the Shareholder get?' by the same author.

shares. If the ploughing back system were abolished, 'the teeth of the campaign for a capital gains tax would be drawn'.[1]

Such arguments deserved serious consideration. But quite apart from the interest of the company in having access to capital conveniently and continuously without elaborate preparations for capital issues, the defender of self-finance could argue that neither the efficiency of the business nor the interest of the shareholder suffered in the way that had been suggested. It was the Chairmen's contention in 1960 that, broadly speaking, 'so long as our policy gives us a return on our capital employed which is not seriously out of line with the performance of business generally, then I do not think we can be said to be treating our shareholders badly.' It might be added that if capital were provided out of income, it necessarily competed for the shareholders' favour with other investment attractions. If a shareholder receiving his capital back in the form of new shares were to find that the yield on these shares (together, of course, with the expectation of future expansion and future advantageous issues) were to add up in his opinion to less than the yield on some alternative investment, then he would presumably sell his shares and other sensible observant people would only be prepared to pay him a falling price. No company, it is fairly safe to suggest, could long survive the effects of falling efficiency if the true facts were disclosed year after year in the published accounts. It therefore seemed doubtful whether the two systems were as disparate in their effects on business efficiency as was made out.

The problem of how capital was to be provided and channelled into industrial investment entered in 1965 a phase of more than usual uncertainty with the new financial and fiscal arrangements of the Labour Government. The effects of the combined Capital Gains Tax and Corporation Tax at once became the economic conundrum of the year. But whatever the long-term effects might be (and as Keynes remarked, 'in the long-run we are all dead'), it was clear that the new rules did nothing to satisfy the critics of self-financing. Indeed, they were designed to encourage more reinvestment of profits in industry, more power to the managerial elbow. Yet many of these supposed beneficiaries were less enthusiastic than they should (in theory) have been, and the most obvious short-term result of the new dispensation was a move away from

[1] These comments were written before the 1965 Budget and Finance Bill introducing a Corporation and Capital Gains Tax.

ordinary shares to debentures as a means of raising new capital. Risk capital was, for the time being anyway, out of favour altogether.

How these variable winds would affect Unilever it is too early to say. One aspect did, however, have immediate implications. The frosty official stare which, for example, in Britain now fell upon overseas investment could have far-reaching effects—if it led to rigid restrictions on any wide scale. Previous chapters have demonstrated that the history and structure of Unilever were dictated in no small measure by those international economic interferences which made export trade in the major articles of production unprofitable and virtually impossible. Local manufacture was the inescapable logic of these (and many other) industries. Hence the need for capital investment overseas on a large scale.

These problems necessarily created certain anxieties. But Unilever had faced and survived many more serious threats. The new provisions still left room for manoeuvre and it seemed likely that the logic of facts would itself in time modify what had at first appeared to be the full rigour of unsubstantiated doctrine. Second, it had to be remembered that the provision of capital for industrial expansion had been achieved in a variety of ways in different countries over the span of modern history. Since the onset of intensive industrialization, it could hardly be said to have been a major problem of economic growth in advancing economies, and there was little that was sacrosanct about method. All in all it seemed unlikely that a well-managed and lively business would find it an insuperable problem. But, for the time being at least, the shareholder seemed likely to be more ensnared than before.

Finally, how did the growth of this world-wide group of businesses look to all the various governments who increasingly regulated or tried to regulate the context within which business operated, at the same time drawing from business profits a sizeable share of the taxation which went to support the spreading activities of welfare states all over the world? In 1945, out of a total gross profit of £22 million, Unilever paid £13 million out in taxation. In 1965 out of a total of £117 million, £52 million was paid in taxation. Throughout the whole of these two decades, out of a total of £1,625 million of gross profits, Unilever had paid £848 million, averaging 52 per cent of total profits. Thus, quite apart from any social benefits which Unilever's enterprise might bring directly to its employees or owners in the form of salaries, wages, pensions or profits, or the amenities which its technology might bring to consumers, it also contributed on a vast scale to those social benefits which scores of governments everywhere were creating not least from the taxation of business profits.

UNILEVER LIMITED

£ million

		CAPITAL EMPLOYED 1949–1965				
Year	Preference Capital	Ordinary Shareholders' Funds		Loan Capital	Deferred Liabilities	Total
		Capital	Reserves			
1949	56·3	13·8	37·1	—	1·4	108·6
1950	56·3	13·8	39·8	10·0	·9	120·8
1951	56·3	17·2	46·6*	24·0	1·4	143·1
1952	56·3	17·2	48·3	24·0	1·5	145·6
1953	56·3	17·2	50·4	24·0	2·2	150·1
1954	56·3	21·5	53·0	24·0	3·1	157·9
1955	56·3	26·8	53·8	23·9	3·8	164·6
1956	56·3	26·8	65·2	23·0	4·7	176·0
1957	56·3	26·8	70·7	22·8	2·9	179·5
1958	56·3	33·5	69·8	22·2	0·7	182·5
1959	56·3	33·5	80·6	22·0	1·9	194·3
1960	56·3	33·5	90·5	20·4	2·2	202·9
1961	56·3	33·8	102·6	19·9	2·3	214·9
1962	56·3	33·8	110·1	19·8	1·5	221·5
1963	56·3	45·0	113·6	18·9	2·3	236·1
1964	56·3	45·0	117·8	18·5	2·8	240·4
1965	56·3	45·4	126·6	32·3	4·0	264·6

* After applying surplus on valuation of shares in subsidiaries and trade investments against the value of shares in subsidiaries.

Figure 8

UNILEVER N.V.

Fls. million

		Ordinary Shareholders' Funds			
Year	Preference Capital			Loan Capital	Total
		Capital	Reserves		
1949	213·1	172·0	182·9	75·0	643·0
1950	213·1	172·0	193·1	75·0	653·2
1951	213·1	215·0	211·8	75·0	714·9
1952	213·1	215·0	162·4*	75·0	665·5
1953	213·1	215·0	170·8	75·0	673·9
1954	213·1	305·4	174·1	0·3	692·9
1955	215·9	381·3	120·0	—	717·2
1956	215·9	381·3	139·7	—	736·9
1957	215·9	381·3	154·4	—	751·6
1958	215·9	476·1	160·1	—	852·1
1959	215·9	480·8	286·1	—	982·8
1960	231·8	482·0	399·8	—	1,113·6
1961	240·9	482·0	479·9	—	1,202·8
1962	243·9	482·5	486·6	—	1,213·0
1963	243·9	642·6	350·2	—	1,236·7
1964	265·1	642·6	368·3	—	1,276·0
1965	265·1	642·6	386·7	—	1,294·4

CAPITAL EMPLOYED 1949–1965

* After applying surplus on valuation of shares in subsidiaries and trade investments against the value of shares in subsidiaries.

Figure 9

UNILEVER LIMITED & UNILEVER N.V.

AND THEIR SUBSIDIARIES

CONSOLIDATED FIGURES

£ million

				CAPITAL EMPLOYED 1949–1965			
Year	Preference Capital	Ordinary Shareholders' Funds		Outside Share-holders' Interests in Sub-sidiaries	Loan Capital	Deferred Liabili-ties	Total
		Capital	Reserves				
1949	76·3	29·6	104·6	18·1	33·9	11·0	273·5
1950	76·3	29·6	128·2	18·3	44·5	12·0	308·9
1951	76·3	37·1	151·4	20·5	58·5	14·3	358·1
1952	76·4	37·2	128·1*	21·5	58·8	13·5	335·5
1953	76·4	37·2	145·9	22·0	56·1	17·3	354·9
1954	76·3	49·9	164·0	22·4	48·8	20·0	381·4
1955	76·6	62·4	186·6	23·1	46·7	19·5	414·9
1956	76·6	62·4	224·2	24·5	45·4	37·5	470·6
1957	76·6	62·4	254·5	24·2	43·4	38·0	499·1
1958	76·6	78·0	270·2	24·0	39·0	38·4	526·2
1959	76·6	78·4	316·7	24·3	39·1	42·0	577·1
1960	78·1	78·5	337·8	24·6	37·8	51·6	608·4
1961	80·1	81·0	362·0	24·2	38·6	56·1	642·0
1962	80·4	73·7	395·6	24·7	56·2	59·3	689·9
1963	80·4	98·3	399·7	25·9	53·3	64·5	722·1
1964	82·4	98·3	437·0	22·2	67·9	66·9	774·7
1965	82·4	98·7	468·6	19·6	84·7	72·6	826·6

* After eliminating Premiums, less Discounts, at which shares in subsidiaries are held, including Goodwill.

Figure 10

UNILEVER
CAPITAL, GROWTH AND DIVERSIFICATION
1951–1965
£ million

	Capital Expenditure (gross)			Acquisitions of new businesses and subscriptions to trade investments			Total		
	1951/55	1956/60	1961/65	1951/55	1956/60	1961/65	1951/55	1956/60	1961/65
United Kingdom	31·8	78·6	89·0	0·2	0·7	47·4	32·0	79·3	136·4
Ocean vessels	2·1	12·9	2·0				2·1	12·9	2·0
Rest of Europe	42·6	67·6	120·6	0·5	11·5	24·0	43·1	79·1	144·6
Europe	76·5	159·1	211·6	0·7	12·2	71·4	77·2	171·3	283·0
Africa	30·0	34·1	34·1		1·3	5·8	30·0	35·4	39·9
North and South America	19·2	20·2	36·3		11·7	11·0	19·2	31·9	47·3
Rest of the World	12·7	14·8	23·8		4·5	6·3	12·7	19·3	30·1
	138·4	228·2	305·8	0·7	29·7	94·5	139·1	257·9	400·3

Figure 11

K

SUMMING UP

THE great corporation, composite of hundreds of diversified manufacturing and other companies, international in its operations, representing the investment of hundreds or perhaps thousands of millions of pounds, is as striking a feature of the economic topography of our times as the joint-stock company was of the seventeenth century, or the factory of the early Industrial Revolution. Striking, not typical. Just as the East India Company dwarfed the thousands of typical partnerships of its day or Arkwright's mill the thousands of cottage handlooms, so the great international companies of the present dwarf the typical, much smaller units of our own day.

As William Lever remarked more than half a century ago, 'the thought of large combinations' in economic life is alarming. Comparatively little has been written about 'big business'. What has been written has often been denigratory, melodramatic, or simply ignorant. The phrase itself has acquired a connotation which the management of large firms have done little to disperse by frank disclosure. Economists brought up on theories of perfect competition (which had never really existed) looked side-long at organizations so large that they must seem by inference to be monopolies against the consumer's interests. The general trend could plausibly be interpreted as one of diminishing compet tion and increasing risks of monopoly of which the large internat onal combine could be depicted as the climax. Thus emerged a supposed dilemma expressed by a distinguished Cambridge economist. Competition, Professor Joan Robinson has said, is surely the main cause of monopoly. But if the campaign against monopoly succeeds, will not the competition so induced create more monopolies? 'Is that what we want? And if not, what *do* we want? What are the rules of the game?'[1]

At first blush the sequence seems plausible enough. Has not the twentieth century seen industry organized into large units, small private firms giving way to a smaller number of public

[1] Joan Robinson, *Economic Philosophy*, Penguin (1964), page 136.

132

companies, here and there to great international combines? Has not the victory gone to the strongest, those with more money, or ingenuity, or knowledge, or stamina? How does a society stop success in enterprise from bringing monopoly? Have we in fact achieved one set of targets—higher production, lower costs, lower prices, more advanced technology—only at the expense of creating monopolies? For centuries monopoly has been a target of moralists and later of economists. Even a loyal Elizabethan parliament barked at their beloved Queen when they suspected her of tolerating the evils of monopoly. Adam Smith himself remarked that wherever merchants gathered together there was a risk of monopoly injuring the public interest. Yet it is far from clear that the true risks of monopoly to the consumer are greater than they used to be. The size of the firm certainly has tended to increase as production becomes ever more complicated and the economies of scale more attractive. Theoretically, it is easier for a smaller number of firms to act in collusion against the consumer's interests than for a larger number.

Against these factors, however, must be placed certain countervailing ones. The old notion of competition was one of large numbers of relatively small producers competing for the custom of consumers of the same kind of article. The dynamic technology of the mid-twentieth century has substituted a different concept. The large firms of today still compete with similar products, but the combined efforts of scientist, technologist and marketing expert mean that the most potent weapon of the progressive firm is the new and superior product that it manages to have up its sleeve. Similarly, as the size of the producing industry has grown, so has the size and influence of consuming organizations. Preceding pages have dealt with the see-saw between the new giant retail organizations in the grocery trade and the producers in industries like Unilever. A period of easy economic growth like the early 1960s might well leave the impression that competition was less sharp than it used to be. It only needs the chill wind of the mid-1960s to remind people at large that competition (mirrored in falling profit margins) is as real as ever. Professor Edwards's study of *Competition and Monopoly in the British Soap Industry* gives a picture of monopolistic competition, competition as sharp and ruthless as any known to the outwardly more competitive and numerous soap-makers of the late nineteenth century.

Those who point to an industry composed of larger and fewer

firms forget that the total number of products competing for the attention of consumers is always increasing. The makers of each type of product are therefore competing more fiercely for the attention of the consumer, though of course at the same time the aggregate income of consumers in the developed countries has been steadily increasing. But even where the problem is that of the amount of competition between manufacturers of the same or similar products, it is far from certain that competition has diminished or monopoly increased. The large and the very large firms are a known fact of economic life. Everybody is aware of their existence, sensitive, perhaps hypersensitive, to the risks of monopoly in their practices. But quite apart from anything which government action and the like may enforce, the risks in this modern situation may well be less than those which were inherent in the older economy with its multiplicity of smaller producers. The first volume of *The History of Unilever* described the agreeable comfort which the Victorian soap-makers were able to enjoy through mutual agreements on prices and the like, an easy-going world shattered by the arrival of William Lever. The era of industrial history before 1914 was one in which secret diplomacy to secure market sharing, quotas, cartels and so on was a characteristic feature of the time. Such devices, which often tended to give the consumer the worst of all possible worlds, still exist. But they have been diminished not only by new and real forms of competition between large firms but by the increasing amount of public criticism and scrutiny to which they have been subjected. By and large the risks of that type of secret diplomacy were much worse than the risks created by a diminution in the number of firms.

Few would deny, nevertheless, that government has a duty to be vigilant on behalf of the consumer and ensure that the public interest is not injured by monopolistic practices.

Fear of monopoly was sharply reflected in the policies of governments in the Old World and the New in the post-war era of popular democracy. Everywhere, a firm as large as Unilever had to take careful account of local attitudes to the monopoly problem. In those countries like the United States, where fear of the political as well as the economic consequences of monopoly had produced the sharpest local weapons against monopolistic practices, the recognition that size in business was essential to progress grew: but so did the vigilance of the enforcers of the anti-trust laws. Germany, which had rarely in its history shown itself sensitive about the faults of monopoly, came under the new articles governing the Common Market which aimed 'to ensure free competition'. The principles came from American anti-trust legislation and ruled out such practices as price-fixing, restrictions on output, market sharing agreements, discrimination, and the abuse by firms of what was described as 'a dominant position in the market'. Elsewhere in Asian and African countries governments invariably armed themselves with powerful weapons against possible monopolistic abuses. In Britain, as in America, restraints on trade were *ipso facto* illegal, but both Labour and Conservative governments also successively introduced legislation requiring the registration of all restrictive practices. In principle such practices were condemned, though they might be allowed if the public benefit could be demonstrated.

A dilemma so complete necessarily produced legal inconsistencies by the score. The solid fact nevertheless remained that governments everywhere felt it desirable to operate a system of checks and balances to prevent the growth of monopoly. Like all systems of government control, this one creaked, groaned, and occasionally broke down completely. Yet the idea of *competition*—however vague and indefinable—persisted as the Platonic ideal. This was especially true of the United States. When Lever Brothers Company was proceeded against by the Anti-trust Division of the U.S. Department of Justice between 1958 and 1963 for acquiring that part of the Monsanto Chemical Corporation's business which manufactured a low-suds synthetic detergent, its defence was highly significant. Charged with restricting competition, Lever Brothers Company replied that it was not merely not reducing competition but actually protecting and increasing it. For both the product it had acquired and its own similar type of business were losing money in the face of rivalry from larger competitors. Such losses could not continue. If the businesses remained separate, the end must be monopoly by the largest manufacturer. By acquiring a competing company, Lever Brothers Company, the third largest detergent manufacturer in the United States, was helping to preserve a more competitive market. Lever Brothers Company won.

There could be no clearer illustration of the faith in the ideals of competition that lie behind the American attitude to monopoly. Many American businessmen would agree that the anti-trust system is a necessary part of the American way of life and government. These twenty years showed that anti-monopoly laws were something the large business must learn to live with. Perhaps it was that much easier to live with because American anti-trust philosophy became clearer and policy a shade more predictable with time. The same could not be said of the British Monopolies Commission whose good intentions rested on no comparable belief in competition *per se* but were hobbled by far more rigid legal definitions. This led one Unilever executive to suggest that the Commission would be better employed 'if it were given the task of ruthlessly eliminating all restraints on competition and were not required, as it is by the present Monopolies and Mergers Act, to waste considerable time and energy in propounding debatable value judgments'.[1]

To the outward eye, the large business corporation like Unilever might seem an engine of great economic or social power, even—in spite of its rigorous policy of political neutrality—of great political power. Surely £700 million worth of economic activity was not to be taken lightly? To whom did it owe its responsibilities?

During the Second World War an enthusiastic body of British businessmen set out what they called 'A National Policy for Industry'. Industry, they thought, had a threefold public responsibility—to the public which consumes its products, to the public which it employs, and to the public which provides the capital by which it operates and develops. The responsibility of management, they suggested, was to hold a just balance between these varying interests of the public, and to make the highest possible contribution to the well-being of the nation as a whole. The formula might sound a little high-minded, but nobody could doubt that the new type of professionally-managed and self-financing industry described in the foregoing chapters must have some such responsibility as was suggested in this definition. The threefold responsibility did exist, and in the nature of things the balance between these responsibilities *must* exist. For if the bias of management went exclusively to the consumer, everything, including wages, salaries, pensions and other benefits, would have been sacrificed to the sole end of minimum prices and perhaps of lower quality. If the business were to become a conspiracy directed by management and labour for their own profit and self-enrichment, a kind of management-labour benefit club, the consumer and shareholder would suffer. If an excessive proportion of the

[1] Mr E. Brough, Chairman of Lever Brothers and Associates, in an address to the Market Research Society on 15 June 1967.

annual resources or the necessary capital accumulation of the business were to be paid out in dividends, consumers, management and employees would all suffer. In the event, by methods that were a mixture of methodical, scientific accountancy, judicious calculation, human judgment and not a little guesswork, a balance was worked out between these different interests. It does not take much imagination to see that any of the alternative forms of disequilibrium suggested above would swiftly bring Nemesis to any management foolish enough to think them a viable alternative.

How, assuming that there was at least a measure of reality in the Victorian caricature of the hard-fisted capitalist, grinding the face of labour, has the transition been effected from the exploiting capitalist to the welfare capitalist? Here, again, the history of management, of the change from private partnership to public company, and the relationship of the capital structure of businesses to the problems of management is still largely *terra incognita*. Only in recent years has the inherent need for continuity in the public company made it plain that management itself must be a continuous process and therefore the object of continuous recruitment and consistent policies of training and education. Here, as in other places, the luck of the draw that went with the private firm has had to give way to deliberate, conscious thought and policy. Yet in some measure each industry must remain a special case and we need far more historical case studies of great industries undergoing this process of transition before we can generalize about the ethics of capitalism. It has been pointed out in this study that the oils and fats industries were an aggregation of consumer industries where more than one entrepreneur saw at an early stage that there was a singular amount of common ground, if not total coincidence, of interest between capitalist, worker and consumer. Hence the conjunction of liberal politics and genuine concern for industrial welfare, that rested not merely on a loose philanthropy which they would have despised but on a union of business-like self-interest and social welfare which seemed to be incontestably valuable to all.

Over a period of time the great owner-manager has been replaced by a group of professionals with little or no stake in the ownership of the companies themselves. Critics have both praised and criticized the manager class. Let us listen again to a word from Mrs Robinson, who has done both. The high-mindedness of this class of men (she has said) is not merely a publicity stunt. There is also a genuine desire for a good reputation and a good conscience in the loyalty which a manager attaches to his firm.[1] The English are particularly prone to these local group loyalties that grow up between individuals and institutions. With the patriotism of the nation goes the loyalty to school, regiment, college, city, church, chapel. In some measure and with local differences this sort of tribal interest is universal. It is this, developing in the case of the public company, which has helped to falsify the prediction made by Adam Smith in relation to the joint-stock company.[2] More recently, the prediction of more modern economists that large limited liability companies would prove a dead-end has been falsified. One of the reasons why the system of self-financing[3] has taken the place of appeals to the public for capital has been the growing emergence of the business corporation as a separate identifiable entity, attracting the closely focused efforts and loyalties of the younger class of managers who direct its fortunes.

The debate on the respective merits of external and internal finance is not yet at an end, but it is evident that in the minds of many managers further investment and expansion do endow the pursuit of profits with a kind of ethical purpose, which it would lack if profits were merely to be paid out in dividends to share-holders. William Lever was apt to regard his preference share-holders as merely moneylenders, entitled to an assured yield on their loans. Some professional managers think of the ordinary shareholders in a similar kind of way. In this new and institu-tionalized kind of business, the pursuit of profits is no longer the entire motive for industrial activity. Mrs Robinson's epigram that industry has become the motive for the pursuit of profit may be more entertaining than accurate, but it contains a measure of truth.

Capital, loyalty, continuity—all these a great business possesses or cultivates. Yet its problems have only been changed, not

[1] *Economic Philosophy*, page 135.

[2] Adam Smith, *The Wealth of Nations*, Everyman edition, vol. II, page 229: 'The directors of such companies, however, being the managers rather of other people's money than of their own, it cannot well be expected that they should watch over it with the same anxious vigilance with which the partners in a private co-partnery frequently watch over their own. Like the stewards of a rich man, they are apt to consider attention to small matters as not for their master's honour and very easily give themselves a dispensation from having it. Negligence and profusion, therefore, must always prevail, more or less, in the management of the affairs of such a company.'

[3] Described in Chapter 6, pages 123-5.

eradicated. Competition remains an essential spur to any business, though it may well be regarded as a problem rather than a privilege by the business manager. Today the nature of competition may be oligopolistic, that is to say, not between a multiplicity of firms but between a handful of giants. In the absence of collusion, which it is the object of anti-monopoly legislation everywhere to prevent, such competition need be no less effective than competition of the older kind. Indeed, it is, by its nature, more exacting, since with it goes the demand for more searching examination of each new capital-consuming project. The burden of each decision grows heavier as time and technology multiply the size and cost of machines and processes.

Again, though size has its advantages, giving stamina in bad times to the less fortunate firm within the group, providing finance for expansion for research and development, and the like, it brings its own problems. Within the advisory departments at headquarters and within each operating unit the ceaseless struggle goes on between those who rightly insist on refining knowledge and perfecting products, and see thereby the need for more perfect organization, longer consideration and more expertise, and those who see that unless the product is marketed at the right time and not a day later the opportunity may be lost for ever. There is, therefore, as in all organizations, a never-ending contest between the need for accuracy and the need for speed.

Size brings also an inclination to think too exclusively in terms of size, to measure and value too exclusively those large and established markets that represent the obvious facts of life. The danger is that the inventions and commodities as yet unborn and therefore not susceptible of measurement may get forgotten. Yet it is here that the future lies. The modern business manager is only human. Awkward brats and their teething troubles are no more attractive to him than to anybody else. But the motto of the former London Passenger Transport remains both old and true: *Ex Glande Quercus*—Out of the acorn cometh forth the oak. Professor Parkinson's Law has its natural momentum here as elsewhere and only the spur of competition can prick a growing bubble of business bureaucracy.

The new forms assumed by competition and technology alike threaten to raise fundamental problems of managerial responsibility for a business like Unilever. On the one hand the growing sophistication of industrial problems, the growing need for

managers who can negotiate with public authorities and present
the right face to the contemporary world, the growing diplomatic
burdens which fall upon private industry, the pioneering problems
thrown up by industrial development in developing economies—
all these and similar problems demand personal qualities in top
managers which were rarely demanded in the simpler commercial
context of earlier times. The new managers must seemingly be
educated to a higher level to understand the contrapuntal relationships between their business and the societies in which
they have to live and operate. But this is not by any means the
whole story. Other powerful forces are working in the opposite
direction.

Unilever is a congeries of companies which may be said to have
coagulated by a kind of centripetal process. In the mid-twentieth
century these were having to compete fiercely with equally large
or larger businesses, often working from a North American base,
that had developed on quite different historical lines. These had
developed centrifugally within an initially vast domestic market,
within which they had evolved highly sophisticated and successful
products, now thrusting outwards into the rest of the world,
backed by enormous advertising and established success in a
prestigious North American market standing for the latest thing
amongst materially less sophisticated consumers. In order to meet
this competition, Unilever was compelled to streamline its own
organization. Local companies, local brands and trade marks,
local national managements and frontiers, a structure once upon
a time determined by the caprice of national tariff systems—
all such historical paraphernalia had to be scrapped in order
to reduce costs in favour of overall marketing organizations
on a product basis. What was to be the effect of this radical
reorganization known for the sake of convenience by the label
'co-ordination'?

Some of those in the middle ranges of management feared that
one effect might be to reduce not so much their financial reward
as their share of personal responsibility. And burdens of responsibility are what the best kind of manager really enjoys. No good
man wants to be paid more for doing less. But while the more
recent reorganization of Unilever has placed a greater responsibility for commercial policy on the man at the centre,
circumstances have enormously enlarged and complicated the
tasks of public, governmental, labour and other responsibilities

which fall on the local manager. The forces which demand a wider range of knowledge and aptitudes amongst managers, and the forces which bundle all the major responsibilities on to a smaller number of men in the highest echelons of management, are therefore nicely balanced. This is not merely a technical problem of management in Unilever; it is a problem of how large-scale industry, seeking its own efficiency in terms of reduced costs and greater competitive efficiency, can continue to offer personal satisfaction of the legitimate ambitions of those beneficiaries of higher educational systems who look to industry for their careers.

As has been pointed out, the 'size' of Unilever is in some sense an illusion. Unilever is not itself a manufacturing company. But it represents the indispensable capital, advice and guidance which enable its constituent companies to make and sell things. Many of these companies are relatively small and operate in fiercely competitive markets. The size of any particular manufacturing or marketing company, research institute or laboratory is dictated by a combination of things—historical circumstances, market conditions and continued experience. These may suggest a small or a medium or a large firm. Each is a special case. At the root of Unilever's problems, successes and failures, lies the old conundrum—to centralize or to decentralize? And to this again there is no single or simple answer. The solution lies in striking the balance between those fundamental decisions (of which finance is often the best and most practical yardstick) which need to be controlled from the centre and can only be made at the centre, and those other decisions which must be left to the man in the field. Much of the comment on problems of size, organization and decision-making made in academic circles and the popular press is really beside the point, for it rests on a failure to distinguish between the differing functions of the holding company, the advisory departments, and the operating unit itself. Equilibrium, division of labour, human judgment and good sense is the answer here, as it is in the problem of Unilever's responsibilities towards its treble tiers of citizens.[1]

To find equilibrium in this and other matters is the business, and the essential business, of management. This is the task to which all the efforts of those who select and train managers must be bent. And in spite of the growing demands of technology and scientific

[1] See Chapter 2 *passim*.

advance, in spite of the increasingly successful search for scientific methods of enquiry to reduce areas of ignorance and uncertainty and to define that hunch which was previously indefinable, there remains a large element of human judgment, sympathy and common sense in the work of the business executive. If this gets overlaid and confused beneath the jargon of the bureaucrat, the consultant presenting the latest fads and fashions in management techniques, or the private vocabulary of the physical or social sciences—if, in short, communication were to break down between the top and bottom of the business or between the centre and the perimeter, the day could be irretrievably lost. Computers and other modern scientific devices can help management to take the right decisions, but in the last analysis business policy and business success is established by discussion and by human judgment.

The working of modern business organizations is not (as has been remarked above) a popular field of enquiry amongst European economists. Yet those economists who have investigated the working of Unilever in recent years have on the whole judged it favourably. Its recent organization, one economist has concluded, successfully rationalized the industry, reducing the number of lines and units of production. Her conclusion was as follows: 'On balance and in the end it seems likely that bigness in this industry benefited the consumer. It did so by a decision drastically to limit the number of lines offered to the consumer, to judge what they needed and could accept and to concentrate production and sales efforts on them.'[1]

Another economist, who has investigated the problems of competition and monopoly in the soap industry more closely than they have ever been investigated before, said of the 1950s that 'Overall the general picture which emerges is one of effective or "workable" competition in the soap and detergents industry. At least during the period reviewed, there have been reasonable profits, expanded output, a progressive technology, improved products, and prices in reasonable relation to the cost of production.'[2] In short, and in so far as Unilever comprised a large part of this particular British industry, management had handled its

[1] P. Lesley Cook and R. Cohen, *Effects of Mergers*, Allen & Unwin, 1958, page 271. The chapter on the detergent industry is by Miss Cohen.
[2] H. R. Edwards, *Competition and Monopoly in the British Soap Industry*, Clarendon Press, Oxford (1962), page 254.

problem of maintaining equilibrium between those to whom it is socially responsible with a considerable measure of success.

In one respect at least, the very commercial and technological progressiveness of a concern like Unilever provoked criticism in some quarters. Was there not something wrong (a certain kind of critic would ask) with the social values and economic priorities of a society which allowed its transport system to run down, its docks to fall into chaos, its housing to be inadequate in numbers and in quality, and so on, while it put an enormous effort of intelligence and money into refining such commodities as toothpastes, washing-up powders and dried peas? Yet this is to think backwards and upside down all at once. It is, of course, characteristic of industrial-ized societies that the nature of the basic industries and services must be transformed by technological progress. Yet basic industries are those which respond most slowly to such changes, tending as they do to break rather than bend. Meanwhile, in all such societies, social demand transfers a growing burden of emphasis to secondary and tertiary industries. It is these which not only constitute the difference between modern and backward economies; it is they who have developed and illustrated most vividly something which is in fact characteristic of *all* industry, that it represents a union of commercial and technological skills, each in its appropriate measure essential to the success of an enterprise. It is in the newer industries that techniques such as those connected with marketing have been most highly developed, yet in some measure again they are applicable even to basic industry. No business sits on a basis of technology alone. It sits on a basis of technology *appropriate to its market situation*. This, broadly, is the lesson which the newer industries can teach to the older ones. Nothing could be more misguided or socially unprofit-able than to put the brake on the progressive 'consumer' industry because it has applied intelligence more successfully to its problems than the older 'basic' industries. The remedy is for society to ensure that those industries which lack the stimuli that urge on the new industries should arrange their affairs so as to catch up with their more advanced neighbours.

The evidence suggests that in a society where more and more people demand a full share in the benefits of production, the needs of mass consumption have been better solved by large firms working under conditions of competition which would not have satisfied the older school of economists than by those which work under conditions of more or less free competition.[1] As regards the shareholders, the evidence of the stock market in this period showed beyond any doubt that they ranked Unilever's shares as amongst the bluest of the blue chips. The record of labour relations was commendably free of major stoppages in the advanced economies, even in years of radical reorganization and increasing automation. The record of productivity may very roughly be demonstrated by a comparison between Unilever's index of turnover and the movement of the Gross National Product. Such a comparison can only be used in very broad terms,[2] but it suggests that in Western Europe as a whole Unilever has grown at roughly the same pace as the national product of the area.

In regard to prices Unilever was able to substantiate convincingly its claim to have passed on the economies of size to the consumer. In 1957 a comparison was made between the rise in price of some Unilever branded products and the rise in the cost

[1] 'The modern standard of life of the mass evolved during the period of relatively unfettered "big business". If we list the items that enter the modern workman's budget and from 1899 on observe the course of their prices not in terms of money but in terms of the hours of labour that will buy them—i.e. each year's money price divided by each year's hourly wage rates, we cannot fail to be struck by the rate of the advance which, considering the spectacular improvement in qualities, seems to have been greater and not smaller than it ever was before. . . . Nor is this all. As soon as we go into details and enquire into the individual items in which progress was most conspicuous, the trail leads not to the doors of those firms that work under conditions of comparatively free competition but precisely to the doors of the large concerns—which, as in the case of agricultural machinery, also cannot have much of the progress in the competitive sector—and a shocking suspicion dawns upon us that big business may have had more to do with creating that standard of life than keeping it down.' J. A. Schumpeter, *Capitalism, Socialism and Democracy*, Harper & Bros., New York, 1942.

[2] The statistical problems of such a comparison are formidable. In the decade 1953–63 Unilever growth seems to have exceeded GNP in some six European countries and in another six to have been somewhat below GNP. The problem is bedevilled by:

    (a) The size of the base from which the comparison starts, i.e. where the starting base is small it is relatively easy to achieve proportionate increments; where the starting base is large it is proportionately more difficult. This applies both to products and to national economics;

    (b) In some situations Unilever has been able to increase the supply of its products far in excess of GNP growth because of unsatisfied demand amongst classes of consumers with high standards of living, whose demand was as yet unsatisfied;

    (c) It may be that once a certain standard of living has been achieved, a further growth of demand for a traditional product will grow less fast than growth in incomes;

    (d) The acquisition of existing companies may give a distorted impression of growth.

of living in the previous twenty years throughout the British, Dutch, Belgian, French, German, United States, Australian and Indian markets. The comparison showed that in eight instances Unilever consumer prices had risen more than the cost of living index. In the other twenty-one cases the increase in price was below the increase in the cost of living index.

Men often speak and write as if large aggregations of capital like Unilever wielded great 'power', political as well as economic. Undoubtedly the modern forms of business association which have replaced those transitory and generally feeble temporary associations of earlier days[1] have achieved a large measure of that *stability* which was amongst their chief aims. Yet their 'power' is strictly conditional upon the practical success they represent and upon the reputation they earn in the opinions of consumers, investors, workers and governments. They must continually change their forms and activities to reflect, often even to anticipate, the changes in the world around them. To relax their vigilance would be to court disaster. Least of all can they allow themselves the luxury (as did John Stuart Mill a century ago) of contemplating the happy arrival of 'a stationary economic state' which would automatically resolve all their problems. In a world where a 'natural state of competition' (if it ever existed) has given way to effective legislation against monopoly and against collusion-to-defeat-competition, such an indulgence would rapidly destroy the bases of economic power, and the organization to which it is conditionally entrusted would disappear into the air, like John Aubrey's fairy, with a melodious twang.

None of this meant that there was any room for complacency. Unilever knew only too well that time and competition were always pressing hard on its heels, and if one effect of serving human beings in very large numbers with their daily wants was to sharpen Unilever's comprehension of human relationships, another was certainly to induce a mood of constant self-appraisal and self-criticism. The prime task was not a new one, but it was one which became no easier with time: to achieve a steady consistency of aim which would balance the unavoidable demand for higher efficiency, greater productivity, greater precision of method, and greater use of automatic production methods with the preservation of human values and ethical standards in all its human dealings.

[1] See *The History of Unilever*, vol. I, chapters V, VI, XX: vol. II, chapters III, IV, XIV.

PART TWO

THE CHRONICLE OF GROWTH

INTRODUCTORY: THE PATTERNS OF GROWTH

THE growth of Unilever in these two decades was not simple but complex; not simply the expansion of existing plant or traditional products, but its expansion and adaptation to new markets, new products and new technologies. It involved not only building new plant and modernizing, sometimes scrapping, old plant, but acquiring plant and businesses from other companies which were brought within the Unilever complex during this period. All this took place against a world background that was changing all the time.

Broadly, the two post-war decades corresponded to two distinguishable phases of economic development. The first ten years were the period of recovery from the war and the destruction and shortages it had entailed. By the early 1950s economic progress in many parts of the Western world was rapid and the quinquennium culminated in the general boom in 1955. In this world expansion even the primary producing countries shared. These were years when demand was still rising rapidly and competition was not yet sharp enough to worry producers unduly. The decade that began in 1955–6 was very different. General economic expansion continued, but it was neither so easy, continuous nor universal as it had been. In Europe and America competition became sharper, and profit margins dropped. In Unilever itself diversified investment became more and more characteristic, but if this offered the most reliable future and the best security against risk, it enhanced for the time being the difficulties of keeping up the return on invested capital.

These external conditions were mirrored in the changing structure of Unilever itself. The 1950s and the 1960s saw Unilever move into another phase of 'acquisitions' which inevitably reminds one of the boom years after the First World War, and was in marked contrast to the period of consolidation which characterized the late 1920s and 1930s. Down to 1958 the number of businesses acquired in any year was never more than could be counted on the fingers of a single hand. But from 1959 onwards the annual number was trebled or even quadrupled. Nothing like it had been seen since the expansive days after the First World War.[1] Yet there was a major difference between the post-war boom of 1918–21 and the last decade. Broadly speaking, businesses were acquired in the earlier period to build up the existing share of the purchaser in some market where he was already powerfully established. Power was to be added to power—some critics thought to the point of monopoly risk. Quite apart from the public safeguards against monopoly which almost every country has built into its administrative fabric since the Second World War, Unilever would probably have hesitated in the post-1945 years to lay out more capital and enterprise on its share of the trade in its original staples, soap, margarine, and oils and fats. The latest extensions and improvements of existing plant were necessary not to increase Unilever's share of the market in these traditional staples but to maintain it, and upgrade quality. Experienced management has learned in the twentieth century (as Lord Heyworth himself said) that monopoly is bad for any business, though it may seem highly convenient to it for a time. Unilever therefore preferred to arrange its capital and managerial skills into a growing number of baskets. The acquisition of existing businesses was overwhelmingly concerned with these new areas of enterprise; almost all the businesses acquired from 1956 to 1965 have been manufacturers of foods or chemicals.

Almost every geographical area witnessed this phenomenon of takeover. Companies were acquired, sometimes because Unilever felt it needed the skill and knowledge which a business represented, and that this was the quickest and cheapest, perhaps the only way of acquiring such a base for a programme of calculated expansion. Often the original approach came not from the purchaser but from the purchased. A company, especially a family business, saw itself running short of money or men or both. It would rather trust its future to a firm of repute already in existence, with terms or understandings that it knew and trusted than wait for decline or for takeover by forces it neither knew nor trusted. 'Perhaps' said the Chairmen in 1964, 'those who sometimes feel critical when they read of our acquiring other companies have a nightmare vision of gallant little independent companies being dragged kicking and screaming into Unilever's maw. Let me reassure them. Acquisitions

[1] See Figure 11, page 131.

are essentially based upon a willing seller as well as a willing buyer and more often than not the overtures are first made by the existing owners of the business because they see very clearly the advantages of becoming a part of Unilever.'[1]

This was especially true of Continental Europe. Here the industrial revolution reached full flood at least half a century, and very often a good deal more, after a similar phase had been reached in Britain. In Britain the move from the family business to the public company reached sizeable dimensions from the 1890s onwards. In Continental Europe it was often another half century before the family business felt the need to change its form. A firm like De Betuwe[2] in the Netherlands joined Unilever voluntarily, for the kind of reason just described. The takeover of the 1950s and 1960s was an instrument not of monopoly, but of growth and diversification.

Yet the pattern of growth and diversification was deliberate, not haphazard. The areas chosen by Unilever came into view not merely because they promised a profitable investment of money. They were in all cases chosen because they represented a form of activity for which Unilever felt it was basically fitted, either by reason of marketing knowledge or close technological affinities. Thus the entire exercise of investment since 1945 formed a broadly coherent whole and not just a collection of expedients. Most of the products were marketed by methods in which Unilever had long been expert. Or they were the result of a congeries of technologies with a broadly common scientific basis. Where, as in Africa, Unilever moved into entirely new fields of manufacture and technology, it did so by utilizing the knowledge of companies long expert in these activities. Unilever entered into partnership with such firms, contributing to the alliance its own marketing skills.

Nor was the process simply one of growth or acquisition. Some businesses were shorn away where they seemed inappropriate in modern conditions. One such was the Norwegian fat-hardening plant of De-No-Fa. Unilever's interest here was nearly half a century old. But it was no longer producing any adequate return and in 1958 it was sold. In West Africa the traditional business of the firms through which Unilever had penetrated the African economy was the buying of local produce. The gradual withdrawal from this kind of business is described elsewhere.[3]

---

[1] 'Investment in Food', a speech to the Shareholders.
[2] Chapter 8, page 202.   [3] Chapter 9, 'Africa', pages 214–15.

These varied facets of change were all in practice interrelated. As one type of production was rationalized and concentrated, the productive capacity rendered superfluous was turned over to other uses. With detergent production concentrated at Port Sunlight and Warrington, Knight's of Silvertown came to the end of their career as soap makers. Henceforth they were to be part of Unilever's chemical enterprises. The old margarine factory at Neuss in the Rhineland, originally acquired by Jurgens' and Van den Bergh's in 1910, was closed down in 1959. In that year it still produced roughly 20,000 tons of margarine. In 1961 a plastics factory was started on the same site for blowing plastic bottles for Lux and carpet shampoo. The former Hartog factory at Oss, originally acquired because of its margarine production, went over entirely to food production. Thus, in one way or another the broad planning decisions taken for Unilever's future made their effects felt in many places in the total production complex. The chronicle of growth, concentration, diversification and adaptation as it evolved in response to market opportunity and scientific change is set out in the chapters that follow.

It would have been a very much more modest chronicle had Unilever not had access to an international corpus of capital, knowledge and, above all, men. It was not least the fact that Unilever's managers operated irrespective of national frontiers that placed great advantages at the disposal of each and every company, whatever its immediate nationality, which was part of this international complex.

UNILEVER TOTAL THIRD PARTY TURNOVER
and sales percentages in main commodity groups

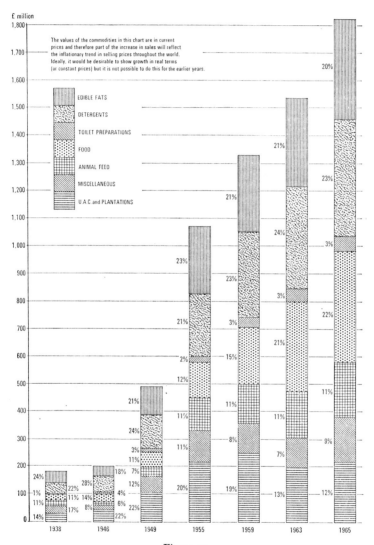

Figure 12

UNILEVER SALES OF DETERGENTS 1950-1965

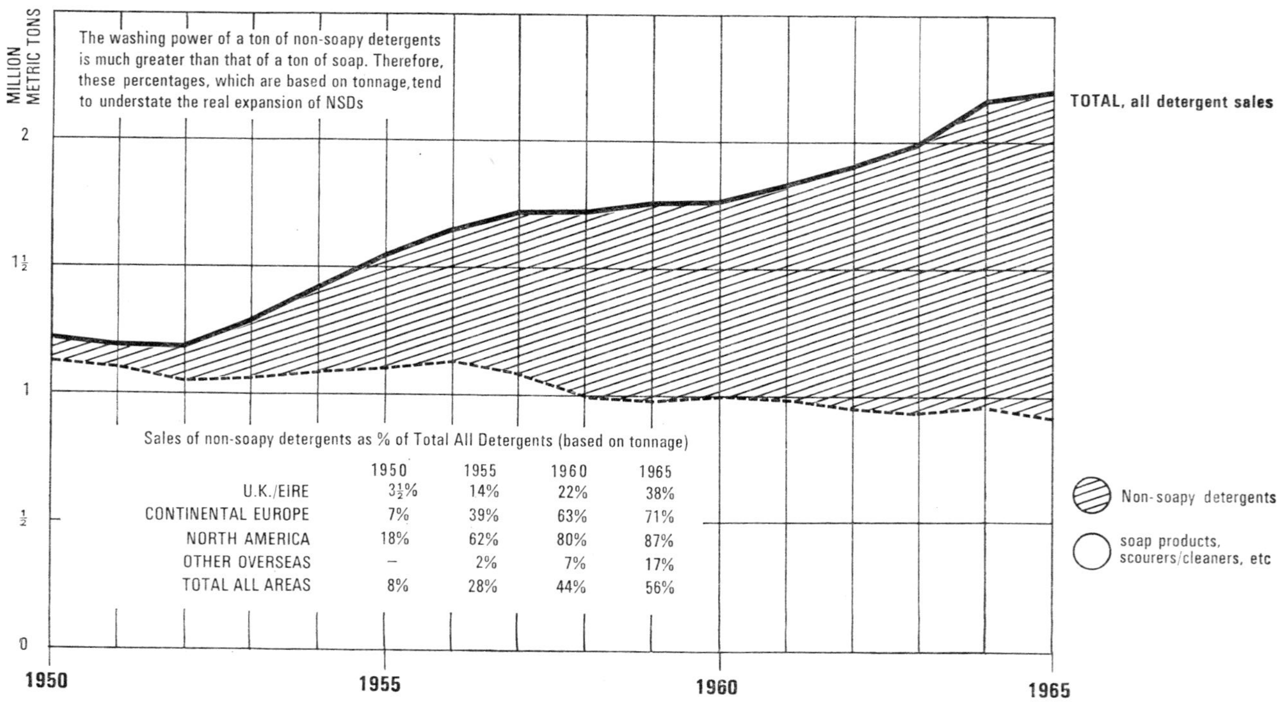

TOTAL, all detergent sales

The washing power of a ton of non-soapy detergents is much greater than that of a ton of soap. Therefore, these percentages, which are based on tonnage, tend to understate the real expansion of NSDs

Sales of non-soapy detergents as % of Total All Detergents (based on tonnage)				
	1950	1955	1960	1965
U.K./EIRE	3½%	14%	22%	38%
CONTINENTAL EUROPE	7%	39%	63%	71%
NORTH AMERICA	18%	62%	80%	87%
OTHER OVERSEAS	–	2%	7%	17%
TOTAL ALL AREAS	8%	28%	44%	56%

MILLION METRIC TONS

2

1½

1

½

0

1950   1955   1960   1965

Non-soapy detergents

soap products,
scourers/cleaners, etc

Figure 13

CHAPTER 7

THE UNITED KINGDOM

Detergents

IN 1931 Geoffrey Heyworth read to a conference of managers a paper on the Unilever soap industry, which contained at that stage 49 manufacturing companies maintaining no less than 48 separate sales organizations. The majority of the companies handled household soap, and the plan of working had so far been utmost competition between companies. The organization was overloaded with far too many products and too many salesmen. His plan for reducing this chaos to order was the basis for the developments of the next twenty years. The shrinkage in the number of factories and products has been described elsewhere.[1] By the time the Second World War broke out three London soap factories had been shut; Hudson's works at Bank Hall and West Bromwich had gone; the New Pin factory, the old Mill Bay Company of Plymouth, and J. L. Thomas of Exeter had all disappeared as soap-makers. The soap production of Gossage's of Widnes had gone to Port Sunlight; their chemical production to Crosfield's of Warrington. The products that the remaining factories made had undergone remarkable changes also. Powders and flakes were improved in quality and had everywhere tended to elbow hard soap out of favour. Even before the war synthetic detergents were treading on their heels. *Total* production by Unilever in the United Kingdom, however, had moved very little between 1930 and the end of the peace. The increase in national consumption had largely gone to competitors.

In many respects, post-war trends may be seen as simple extrapolations of pre-war trends. The number of factories was further reduced. So was the number of products. Qualities improved as more was spent on research and development. Yet the general economic background was very different. British consumers went on buying and using more soap and detergents. By 1958 total consumption had reached a figure of 638,000 tons. This was not only an advance of nearly 130,000 tons on the last figure pre-war,

[1] *The History of Unilever*, vol. II, pages 345–7.

but represented products of far higher detergent power. Within this total Unilever's production likewise moved up much faster than it did in the 1930s. By 1962 Unilever in the U.K. and the Republic of Ireland were selling a total of 326,000 tons. This included soap powders, synthetic powders, liquid detergents, toilet soaps, hard soaps, soap flakes and scouring powders, as well as specialized industrial soaps. Thus Unilever's production had increased in volume by some 23 per cent since 1938. But Unilever's share of the total United Kingdom market remained almost exactly what it had been in 1938.

The early years after the war found seven of the early starters still in the soap race in spite of earlier rationalization. They were: Lever Brothers, Port Sunlight; Joseph Crosfield and Sons of Warrington; Joseph Watson of Leeds; Christopher Thomas of Bristol; John Knight's of Silvertown; T. H. Harris of Stratford, London; Edward Cook of Bow. Some of their makes were old and famous, like Knight's Castile and the Christopher Thomas Puritan Soap. They owed their place in the Unilever family partly to the general process of concentration that the soap industry had undergone in the twentieth century and more particularly to William Lever's dogged determination to justify himself and his policies in the matter of the abortive Soap Trust of 1906. They survived so long as the concentration process seemed to have gone far enough: in practice that meant so long as the soap-making process did not undergo more radical technological transformations than it had done by 1939. The coming of continuous processes and of non-soapy detergents thereafter marked the new watershed. The first soap-makers to go were Christopher Thomas and Brothers, T. H. Harris and Edward Cook. They were followed by Joseph Watson in 1952.

The core of the problem nevertheless remained. Port Sunlight, that bold and progressive late Victorian essay in enlightened industrialism, had always been the heart of the soap industry for Unilever. Its inescapable paternalism was now out of fashion as the State elbowed out all other competitors for the paternal function. Its administration was overburdened with other factories, including the Stork Margarine Works and hydrogenation plant, the British Extracting Company, Price's Bromborough, a research department and several other service departments. Its production costs were high and some thought its management too comfortable in its outlook; yet the value of its site was inestimable. Its capacity was not fully extended. Everything pointed to the reorganization of Port Sunlight as one of the major necessities of the Unilever detergent industry.

In 1959 a study group under the chairmanship of Dr E. G. Woodroofe reported on its future. It remarked that during the three-quarters of a century since its establishment, the products and techniques of the industry had been revolutionized. Yet Port Sunlight had only been adapted partially and piecemeal to keep up with change. Foreseeing continued population growth and increased income per head for another twenty years, they believed that Unilever should plan to maintain its share of the growing national market in detergents. There would be improved and more costly products and more specialized products requiring new plant. They therefore recommended a further concentration of production. John Knight's of Silvertown was to be the first victim of the new progress. Its soap manufacture was to be transferred to Port Sunlight, for the site at Silvertown was not suitable for large-scale development, and production there was in fact uneconomic. Secondly, there should be a rearrangement of production between Port Sunlight and Crosfield's factory at Warrington, only nineteen miles away. Warrington would concentrate on soap and white synthetic powders. Port Sunlight would be responsible for all hard soaps, flakes and blue synthetic powders. To facilitate this the Port Sunlight administration, saddled as it was with extraneous responsibilities, should be relieved of these by a separate 'service company', which would administer the whole site.

Other conclusions followed from these. The glue business at Silvertown should be sold if an adequate price could be obtained. A new detergents factory in the south of England might be necessary if Warrington had to develop largely as a chemical producer, and if new capacity were needed for the expanding liquid detergents production.

Not all these decisions were to be carried out in their entirety. The recommendations of the Woodroofe study group were nevertheless the essential basis for radical reorganization in the following five years. And its repercussions were to be felt at many points in Unilever besides the soap industry itself. Behind the need for change two kinds of pressure were building up. One was the technological change already referred to, which pointed to the economies of further concentration of production. But the other was the changing nature of competition in the soap market. As the major competitive struggle became one between Unilever and a single major rival (Procter and Gamble Limited), unhindered by a history of multi-company relationship and able to draw immediately on the latest knowledge of their parent company in the United States, the need to streamline Unilever's own operations was plain.

The situation was the more urgent in that the market itself was showing some signs at this stage of slowing down. The major factor in the campaign was thus becoming the ability of the company to develop and market a new or improved product rapidly. And here Unilever felt hindered by an over-complex relationship between its multiple production system and a multiple marketing system. For Knight's, Lever Brothers Port Sunlight and Crosfield's were not only producing separately. They were marketing and selling through research and marketing executives spread over three different marketing companies—Lever Brothers Limited; Crosfield's, Watson's and Gossage's, and Hudson and Knight's.[1] If the new arrangements for soap production were to be effective, a single Unilever strategy would have to be developed for marketing and selling their products. This meant a single company to co-ordinate marketing, sales, development, advertising services and commercial problems. The natural sequel to the Port Sunlight plan was therefore the formation of Lever Brothers and Associates, announced in April 1960. Its directive was that it was to make policy for the soap producers, to strengthen communication with research and other service divisions, to concentrate marketing policy of all brands under a unified command, and to consolidate advertising for the soap group.

The recommendation that Crosfield's should concentrate on soap powders and white synthetic powders at Warrington, while Port Sunlight should concentrate on soap flakes and blue synthetic powders was changed in practice, so that all synthetic detergents were concentrated at Port Sunlight. A powerful factor in bringing about this change of emphasis was the growing importance of research into the new processes which was being developed at Port Sunlight. Correspondingly, as the plans for chemical expansion became clearer in the years following the Port Sunlight study group's report, the need to envisage a purely chemical future for Warrington emerged. The estate service, on the other hand, under the name of Unilever Merseyside Limited, came into

[1] For the creation of this marketing company complex, see *The History of Unilever*, vol. I, page 310.

being in 1960 and took over the task of administering and making more efficient such services as Bromborough Dock, the internal railways and waterways, the Merseyside Power Station, the water and health services, training facilities, Port Sunlight Village, and the surrounding buildings, roads and lands.

The condition imposed on the suggested sale of John Knight's was not realized. No purchaser willing to pay an adequate price turned up to buy the old fat and bone business. It was accordingly retained, together with the glues and adhesives business; its story is told elsewhere.[1]

The results of the changes were nevertheless impressive. During the period between 1959 and 1963, Port Sunlight enjoyed what its Chairman described as 'an explosive expansion'. Its total production rose from 199,000 tons to 223,000 tons between 1959 and 1962. The biggest increases were registered in the manufacture of synthetic detergents, toilet soaps and hard soaps. The total output of all Unilever soap and detergent products now increasingly concentrated in Port Sunlight and Warrington increased from 349,000 tons in 1952 to 387,000 tons in 1962. More important was the rising proportion of this total represented by new non-soapy detergents. From 14,000 tons in 1952 it had risen to nearly 100,000 tons by 1962.[2] Critics might feel that production was still too much fragmented. Port Sunlight, for example, still manufactured more than 1,400 packs, even after all the streamlining that had gone on for many years. But it had to be remembered that Port Sunlight worked for a world export market. Nevertheless the manufacture of large numbers of specialized lines was often unprofitable, for they involved a disproportionate expenditure of time and reorganization of plant. There was, therefore, pressure for further streamlining. Some time-honoured old brand names like Knight's Castile and Puritan Soap lived on, even though the firms that created them fell victim to economic law.

Another measure of acquisition and concentration came to its natural conclusion in 1965 with the transfer from Newcastle-upon-Tyne to Port Sunlight of the production and distribution of the Domestos business. Domestos was really an outgrowth of the traditional chemical industry of the north-east. It was founded in

[1] See Chapter 3, pages 58–9 *et seq.*, and below pages 176–7.
[2] These tonnages are not entirely comparable because of the smaller washing power per weight unit of soap compared with the new synthetic powders. The washing power of the latter varies, moreover, quite considerably from country to country, according to the hardness of the water.

1930 by W. A. Handley, who manufactured from raw materials readily available from the local chemical industries a powerful disinfectant and sterilizer. To this he added other disinfectants, liquid detergents, shampoos and polishes. Domestos itself was used as a sterilizer, a deodorant, a germ killer and a bleach, and it found its customers both domestically and in the catering industries. Stergene was specially designed for washing woollens and for large-scale use in industries like laundries and garages. A variant, Hytox, was used in hospitals and food processing plants. Here was an energetic little company which needed greater resources of capital and management. In 1961 it became part of Unilever and four years later part of the Port Sunlight group.

Toilet Preparations

The concentration of soap and detergent production at Port Sunlight and Warrington had other consequences. At Leeds was the old-established firm of Joseph Watson's. Before 1906 Watson's had ruled the soap market of north-east England. Then in 1912 Lever's had first acquired a shareholding in Watson's, completed in 1917. In 1952 they were still making Puritan Soap on a sizeable scale. Thereafter soaps and detergents were steadily moved to Port Sunlight. Another component in the crossword puzzle was D. and W. Gibbs, which Lever had acquired in 1919 when he bought Price's Patent Candle Company with which it was associated. Gibbs's, together with Atkinson's, Pear's and Vinolia, formed the toilet-preparations centre of Unilever.

As detergent production was moved over to Warrington and Port Sunlight, a twofold concentration took place at Leeds. Joseph Watson's factory became the production headquarters of toothpastes, shampoos, hair dressings, skin cream, shaving preparations, and the like. These were manufactured under the name of Gibbs Pepsodent Limited, exploiting the reputation of the long-established Gibbs name in this kind of market. At Leeds, increasingly from 1952 onwards, and completed under the terms of the concentration plans for 1959, Unilever concentrated the former toilet products of John Knight's of London, Christopher Thomas of Bristol, Lever's of Port Sunlight, Atkinson's of Bermondsey, Seward's of Vauxhall, and Pear's of Isleworth.

Leeds probably produced a greater variety of brands, packs and products than any other Unilever factory. It acted as a centre of knowledge for other Unilever toilet preparations companies all over the world, it collaborated with European companies in its soap products and, to do all this, it was given an increasing measure of freedom to carry through the total development of new products from the research to the marketing stage. The so-called toiletries market was far from an easy one. The world turnover was enormous—almost £750 million by 1959 and more than £1,100 million by 1965. Unilever's share of this total world market was still small. There was plenty of room for expansion, but a survey made in 1959-60 suggested that Unilever should concentrate on 'utilitarian' preparations, like toothpastes, shampoos and hair dressings, for research expenditure was high and products were apt to be short-lived. But already between 1949 and 1963 a substantial measure of concentration had been achieved. The eight production centres working in the 1940s had been reduced to the single centre at Leeds by 1963. Turnover in the same period had roughly doubled.

Margarine and other Edible Fats

The margarine and edible fat trade developed in a markedly different way from other branches of Unilever's business in two respects. First, in the 1950s and 1960s it was expanding only very slowly and with great difficulty. Once Government control of edible fats was lifted in 1955 Unilever's sales levelled off at a figure of about 377,000 tons; and there, for the next ten years, it stood, subject only to temporary ups and downs. Saturation point was obviously being reached, and in this constricted market manufacturers were competing still with natural products—butter and lard—the prices of which controlled the prices of margarine and cooking fat. Secondly, this was a branch of production where great economies of scale had already been achieved through concentrating production before our period opened. By 1949 Unilever had concentrated its production in two major factories in the United Kingdom—one serving the north from Bromborough, another serving the south from Purfleet—and a smaller one in Ireland. The combined output of these factories represented something like 20 per cent of the total United Kingdom butter and margarine market before the Second World War. By 1966 this had risen by 5 per cent.

The more or less static condition of the market nevertheless concealed changes of great importance in the quality of production. For though the *volume* of production had increased by only a small amount, the *value* was very much larger—in fact by some 50 per cent. At both the major United Kingdom factories large amounts of capital had been injected into the plants to convert them to the most modern methods of production. At Purfleet over £3·25 million was spent to introduce continuous methods of production, to add a new hardening plant, an improved oil refinery and various other new and improved ancillary plants. At Bromborough a £3·5 million reconstruction plan provided a new laboratory, health centre, dairy, oil blending plant, and so on. These new methods of production, the technology of which is described elsewhere,[1] enabled the Unilever Margarine Group to market through Van den Bergh's Limited, the marketing company responsible, much improved products which incorporated all the knowledge won by research in the laboratories at Vlaardingen and elsewhere. Each of the new brands marketed under the names of Stork, Summer County, Blue Band, Echo, had qualities which had escaped earlier technology. Some spread more easily, even when taken straight out of the refrigerator, all remained firm in hot weather, and had better texture and consistency. Each might in fact be properly said to compete with the natural product of which margarine had originally only been a poor imitation—butter. Not all aimed to taste like butter, but the manufacturer of brands that did could now go out and with some confidence ask the housewife whether she could distinguish between margarine and butter.

All this suggested genuine progress, not merely in marketing but in the real technological improvements which created the market man's confidence. But, in a market that was plainly reaching saturation point, manufacturers could not remain complacent. There was for them no obvious logic of diversification born of higher living standards such as was open to the soap companies. No new product emerged obviously from margarine as the new detergents had done from soap. The problem therefore was to determine the direction which diversification should take. Cooking oil was one possibility. Another was soft drinks, a symbol of twentieth-century life so characteristic that it had been already immortalized in verse by Mr John Betjeman.[2] Another was cheese.

---

[1] See Chapter 4, pages 78–80.
[2] See 'Margate 1940': *Selected Poems* (1948).
>Oh then what a pleasure to see the ground floor
>With tables for two laid as tables for four
>And bottles of sauce and Kiaora and squash
>Awaiting their owners who'd gone up to wash.

In short, while there might be no technological links that bound these various food products together, the knowledge of food marketing gave a sort of logic to them as a group.

Oil and Cake

When the Margarine Union and Lever Brothers came together in 1929, the new combine spanned everything from growing coconuts and catching whales to selling a wide range of manufactured products for the home in thousands of shops. In between came large numbers of factories all over the world, using up oils and fats and making products which were sold through chains of shops. Drawn out on a diagram, these all had the neat appearance of a vertical organization into which primary products were fed at the top, falling into the customer's lap at the bottom. Many commentators on the new combine in 1929 and later assumed that this was an accurate picture. In reality it was highly over-simplified. Long before 1929 the economics of verticality had been severely modified by experience. Most, if not all, of the companies within this apparent vertical combine regarded themselves as straightforward marketing companies, selling their product on the open market at market price.[1]

One of the middle processes of manufacture to which both Dutch and British precursors of Unilever had committed themselves deeply was the manufacture of oil and cake. Both sides needed the same oils and fats, largely obtained by 1929 from the crushing and processing of oil-bearing seeds. The control of these sections of the two industries proved one of the most difficult points in the bargaining of 1929. In the United Kingdom the roots of the oil-milling industry were deep. Port Sunlight had had an oil mill to process tropical oil seeds for soap-making. It had manufactured cattle foods as a sideline since 1896. Then in 1925 Leverhulme had bought a controlling interest in the British Oil and Cake Mills, an amalgamation of twenty-eight mills and twelve oil refineries, mainly in Hull, Liverpool, Glasgow and London.[2]

To this had been added in 1929 the Olympia Oil and Cake Company of Selby, Yorkshire, and the Erith Oil Works near London, which had been part of the Jurgens contribution in Britain to the Unilever alliance of 1929.

In 1949 Unilever still owned twenty-two separate oil and cake

[1] See *The History of Unilever*, vol. II, pages 202–3, 322–3.
[2] Ibid., vol. I, page 278.

M

mills, carrying out the various processes of their trade—seed extraction, oil refining and hardening and compound manufacture. They were grouped mainly round the Thames basin, the Avon, the Humber, Liverpool and the Mersey, the Clyde, and Belfast, for access to the sea was essential to an industry which depended on bulk shipments. In addition to the British Oil and Cake Mills, with its factories at Erith, Silvertown, Avonmouth, Hull, Manchester, Selby, Greenock and Renfrew, there were now Loder's and Nucoline of Silvertown, the British Extracting Company at Port Sunlight and Bromborough, Lever's Feeds Limited, and R. Silcock and Sons Limited, a manufacturer of compound animal feeding-stuffs, with factories at Liverpool, Hull, London, Avonmouth and Renfrew. Unilever was later to take an interest in Associated Feed Manufacturers in Belfast.

Here again was an industry hard pressed by world competition. For the great majority of the seeds and materials that formed the raw material of the oil-miller and cake-maker came from overseas, often from developing countries. Inevitably, economic development in the producing regions brought with it the ambition not merely to produce primary products, but also to process them. An increasing proportion, therefore, of these products was exported to the consuming areas in the form of oil rather than seeds. The total amount of oil produced in the United Kingdom tended to fall, the production of feeding-stuffs to rise. This dual process made more urgent the rationalization of the whole industry, especially on the oil-milling side. By 1963 six of the factories operating a decade earlier had been closed down. The remaining plant had been reconstructed and reorganized so that it could deal more flexibly and efficiently with any type of seed which might come to hand at a given moment. By 1950 four mills had ceased crushing altogether. Avonmouth closed its crushing mill and doubled its expeller-mill capacity in the following year. In the same year the Bromborough mill of the British Extracting Company launched its continuous solvent extraction plant. The crushing mills at Gloucester and Glasgow closed in 1953. In a number of cases crushing was replaced by expeller plant or solvent extraction plant. But at Hull and Warrington solvent extraction plants were closed in 1953 and 1956 and expeller plants were shut down at Silvertown and Selby in 1963.[1]

[1] For technological details of these changes, see 'Research and Technology', pages 78–9.

The more concentrated and efficient oil-milling industry that remained was still essential to Unilever. But more and more its future turned on its success in exploring the market for animal feeding-stuffs in Britain; it was estimated that in 1965 British farmers were spending £450 million a year on feeding-stuffs—an increase of nearly 40 per cent in ten years, which had accompanied the rapid increase of livestock on the nation's farms in that period. Compound feeds for cattle had increased by 23 per cent. Poultry compounds had nearly doubled. To help in exploring this market the Unilever Milling Group had developed a number of demonstration farms, where farmers could watch the results of research into animal nutrition and livestock development. British Oil and Cake Mills had five such farms, Lever's Feeds one, Silcock's two. At Barlby, in Yorkshire, British Oil and Cake Mills were carrying out enquiries into the breeding of bulls, pigs and poultry. As farming itself became more and more industrialized, the Unilever organization harmonized its processes with those of its customers. Through the research laboratories like Colworth, through the demonstration farms, through the factories like Avonmouth with its concentrated 20,000 tons a week of animal feeding compounds flowing to the farms in the West Country and South Wales, the entire oil and cake industry was geared to faster, larger and more efficient production. New feeds meant a sow which could produce five litters in two years instead of two litters in one year. Silcock's concentrated feeds for broiler chickens produced a $3\frac{1}{2}$ lb bird in ten weeks on less than 9 lb of food. In a competitive industry these were essential changes. And the search for new markets and new products was still in progress.

Foods

The growth of the market in preserved or processed foods was one of the socio-economic phenomena of the 1950s and 1960s. To take the frozen-food market alone, here was an invention new in the 1930s. As late as 1955 the market in Britain was worth only £7·5 million. By 1963 it had swollen to £75 million, included vegetables, fish, meat and cakes, and accounted for one and a half per cent of total food expenditure. In Unilever alone, sales of frozen foods rose from £2·5 million in 1953 to nearly £45 million in 1965. Food sales now covered canned foods, frozen foods, dehydrated foods, sausages, ice-cream, fish, cheese, fruit drinks and many others.

Into this strangely assorted company, Unilever had originally stumbled more by accident than design. Mac Fisheries originally formed part of William Lever's adventures in the Hebrides which passed into the company largely because their originator could no longer afford in the dark days of 1922 to retain them. Mac Fisheries by this time had capital invested in retail shops, trawling companies and Wall's sausages. And this happened to be the year when Wall's, looking for something to make good summer slackness in the sausage trade, took to ice-cream and the 'stop me and buy one' tricycle. The same year financial stringency attracted another of Lever's private interests, Angus Watson's, into Lever Brothers, and Lever Brothers found themselves the unenthusiastic owners of Skippers and tinned salmon.

These, then, were the fortuitous bases of the enormous developments of the 1950s and 1960s, when what had been accident became by calculated design a new facet of the Unilever business empire. This essay in diversification grew by acquisition (for Unilever still felt itself very short of the technical knowledge required to enlarge its food interests). Expansion and concentration followed in varying degrees. A fivefold increase in turnover was not achieved free of all trouble. Competition in the food industry was more complex than in soap, for the competitors and interveners included not only rival firms but Nature herself. A bad summer could make a nasty mess of Wall's plans. A bad winter could restore the faltering fortunes of Birds Eye, and a shortage of fresh vegetables convert millions of suspiciously conservative housewives into permanent customers for frozen foods. It was hardly surprising that, faced with problems not only of principle but of personalities too, the decision-makers did not always tread quite as sure-footedly as they did along more familiar paths. Nevertheless, turnover grew, business prospered, and profit margins in general slowly rose to respectable levels.

Historically, the story of Unilever's food interests (distinct from its traditional bases of edible fats) began with Mac Fisheries. Even after the Second World War, traces of a 'vertical' organization still remained in this part of the Unilever structure, reminiscent of the days when Lever had foreseen prosperous fleets of trawlers shovelling their catch into chains of Mac Fisheries' shops and perhaps even producing oil for the soap-maker.[1] This vision, with the Hebridean islanders hard at work in the centre, fishing and canning

[1] See *The History of Unilever*, vol. I, pages 261–2.

fish, had quickly faded. But the shops remained and so did the trawler fleet. Even in the 1950s Mac Fisheries still not only owned trawlers but could claim to have renewed the Aberdeen fishing fleet. But by 1956 there were increasing doubts whether it was worthwhile or advisable to retain the trawler interest. Managing trawlers was a highly specialized business, and there were those who felt it was not Unilever's *forte*. Moreover, the end of food shortages revealed a very marked downward trend in fish consumption in Britain. One of the first effects of the returning power to choose, combined with growing affluence, was an increasing preference for almost any form of meat rather than fish. All this was in marked contrast to the German market, where fish was becoming more popular in the post-war period, and where Nordsee, a company in which Unilever had a major stake, was to be in the forefront of technological developments connected with catching and preserving fish. Maybe it was something to do with the passing of the cloth-cap working-class conception in Britain. Fish-and-chips was indissolubly bound up with that conception. Bourgeois aspirations went perhaps with the determination to leave the fish and chips behind, though few reflected that at its best it was a better food than much that was associated with middle-class catering.

One thing seemed clear. As fish eating became less popular, a question mark hung over the future of the Mac Fisheries shops. The way in which the challenge was met and the breakthrough into the supermarket world is described elsewhere.[1] Mac Fisheries themselves were not prominent as manufacturers or processors by tradition. In 1958, however, they had equipped their Finsbury depot as a processing factory for preparing foods and manufacturing branded goods under the Mac Fisheries name for distribution to their own and other shops, exploiting the Mac Fisheries' reputation for high-quality food. Their Five-Year Plan evolved by 1961 had to undergo many modifications. By 1963 there were twenty fewer Mac Fisheries' shops than in 1962. Some ambitious plans for grouping satellite stores round great parent stores had had to be abandoned. The optimum size for a Mac Fisheries supermarket had been worked out by experience, and some careful thought had gone into defining the district where this kind of supermarket was best established. Shop managers were trained with considerable precision in the arts of marketing special

[1] See Chapter I, pages 19–21.

commodities, and Mac Fisheries had emerged as one of the largest retailers of fruit and vegetables in England. Like the butcher, the baker and the candlestick-maker, the fishmonger was plainly marked out to be a victim of the new economies of scale in the retail trade, but by 1965 it looked as though Mac Fisheries might well have survived the worst of the storm.

A natural connection in the early days of Mac Fisheries was the Angus Watson Company. Angus Watson had set up a canned fish business in Newcastle in 1903. His business brought brands like Sailor, Skipper, and Tea Time into the Lever business. Tinned salmon had become by the inter-war years a familiar delicacy of working-class domestic life. Industrial workers in the North and Midlands used a can of salmon and a bag of tomatoes as a bite at the coal face or the foundry. (The biggest sales of tinned salmon in Britain are still in the areas of heavy industry.) Richard B. Green and Company, the Liverpool firm founded in 1870, also importers of tinned fish, were likewise swept into the empire. So were Pelling Stanley, in which William Lever had acquired shares which he transferred to Lever Brothers Company in 1924. Here again was a firm which went back to 1861 and was to survive until 1963, when, together with the other canning firms just mentioned, it was reorganized under the umbrella structure of John West Foods Limited, with its headquarters near Stanley Dock, Liverpool.

John West was the name of the American who first salted salmon at Westport, Oregon, in 1857. To this export trade was added the salmon canning industry in the 1870s. Two Scotsmen, William and George Hume, pioneered the business on the Sacramento river, and William's nephew Robert Deniston, 'the salmon king of the Oregon River', sold his product through Pelling Stanley. Hume bought the exclusive rights to use the name John West and sold them to a Liverpool firm who re-sold them to Pelling Stanley in 1888. In 1963 John West was disinterred to preside over a vast business in imported foods—salmon and tuna, peaches and mandarins, shrimps, crabs and prawns from Japan; dried fruit from Australia; asparagus from New Zealand; from Malaya, pineapples; fruits and pilchards from South Africa; currants from Greece; tomato juice from Italy; sardines from Portugal; tuna from Peru; salmon, shrimps, prawns and fruit from the United States; brisling from Norway; salmon from Canada and Alaska. But, as in the past, salmon still dominated the business of John West.

'Meat' for Unilever in Britain meant Thomas Wall and Sons.

Thomas Wall, who inherited an eighteenth-century family business in 1840, was characteristic of the type of entrepreneur in light industry who proliferated in late Victorian England. (A plaque in London's Jermyn Street, where Wall's still have an establishment, pays tribute to his philanthropy and educational work towards the end of the nineteenth century.) Wall's sausages and pies were still famous in the post-war world. In 1951 their turnover was between £2 million and £3 million. The next year, as supplies of meat returned, Wall's turnover topped £4 million. A decade later, it was over £26 million: in 1965, £40 million.

This astonishing growth, comparable to the growth of quick-frozen foods, was based on an ambitious programme of co-operation with the farmer and the agricultural scientist. Originally, Wall's factories had concentrated on bacon-curing and sausage-making. After the war, Wall's led the way in devising the best ways of producing efficiently the heavy pig. The research was financed out of profits made by employing the most scientific methods of feeding and breeding. Here was a piquant debate with another Unilever firm, British Oil and Cake Mills, for whereas Wall's were concentrating on the heavy hog, British Oil and Cake Mills were developing at their own experimental farm at Stoke Mandeville a lean pig to produce both bacon and fresh pork. The expanding meat business of Wall's needed more capacity. In 1949 their business was based on the part use of a factory at Godley, Cheshire, and another at Willesden, serving the South. By 1963 Wall's meat had taken over the whole of the Godley factory and there were others at Hayes, Isleworth, and Wembley. The factory at Southall, whence Otto Mønsted, the Dane, had supplied the Maypole shops with margarine in the early days and which in its time played many parts, was likewise pressed into service by Wall's.

Meat, however, was by no means Wall's only care. Their other was ice-cream. Until 1960 this was manufactured at Acton, at Godley and at Craigmillar in Scotland. In 1958 Walls, whose turnover had risen from over £10 million to £13 million, were pressing for new factories. Acton could no longer cope with the demand that existed, much less with the expanding demand which seemed to lie ahead. The small local manufacturer seemed to be disappearing; a big future was foreseen for mass-produced ice-cream of the hard type already popular in North America. A bold capital investment was assured of a good long-term future here.

The Wall's management did not get quite all they wanted, but they did get a new factory at Gloucester, costing £4·5 million—£500,000 short of the capital allocation for which they had originally asked. The new factory went into production in April 1960, two months ahead of schedule. Craigmillar was shut down.

The Gloucester factory was a model of advanced technology. The manufacture of ice-cream is a delicate operation which has to be carried out with the maximum attention to hygiene. The factory was therefore highly mechanized and in some departments entirely automatic. Labouring jobs were few, but the technicians and mechanics needed to be of high quality. The disappearance of the aircraft industry in the neighbourhood had left a pool of suitable skilled men. But it was fundamentally shortage of general labour which forced automation on Wall's, and automation was crowned by the employment of a computer for a large variety of tasks which would otherwise have absorbed vast quantities of labour in a company engaged in transactions running into many millions, each carrying only a marginal profit.

The new factory in Gloucester supplied an area representing more than 30 million people in Wales, West and North England, Scotland and Northern Ireland—more than 60 per cent of the British population. In layout and method it was the largest and (with the Heppenheim factory in Germany)[1] most modern factory of its kind in the world. It ran twice into a trade recession which faced its management with very serious problems. 1960 sales fell by nearly £2 million from the 1959 peak of £16 million. In 1962 they had fallen again. Total production in 1959, before Gloucester came into production, had run at 23 million gallons. By 1964 Acton and Gloucester turned out 19 million gallons. This was a long way below full capacity, and until that capacity could be fully occupied there was little profit to be had. Meanwhile competition, especially from smaller firms, specializing in a different kind of product—the so-called 'soft' ice-cream—had sharpened markedly. The energies of the Wall's management were therefore mainly directed into securing a bigger share of this particular market, which seemed to be the one lively area in a declining market. This in turn meant economizing on other costs, and utilizing the undoubted advantages of the new Gloucester factory to the greatest possible extent. If more varieties of product could be launched and popularized, if refrigeration could be spread more

[1] See page 204.

widely than it was in Britain, and if British housewives could be persuaded to emulate the Americans and treat ice-cream as a food course to be taken with a meal, the era of what one Wall's executive called 'profitless prosperity' could be brought to an end. By 1964 the figures suggested that the tide had turned. By 1966 the profit figures were to reflect the economies achieved by reorganization.

Perhaps the most remarkable post-war phenomenon was Unilever's development of quick-frozen foods. Most people in Britain live in towns where really fresh food is not always easy to come by. A similar problem in the United States had produced the invention of quick freezing. The effect of quick freezing was to stop decay and preserve food in exactly the condition in which it entered the freezer. Clarence Birdseye, an American scientist, had worked out a particularly effective method in the 1920s and 1930s. He brought the food into contact with intensely cold metal plates. His was not the only process. There were others. The Birds Eye process was a good one, though it was not cheap. Nevertheless it had been successful in America and in 1933 Unilever was discussing samples of Birds Eye frozen foods from America. The company which was formed in 1938 to run the Birds Eye business in the United Kingdom was an independent company, Frosted Foods Limited, who quite early on had had contacts with Mac Fisheries, for it was interested in freezing both fish and vegetables. (Similar small ventures in frozen foods took place about the same time in German Unilever in conjunction with Birds Eye.) It did not get far, for the war brought this kind of thing to an end. Nevertheless, negotiations went on between Birds Eye and Unilever. Geoffrey Heyworth, then Vice-Chairman and later Chairman of Unilever Limited, was impressed by the possibilities, but he warned his Board, 'It must be realized that if we went into the business it would have to be in a big way.' The negotiations went on and by 1943 Lever Brothers had taken the majority of the shares in the Birds Eye company in the United Kingdom.

Its early days were far from prosperous. Food was still short, rationing persisted and it was not easy to persuade the conservative British housewife that these apparently costly foods were worth the saving in labour they represented. On the other hand, there was a growing desire to get rid of the dreariness of wartime rationing and restrictions and a willingness to pay for novelty and variety.

Between these twin poles of opportunity and obstacle the new company had to operate. It went ahead with growing peas in the Spalding area to be frozen at Sheffield (in a factory belonging to another Unilever company, Batchelor's) and at Southall (in the old Otto Mønsted factory). It was still talking about frozen herrings for Mac Fisheries in Scotland and at Great Yarmouth, where there was already a cold storage plant belonging to Mac Fisheries. By 1945 attention was increasingly focused on Yarmouth, for in the nearby countryside fruit and vegetables could be produced to be processed between the fishing seasons. Government planning permission for the new factory at Yarmouth came early in 1946. Contracts were worked out on principles, which still hold good, for encouraging the farmers to take an interest. The contract virtually hired the farmer's land and labour for the growing of peas and beans. The seed was bought from Birds Eye so that the strain and quality could be controlled. The harvesting was timed by the contractor's field man. The farmer knew that he would be paid on the nail at a time of year when there was little cash coming in from other crops.

First harvests began to come in in July 1946. The total year's turnover came to £59,000 and there were a hundred shops selling Birds Eye goods. Distribution and marketing were still largely improvised. Frozen foods demand cold storage buildings and insulated transport. There was still nothing like enough, but in the years that followed, Unilever's transport company, S.P.D. (Speedy Prompt Delivery) was increasingly drawn into the problem. They developed their cold storage capacity and added insulated vehicles to get the goods to the shops. The next problem was to induce the shopkeepers to buy the cabinets for keeping and displaying the products.

By 1948 there were 900 shops stocking Birds Eye goods. Output and sales were rising, but profits became correspondingly harder to earn as the competition of more plentiful fresh foods increased. It was plain by 1949 that Birds Eye was facing something of a crisis. It began to look as though to some housewives these foods were a luxury, and the Special Committee was nervous lest they might remain 'an exclusively upper-middle class trade' with few prospects of wider expansion. Costs seemed likely to remain high. There was cause 'for some little nervousness'. Even the original plans for developing research at Colworth House might have to be modified in view of 'the company's diminishing interest in the frosted food business'.

In retrospect these hesitations seem curious. Yet there certainly was cause for hesitation. There was a bad pea harvest in 1949. Competition was forcing advertising expenditure up and there was labour trouble at Yarmouth which ended with a go-slow strike. Yet those most closely associated with the schemes remained optimistic, and from 1951 onwards their optimism was justified. Thereafter progress was rapid. The old factories at Southall and Sheffield gave way to modern plants at Yarmouth and Lowestoft. Then came a new factory on an industrial estate at Kirkby, nine miles outside Liverpool. This was still an era of ingenious improvisation, but it saw Birds Eye through until the 1960s. By then, further factories had been added to the group. By 1963 there were in all six Birds Eye plants—Great Yarmouth, Lowestoft, Kirkby, Grimsby, Hull and Eastbourne. Cold storage space had increased steadily, with buildings more and more advanced in their design. Depots were run in close conjunction with S.P.D. and increased to a point where Birds Eye could store about 50,000 tons of frozen food. Birds Eye and its competitors had not only brought about a revolution for the housewife. They had had a considerable impact on Britain's farmers and fishermen. The pea now ranked with wheat-growing in importance. Over one-third of the white fish catch now went to the freezers and the proportion was growing every year. Fish contracts were tending to replace the old open auction at Grimsby fish market.

In a highly competitive business Birds Eye managed to seize and retain first place. The sales of quick-frozen foods had risen between 1951 and 1965 from £1 million to £45 million. Yet the market was becoming ever more competitive. Competition came not only from other frozen-food manufacturers but also from other types of processing. There was, for example, accelerated freeze drying, which produced foods that needed no refrigerator, though there were serious problems both of quality and marketing with these competing methods.

Doubts and hesitations were not the prerogative of those who, like Birds Eye, had to operate a new technology with all its attendant problems. They afflicted also the representatives of older types of processed food businesses. They afflicted in particular the management of Batchelor's. When this firm was purchased by Unilever at the end of the Second World War it was probably the leader in the British vegetable canning industry, with resources of technology and manufacturing experience which Unilever was glad to purchase along with its fixed capital assets. In the artificial conditions of scarcity and control which lasted for a long time after the war, the Batchelor's business boomed. Even after de-control, in fact until 1954, their turnover in canned processed peas went on expanding generously, and in this expansion they were assisted by the new capital which the Unilever connection provided, for this meant innovations like hydrostatic cookers which extended their lead in this particular type of product.

Batchelor's continued to be controlled by its former management until 1948. To its traditional location in the Sheffield area had been added a new site for development near the Kent vegetable and fruit country at Ashford. Until 1954 Batchelor's were satisfied that their major problem was to expand production; yet no sooner was the Ashford project under way than it became clear that it was bedevilled with difficulties. Controls on the import of canned fruits were suddenly lifted. Labour proved to be short in the Ashford area. The disposal of effluent raised apparently insuperable difficulties. Transport costs between Ashford and London proved to be heavier than those between Sheffield and London. By 1957 Batchelor's weakness became increasingly clear. Their turnover dropped below the 1954 figure, while costs continued to rise.

Batchelor's salvation came in the shape of variants of the dehydration process. First came a range of dried soups earlier developed in the United States by Lipton's. Then a new invention in the form of a dried, pricked pea which had been developed to the pilot plant stage at the research laboratory at Colworth House.[1] By 1957 a similar plant was installed at Batchelor's. It came into production in 1961 and immediately attained a sales value of nearly £500,000. Heavy capital investment was pressed on. New, improved or modified plant was installed at Sheffield, Huntingdon, Worksop and Ashford. Sales increased astonishingly, until by 1965 they reached £3 million. Other vegetables were added to the range, which was marketed under the name of Surprise. Another product was also developed and introduced—dehydrated complete meals. A new management at Batchelor's showed itself ready to investigate a range of curries, spaghettis, and chow mein, all of which could be quickly served up at a few minutes' notice, in the home. The idea of a completely prepared meal offered advantages not only to hard-pressed housewives but to canteens and

[1] See supra, Chapter 4, 'Research and Technology'.

institutional caterers. Thus, by drawing on the experience gained with other types of food processing, by utilizing the research capacity of Colworth House, and by reorganizing their business administration, Batchelor's came back into a new and remarkable phase of prosperity.

A feature of all these Unilever ventures into food processing was a centrifugal movement of production outwards towards the points at which supplies could be most easily obtained, and away from the growing congestion of London and other large cities. Ports like Great Yarmouth, Grimsby and Hull, places like Worksop, Ashford, Huntingdon and Gloucester, were the beneficiaries of the new policy. Birds Eye moved their headquarters out of London to Walton-on-Thames. Mac Fisheries went to the 'New Town' of Bracknell. Basic research continued at Colworth House near Bedford. Development work was shared between Colworth and the development laboratories and plants at Ashford, Yarmouth and other centres.

These developments did not exhaust the possibilities of the food market. In 1964 came an agreement with a Norwegian firm, Vik Brothers, which gave Unilever the right to operate a new process for the breeding and rearing of salmon and trout. This was placed under the control of the Unilever Milling Group which had purchased the share capital of a firm marketing trout food, and two freshwater trout farms in Lincolnshire. A new firm to operate these activities, Marine Harvest Limited, established an experimental fish farm for breeding salmon and trout at Loch Ailort in Scotland in 1965.

Thus, the resources of the factory and methods of mass production were applied to jobs which had previously been carried out in the domestic kitchen. Quick freezing, canning, dehydration, took back into the factory tasks which the housewife had previously done for herself or had employed servants to do for her. In this, the new processes were extending what late Victorian entrepreneurs had begun with mass-produced jams, preserves, fish, and the like. The market was still capable of enormous expansion, but it had its own peculiar problems. It was highly competitive, technologically complicated, and it called upon all the arts of both scientific and marketing expertise. Not all the skills of the technologists were likely to engage the interest of the housewife unless they could produce the foods she liked at a price she could afford to pay. The debate continues.

Chemicals and Packaging

The history of the oils and fats industries in the twentieth century has been dominated by the spectacular achievements of the Lever's, the Jurgens, the Van den Berghs, and the Schichts in matters of marketing and salesmanship. These, and the great mergers, tended to obscure the essential basis of science, and especially of chemistry, upon which industries like soap-making were founded. Nineteenth-century chemists showed that soap-making was essentially a chemical process. The soap-maker needed chemicals like caustic soda. He produced by-products like glycerine. The coming of fat hardening involved him again in chemical technology. The soap industry had for all these reasons always been highly involved with the chemical industry. The involvements multiplied as a result especially of Lever's business strategy. His concern to secure his raw material supplies led him into complex diplomacy which eventually brought into the Lever family great firms like Crosfield's, John Knight's, and Price's, all of whom had or were to develop chemical interests. For similar reasons he likewise acquired a large stake in Thames Board Mills, to secure his supplies of packaging. Thames Board Mills were not in themselves a chemical firm, but they might be said to have been the cause of chemistry in others. For they in turn needed large supplies of adhesives. Hence an area of mutual demand and growth.

This then was the older area of chemical interests in the Unilever family. Crosfield's of Warrington were still the largest chemical company in the group. It still employed some 2,500 people and its business still remained partly soap and partly chemicals. Crosfield's were the largest manufacturers of silicates in the United Kingdom. This was their original chemical product, and the simplest. Thousands of tons of sodium silicate used as an adhesive went to the making of packaging board, cardboard boxes, tubes, and so on. Crosfield's were therefore important as a supplier to other Unilever industries as well as to a growing number of outside users. Silicates went to make cores and moulds in foundries, into alkaline products for cleaning bottles and fabrics, water softeners, coating for cathode ray tubes. The plastics and paint industry bought fine silica. From the days of hydrogenation Crosfield's manufacture included catalysts for use in that process. The technology of catalyst manufacture took them in 1951 into the manufacture of special catalysts for cracking hydro-carbon oils.

Another company that came into the Lever group in the same

year (1920) as Crosfield's was John Knight Limited of Silvertown. By 1912 they had begun to manufacture animal glue. When the Unilever soap industry was reorganized in the 1960s the fat and bone processing industry of Knight's was retained. Edible oils, greases, bonemeal, bone for making bone china—all these went to other Unilever companies and to outside buyers. The most vigorous development was in synthetic adhesives, again directed towards the packaging industry. In the early 1960s the John Knight group came to include a number of formerly independent firms (Fixol and Stickphast, Gloy and Empire, and Surridge Patents). By 1965 the John Knight group was manufacturing 8,500 tons of adhesives a year, mainly for industrial users like the furniture and building trades.

Another area of interacting demands and technologies was that of packaging and board, which grew every day more important as Unilever expanded, especially into the food industry, one of the largest users of modern packaging. From 1920 to 1964 Unilever had only had a stake in Thames Board Mills. In May 1964 it took complete control at a cost of £22·5 million. Thames Board Mills were the world's biggest converter of waste paper into packaging board. In the 1960s they were in the middle of the consequences of the packaging revolution. At Purfleet they installed a £6 million board-making machine, capable of producing 100,000 tons of board annually. At Workington in Cumberland they were developing a £6·25 million integrated pulp and board mill, in order to compete with countries like Sweden which had the benefit of local supplies of timber. At Cumbernauld, a 'New Town' near Glasgow, Thames Board Mills set up another factory conveniently placed to meet the needs of its biggest customer—the whisky industry. By 1965 it was producing 250 tons of packing materials a week.

Other acquisitions in the 1960s helped to round out this area of technology, to provide for the needs of Unilever itself and to extend trade with the outside world. In 1961 E. R. Holloway Limited was acquired. Holloway's were one of the three largest makers of plastic containers. Their sales had more than trebled in the previous five years. Starting in a small way in Barnet they had expanded into a market dominated before the war by the Germans —for plastic combs, hairslides and the like. By the 1950s they were using new and sophisticated plastic materials in a wide variety of manufactured products. There were two reasons behind the merger. Holloway's expansion had outrun their resources of capital. To

Unilever, liquid detergents and the plastic bottles which they bought from Holloway's were simply two sides of the same problem.[1]

If the acquisition of Holloway's could be seen as part of the logic of Unilever manufacture, the acquisition of Commercial Plastics Industries Limited was a different story. Commercial Plastics was mainly engaged in converting plastics into materials for such items as refrigerators, upholstery, furnishing, packaging and rainwear. It had achieved a spectacular growth rate of about 20 per cent annually. Fablon, its best-known product, was a self-adhesive plastic covering with a promising future. Commercial Plastics needed capital. Unilever needed the special technical knowledge which Commercial Plastics could bring into its whole range of packaging industries. The union was therefore a natural commercial marriage.

Meanwhile, pressure from an entirely different direction was also pushing Unilever more deeply into chemical technology. The new synthetic detergents that began to dominate the markets in the 1950s brought the chemical industry into partnership with the older soap industry and gave soap manufacturers the opportunity to extend into chemical manufacture. For many years it had seemed that the chemistry of washing products had been so thoroughly explored that there was little scope for the scientist. Now things were to change. 'The new products' as Lord Heyworth and Dr Rijkens remarked in 1953, 'have introduced a more balanced perspective to the industry and the scientist can look forward to a future as absorbing and exciting as can be found anywhere in the chemical trade.'

The chemist and, to a lesser extent the physicist, became vital to the manufacture of the new products. But there were wider implications too. Synthetic detergents seemed to threaten repercussions in the whole world market for oils and fats. They reduced the output of glycerine, which was a by-product of soap manufacture, and led to urgent enquiries into methods of making synthetic glycerine. Contrariwise they seemed to threaten a superabundance of fatty acids. These arose as residues from the refining of oils, especially from margarine. They were thus inedible, but they made admirable soap-making material provided they did

[1] In September, 1966, the name of E. R. Holloway Limited was changed to Holpack Limited, and the new company retained only the packaging interests of the Container Division. A company, independent of Unilever, was set up to make and market combs, sunglasses and certain other preparations under the name of E. R. Holloway Limited.

not exceed a certain percentage of the total. Rising margarine production meant more fatty acids at a time when the soap-maker seemed likely to need less fatty acids. Hence a surplus in Europe and a fall in price in the early 1950s.

The prospect of a serious superfluity of fatty acids which seemed to threaten in the early 1950s never quite materialized as the prophets feared. New methods of oil refining reduced the amount of fatty acids thrown up by these processes. New methods of soap-making absorbed larger quantities of fatty acids. And the demand for hard soap, especially in the less sophisticated markets of the world, held up longer than had seemed likely. All these factors combined to mitigate the effects of the new technologies which had seemed to threaten a complete upset in the oils and fats world. But they only mitigated it. They did not cure it entirely. Hence again a series of moves within Unilever to raise the degree of profitability of this aspect of the industry.

The obvious path here was to upgrade to the maximum the quality of the fatty acids becoming available within the Unilever complex. Here Unilever already had a valuable instrument at hand. Price's of Bromborough had originally been part of the great Victorian candle business. This had been separated off and remained at Battersea, independent of Unilever. Bromborough was dissociated and brought into the Unilever organization in 1936 and from then Price's (Bromborough) Limited had been developing the upgrading of fatty acids, production of fatty alcohols and the manufacture of other oleo-chemicals. Their products were sold to the textile industry, especially to the finishers of synthetic fibres. They were embodied in lubricants, soaps, disinfectants, synthetic rubbers, duplicating stencils, cosmetics, polishes and scores of other industrial products. By 1965 Price's production of chemicals from oils and fats had risen to 67,000 tons a year, five times the pre-war figures. But more important even than volume was the increase in diversity. By the 1960s Price's were making 200 final products and selling in 120 different industries.

By 1965 Unilever progress in chemicals had thus acquired a momentum of its own. Investment in chemical technology was costly. All the more important, therefore, that knowledge expensively acquired should be put to the widest and most profitable use. Equally, that Unilever should acquire control of knowledge which seemed complementary to what Unilever already had. In 1963 the Walker Chemical Company, manufacturers of synthetic tanning

N

agents and formaldehyde, was acquired. Formaldehyde was used principally in making synthetic resin. The rest went to industries treating textiles, paper and leather, and the makers of chemicals, explosives and disinfectants. The following year saw another smaller company also added to the Unilever chemical empire; Charles Lowe and Company, of Manchester, distilled tar and made resin as adhesives for the plywood and plastics industries.

Other developments in the chemical-manufacturing area were more a matter of internal reorganization to meet Unilever's needs and provide profitable third-party trades. Proprietary Perfumes Limited, formed in 1960, represented a concentration of perfumeries that had previously been attached to individual Unilever companies and had supplied many of the scents and flavours used by Unilever in washing products, toilet preparations, even in animal feeding-stuffs. Proprietary Perfumes Limited, in their new factory at Ashford in Kent manufactured hundreds of different blends of perfume based on more than fifteen hundred raw materials. At Grasse, in the Alpes Maritimes, long the centre of the French scent industry, an interest was acquired in the firm of Bertrand Frères, manufacturers of natural essential oils. Many raw materials, however, were now manufactured synthetically. The technology of perfume meant that here was a growth area where the chemist and the perfumer worked in close co-operation.

Vitamin manufacture was another chemical industry that had long and close connections with the oils and fats side of Unilever. Advita Limited was founded in 1946 specifically to supply the margarine industry with vitamins, colourings and flavourings, but it had developed far beyond this to provide a large variety of products for both human and animal needs. With Advita, in a new headquarters at Walton-on-Thames, were grouped four newly acquired firms, all manufacturers of food flavours and essences: the Birmingham Chemical Company of Lichfield, C. W. Field of Liverpool, Cumming Parsons of Manchester, and William Hay of Hull.

Glycerine, freed during the soap-making process, has always been a valuable by-product. Its refining and sale was now placed in the hands of a central company, Glycerine Limited, which sold to paint-makers and lacquer-makers, explosives manufacturers, and tobacco and drug manufacturers who used it as a solvent and a lubricant.

Unilever's diversified investment in chemicals was no mere haphazard process. Each acquisition represented a logical move into some industry that was either important to Unilever from a marketing or a technological angle. The whole was held together by a logic of products. Development was organic, product by product, as traditional skills were retained, developed and diversified. All this diversification was designed to bring increased sales to third parties and increased usefulness to other Unilever businesses. By 1960 the total size of the interests involved suggested the need for a more articulate policy of expansion. The chemical industries of Unilever in Britain were combined into the Chemical Group in 1960.

Unilever was expert in the mass domestic consumer market. Marketing to other industries was a very different matter. Here a major problem was not only to improve communication between the different Unilever chemical companies, but between them and the management of the customer companies. Chemical products were highly technical and their use involved complex technical problems. Their sale therefore demanded not only salesmen but technicians and engineers capable of giving specialist advice to consumers and providing after-sales service. Products used in other industrial processes had to provide continuous satisfaction and to be adaptable, as the production processes themselves might have to be adapted. The fulcrum of every transaction was the proof that the chemical product was of the correct quality for the production process to which it was directed.[1]

There were important new problems of research and technological development too. In the relative technological torpor of the inter-war years, the old historic connections between the soap and chemical industries had been obscured. The new and sharper competition revived technological progress once more in the post-war years. Unilever became more sharply aware than ever before of an area of chemical, physical and biological knowledge that was vital to its competitive efficiency. The problems of disposing of the effluent from synthetic detergents aroused the widest possible publicity. The detergent-maker found himself involved *inter alia* in problems of the fundamental properties of dirt particles, which arose from effluent disposal. Unilever scientists investigating it found that they were engaged not on an isolated technical problem but operating in a coherent area of surface physics and chemistry.

[1] See also pages 196–7.

Scientific knowledge and technology thus became more indispensable as they themselves progressed. They also became very much more costly. If they made a larger turnover possible, they also in turn demanded a larger turnover to support the costs which they themselves entailed. Unilever's chemical developments illustrated in fact the simple logic of size in modern industry; not size for its own sake regardless of the logic of knowledge, but size suggested by a balance between turnover, profits and costs. Such were the dynamics of growth within the Unilever chemical group. In 1952 Unilever chemical sales in Britain were valued at about £8 million. By 1965 they had more than trebled. To a casual observer the decision to launch into plastic or glue manufacture might suggest that the shoemaker was leaving his last. A closer look confirmed that he was in fact sticking to it remarkably closely. Far from being a matter of random choice, diversification here, as elsewhere in Unilever, followed out closely the implications of technological logic.

CHAPTER 8

THE WEST EUROPEAN CONTINENT

The Recovery of Continental Europe

THE motives behind the final Unilever merger of 1929 were many and varied. They were never stated with unimpeachable clarity at any stage in the negotiations, and indeed they changed during their course. One fact nevertheless stood out to all the participants. There might well be imponderable advantages, such as the pooling of skill and knowledge, or through economies in those areas of raw materials and raw-material processing common to both Dutch and British sides. There might even be savings where operating companies from both sides confronted each other with similar products in the same markets. But in the last analysis the Dutch and British drew their strength from different manufactured products sold in different geographical areas. The Dutch group was based principally upon the margarine trade in Europe; the British upon the soap market in the United Kingdom and Commonwealth areas overseas as well as on the Continent. The British group was also by tradition more deeply engaged in raw-material trades in the tropical areas.

It was possible to envisage a situation where both businesses in different areas were equally prosperous or equally hard-pressed, but it was more probable that there would be differences and fluctuations in their respective fortunes. Union would even out these fluctuations and enable the more fortunate partner to assist the other until the fortunes were reversed. This indeed proved a major feature and justification for the merger and for the equalization arrangements arrived at. By 1937, when Unilever had slowly reorganized and concentrated its energies, after the costly adventures of William Lever in his later years,[1] the Continental markets, Germany in particular, were creating insuperable problems for Unilever N.V. In the great German market which was their largest single source of business, Nazi economics placed guns not only before butter but before soap and margarine and many other things. The war followed, and to all intents and

[1] See *The History of Unilever*, vol. II.

purposes the businesses on the Continental mainland disintegrated for five years or more.

The following years were the years of recovery, the European miracle, and not the least of the phoenixes which arose from the ashes was Unilever itself. By 1955 the scales were once again weighted in favour of N.V. and by 1965 the Dutch group provided over £62 million of profits before tax, while Unilever Limited provided nearly £55 million. Within these figures of recovery and expansion were encapsulated the total loss (subject only to the patchy incidence of compensation) of formerly valuable businesses in Czechoslovakia, Hungary, Poland, Rumania, Yugoslavia and in East Germany that mainly derived from the Schicht organization; the dramatic recovery of the German market, especially the world's largest margarine trade; the unprecedented progress of the detergent market in France; steady progress in Scandinavia; the striking growth of smaller but progressive businesses in Italy; and the emergence of new enterprises in countries like Spain and Greece, which were only just beginning to experience the transition from agrarian to industrial economies.

Unilever was no longer restricted to its original trades in margarine and detergents. By 1963 it had invested £158 million in enterprises that manufactured a wide variety of prepared foods, from meat and fish to ice-cream, jams and vegetables. Between 1955 and 1963 it also put nearly £29 million into its various printing and packaging enterprises. The story was not without its hesitations and failures, but by and large it was a broader-based, more diversified and stronger Unilever that faced the combined challenge and opportunity of the new Europe.

Edible Fats

The margarine industry in Continental Europe had risen with the rise of industrial society. In Germany in particular it was almost exactly coeval with the emergence of heavy industry and town life. In the post-war world this connection with industrialization was still strong. The majority of Unilever's Continental margarine factories were strung out strategically along the seaboard of Western Europe, from Lisbon and Bilbao, through Northern France, the Low Countries and North Germany, via Copenhagen, Kalmar in South Sweden, up to Stockholm and Helsinki. This was traditionally the European area of industry and trade, and it had become ever more so as shipping and ports had become increasingly essential to industry's bulk supplies of raw materials. Margarine was by tradition Unilever's principal Continental product. At the time of the merger in 1929, Unilever was selling just under 900,000 tons of margarine and edible fats in Europe. Equally by tradition Germany was far the largest market for margarine, consuming just under half of this total Unilever output in Europe, roughly twice as much as Britain.

The Second World War had very largely wrecked Unilever's industrial plant in Germany. The biggest plants—Hamburg–Bahrenfeld supplying the north, Kleve supplying the west, Mannheim the centre and south—had all been heavily damaged. The former Jurgens' factory at Goch had been entirely destroyed. Not only the margarine plant itself but the complex of oil mills and extraction plants which formed the lifeline for the margarine manufacturers were heavily damaged, and in some cases entirely destroyed. Nor was the physical destruction of machinery and buildings the only problem. Management and staff had been broken up and dispersed. Many of the older generation were dead or retired, but Unilever was fortunate in regaining swiftly the services of a handful of top managers from pre-war days. At considerable personal risk they left Berlin to restart the business at Hamburg. It was not easy for a year or two to start recruitment and training. The skeleton management (supported by temporary help from Britain and Holland) faced extraordinary difficulties. Germany was still divided amongst the different Allied zones. Between these it was difficult to get permission to travel freely and negotiations for raw materials, for example, had to be undertaken with three separate Allied control offices.

In spite of these daunting problems, German Unilever set about the work of reconstruction with a determination which swiftly made the revival of this industry in Germany not the least spectacular aspect of the German economic miracle. In 1948 the first group of new trainees were being absorbed into the business. In subsequent years the supply of oils and fats was freed from control, and open market conditions in Germany were restored. Reviving industry and currency reform released the first of the great waves of consumer demand which were to characterize the post-war German market. Quite early the German management had set themselves a target of an annual capacity of at least 300,000 tons. Their optimism was justified. By 1951 the West German market was absorbing in all nearly 470,000 tons of margarine, and by 1955 the figure had risen to 641,000 tons. Unilever factories were supplying about half of this total.

No less striking than the restoration of tonnage was the restoration and improvement of quality. For several years after the war no brands were allowed on the market. They came back in 1949, but it was 1954 before Unilever was ready to launch a really high-quality product, Rama margarine. The success of this new brand went hand in hand with a necessary reorganization of German production, for it was itself produced by the new continuous enclosed system of manufacture.[1] The technical demands made by the new qualities on plant, and the need for economies of scale to reduce costs, brought about an almost complete reorganization of the factory planning and lay-out. Five pre-war factories were either closed or converted to other types of manufacture. One at Wunstorf became a frozen-food factory. Another at Neuss was converted to plastic-bottle manufacture. The main production for Germany was now concentrated in three large factories which came to include the most modern plant in the world—Kleve, Bahrenfeld and Mannheim—each with a capacity approaching 100,000 tons. The German margarine business had re-established its old claim to be Unilever's biggest Continental enterprise. Out of a total Continental turnover of £731 million, £170 million came from margarine and edible fats, £118 million from foods, and £103 million from detergents. The biggest single market was once again Germany, which supplied £316 million of the total, including £73 million for edible fats and oils, £66 million for foods, and £29 million for detergents.

In the Low Countries the dimensions of the post-war problems were smaller than in Germany. Wartime damage to the margarine plant was negligible both in Holland and in Belgium. Here the problem was simply to restore the situation as the post-war shortages were overcome, and steadily to improve the lay-out and operation of plant which, both at Rotterdam and Merksem near Antwerp, dated from before the war. There was little that was spectacular to report in Belgium, where the market for margarine seemed to be stabilizing by 1960 rather than expanding. On the other hand, out of its total sales figure a rising proportion was for the new, improved and more expensive brands. In the Netherlands sales were back to nearly 100,000 tons by 1949. They increased by another 50 per cent by 1960, and, as in Germany, much of the

[1] See Chapter 4, page 80.

expansion was of the new high qualities developed with the assistance of the scientists and technologists at Vlaardingen. Production had long been concentrated in the single factory at Nassaukade, Rotterdam. To produce the new qualities this was reconstructed in 1953, using the most modern machinery and processes. Practically all of its 3,000 tons a week output was directed to the Dutch market.

A different and less encouraging story came from Switzerland. Here the factories were, of course, untouched by the war. But if Switzerland was a prosperous industrialized market it was also the stronghold of a powerful and highly organized dairy agriculture. Margarine output was accordingly hampered by restrictive legislation in favour of the dairy industry. In May 1961 the government increased the import levies on fats for human consumption, edible oils and raw materials for such products. So long as over a quarter of a million small dairy farms were the heart of the Swiss economy, the margarine-maker could not expect life to be easy.

By contrast Scandinavia was traditionally a prosperous market for margarine. But in Sweden, Norway and Finland particularly, the combination of great distances and numerically small population had left Unilever with relatively more factories than in most other countries, where production had been concentrated before the war. In 1946, for example, there were still three plants in Sweden—two in Stockholm and one in Kalmar. These dispersed factories were now subjected to a vigorous process of concentration. By 1960 both the Stockholm plants had been closed and production transferred to a completely new factory using the most modern techniques on the island of Lidingö near Stockholm. Production of the Kalmar plant was gradually transferred until by 1963 it had also ceased production. Lidingö's production of 47,000 tons in 1965 was double what Unilever had been producing twelve years earlier. Over the years the whole programme of concentration in Sweden represented a major exercise in industrial reorganization involving the removal of production over great distances. It had been necessary if Unilever was to meet competition both from the co-operatives and other private producers in a market where natural conditions still created uncommon difficulties for the producers.

Similar reorganization went on in the other Scandinavian countries. The factories at Sønderborg in Denmark and at Oslo in

Norway were entirely reorganized, as were the selling arrangements. In Finland, at Lahti and Helsinki, the old factories were
closed down and replaced by entirely new plant at Hertonäs, near
Helsinki, designed to produce 6,000 tons of margarine a year.
Its efficiency was summarily improved by a tunnel blasted through
an offending cliff of rock so that the oil tankers could supply the
factory direct.

In France the way of the margarine maker had never been easy.
The French, like the English, were butter eaters, and France was a
great butter-producing country. The French housewife in the
northern half of France preferred to cook with butter. Towards the
south she used oil. Nevertheless, as earlier accounts have shown,
Unilever had pioneered margarine production in those heavily
populated and industrialized areas which seemed more likely to
follow the patterns of industrial Europe elsewhere. By 1930 they
had reached the point where a large modern factory was set up at
Asnières. Asnières gradually absorbed the production of the other
four factories in the Paris area. Only Béthune in the north-east
remained to supply this highly industrialized area. The war and
the occupation dislocated this steadily growing industry. Asnières
itself was badly damaged in 1944, but by 1948-9 progress was
resumed again, in spite of official price controls and other government regulations. The damage at Asnières was swiftly made good,
and in the 1950s production was completely reorganized. Technologically, French Unilever forged ahead in these areas to achieve
a formidable reputation for quality. But the future for margarine in
France remained obscure. A useful, if limited, market was beginning to emerge for the first time. But the dairy farmers remained a
powerful force in France, and much continued to depend on Common Market policies with regard to butter and margarine.

Italy, like southern France, had never been a very promising
area for margarine. Indeed, until the middle 1950s little sign of a
significant market began to emerge. Then in the industrial north
there were signs of a change. Out of a total consumption of some
12,500 tons in 1955, Unilever was producing about one-third.
By 1960 total consumption had risen to 34,000 tons and Unilever
had pushed its share up to nearly half. By 1965 it was over half.
Part of its successful strategy was made possible by the acquisition
of a new plant at Crema, near Milan, which replaced an older plant
at Villastellona destroyed during the war.

Thus everywhere in the old Continental markets production had been restored to levels higher than pre-war, qualities had been vastly improved, production and technology revolutionized. Since the production process itself had already been considerably rationalized before the war, these latest innovations had been made possible by the modification of existing plant at existing sites. But where new markets were being entered, new plant was necessary. In Spain the new Agra plant was acquired at Lamiaco-Lejona, near Bilbao, and by 1965 was producing nearly 12,000 tons of margarine and other products. In Portugal a new plant was set up at Lisbon.

Margarine thus retained its place as the most important sector of the business on the European Continent. Its production and sale did not, however, cease to demand complex diplomacy. It continued to involve Unilever, as it always had done, in negotiations with governments, in complex problems within the new body of law within the Common Market and in delicate relationships with the farmer everywhere and especially in France. By the 1960s the increase in the volume of sales was certainly slowing down in the older markets. This made it all the more important to concentrate research and technological effort upon the improvement of quality. Already research into flavours and properties had produced a product very different from what had been once the poor man's substitute for butter. Different parts of Europe still liked different flavours. Medical enquiries suggested that certain types of margarine were even preferable to butter from the point of view of health—a consideration which began to affect the margarine market in Germany, just as it had done in the United States. Elsewhere, opportunities seemed to lie more in such fields as cooking oil. In France an attack had begun on this market, but failed dismally. Meanwhile the study of the future location of the margarine industry continued. In the existing political condition of Europe margarine production was probably as concentrated and rationalized as practicable. But continued progress towards a totally unified Common Market would certainly inaugurate a new phase of intensification.[1]

[1] The peaceful development of the margarine market was rudely shattered in the 1960s by the Planta Margarine affair. Planta, a vegetable-oil margarine containing a new emulsifying agent, was marketed in the Netherlands. Soon afterwards a skin disease, which affected a large number of people, was attributed to consumption of this new margarine. Manufacture was stopped and stocks withdrawn. At the same time the Board of Unilever N.V. decided that, irrespective of liability, all who had suffered from the skin disease would be

Oil Milling

The ownership and possession of oil mills had provided one of the most intractable problems during the negotiations of 1929 that led to the formation of Unilever. British and Dutch might agree to divide their interests of soap and margarine, but both sides were inextricably entangled with the oil-milling industry which provided indispensable raw materials for both. Just as William Lever had bought his way into the British oil-milling industry, so the Margarine Union had inherited a vast legacy of oil mills from Van den Bergh's and Jurgens'. Statistically its concentration of mills was most dense in Germany, though there were lesser concentrations also in France and in the Netherlands.

In Germany the Second World War seriously disrupted the oil-milling industry. Yet oil mills like steel mills seemed to be too vital an element in the national economy to be left in ruins. During the 1950s it was a major point of reconstruction to rebuild the oil-milling industry.

Amongst the Unilever plant the great extraction plant at the Thörl's Harburg factory had been completely destroyed. The Bremen Besigheimer oil mill had its capacity reduced by two-thirds. At Mannheim the damage was less serious and more easily restored. As reconstruction went forward, production rose again.

The Nazis had reduced oil production by half. Even in 1949 the Unilever mills in Germany were still only crushing a tiny fraction of the pre-war volume of seed. By 1965, oil production in West Germany was four times the figure of 1950 and equal to the total for the whole of Germany in 1931.

These figures of growth, however, concealed an important

compensated. More than 8,000 claims were dealt with and approximately £125,000 paid as compensation. Meanwhile the Public Prosecutor at Rotterdam had opened an enquiry. When, three years later, he served a notice of prosecution, Unilever lodged a statement of objection. The Rotterdam District Court decided that there was no case to answer and that the prosecution should not be proceeded with. This decision was subsequently confirmed by the Appeal Court at The Hague and by the Dutch Supreme Court. Charges against Unilever were therefore finally dismissed. After the decision of the Supreme Court it was explained at a Unilever Press Conference that extensive tests over five years had failed to reveal any injurious element in the margarine. It had proved impossible to reproduce the disease and no scientific test had proved that the emulsifying agent by itself had caused the disease. Thus ended the Planta Affair. Damaging though it had proved temporarily, it had drawn attention in dramatic fashion to the potential dangers that might lurk in modern food manufacture, and to the need for utmost vigilance in dealing with such matters.

technical change. As explained elsewhere,[1] the soyabean had become the largest single source of oil, being many times as great in volume as that of copra or rapeseed. Like all the German oil mills the Unilever mills were bound by law to contribute to German agricultural prosperity by crushing a certain percentage of German rapeseed each year. All in all Unilever's German mills accounted for about half the total seed crushed in West Germany. But whereas the reconstruction programme had in general produced over-capacity in this industry, the Unilever mills were able in one way or another to keep most of their capacity working. It was now concentrated in three main mills. Hamburg supplied the north, Mannheim the south, while Spyck helped to supply the industrial centre of Germany.

In the Netherlands there had been far less damage to the oil-milling industry, but here as in Britain the crushing industry was becoming less important, while figures of oil produced by the extraction process nearly doubled between 1949 and 1963. Within this total picture soyabeans had established their position as the dominant raw material.

In France Unilever's oil-milling interests had centred principally upon the Calvé-Delft company in which Unilever had acquired an interest in 1928. Although this was a Dutch company, it had arisen from a merger with the French firm of Calvé of Bordeaux whose connection with oil milling in France was half a century old. They owned one factory at Laubardemont near Bordeaux, another in Marseilles and a small mill at Nantes. In the 1930s the original Marseilles mill was closed, but more modern mills were acquired and to these was added a newly built oil-milling, refining and hardening plant at Asnières. In 1948 the French oil mills were merged together under the control of a single Calvé-Delft company.

By 1950 a new vigorous industry had taken shape. An extraction plant was transferred from Valabrègue to Laubardemont and its capacity doubled. Another was built at Croix-Sainte and in 1950 another new extraction plant was completed at Asnières. This brought Unilever's share of the oil-milling capacity of France back to about 15 per cent of the total. Throughout France a large proportion of Calvé's edible oils was distributed by drums or tank wagons to the multiple shops and wholesale grocers of France. But like many other bulk industries this one was also succumbing to the

[1] Chapter 4, pages 71–2 and 230.

economics of the branded product. Although the Unilever oil industry in France was growing, it was still only making slow progress in penetrating this very profitable part of the market.

Both in France and in the Netherlands, however, much more rapid advance was made in another related branch of the industry —the animal feeding-stuffs trade. In general the farming industry on the European Continent was slower to adjust itself to the new economics of production than in Britain. For one thing, it had lacked the stimulus which wartime needs had given to commercial farming and the growth in the size of farms. For another, the small peasant owner-farmer remained in much of the Continent a characteristic figure long after he had virtually disappeared from the English scene. Thus Continental farming was less capitalized, less commercial, more apt to rely on its own resources of feeding-stuffs and less on commercial products. Everywhere in Europe agricultural interests were politically powerful. The margarine manufacturer entering the animal feeding-stuffs industry was therefore engaged in a delicate diplomatic exercise. Existing manufacturers of feeding-stuffs who traditionally bought their materials from Unilever oil mills might be antagonized for the sake of a relatively small stake in an industry with prospects which might well have proved limited.

In spite of these problems, however, Unilever went ahead. In France the feeding-stuffs business was expanded and reorganized. The production of oils and cakes was concentrated at Bordeaux, Asnières and Croix-Sainte; compound foods (that is, balanced rations for pigs, cattle and poultry containing scientifically regulated proportions of cake, meal, cereals, minerals, vitamins) were manufactured at Laubardemont, Nantes and Marseilles; these and other mills making poultry and cattle foods were regrouped under the Compagnie Française de Nutrition Animale, based on Tours. In the Netherlands as in France animal feeding-stuffs production was concentrated and developed in four factories. The two major ones were those belonging to Calvé and Twijnstra. Between 1950 and 1965 the total production trebled.

The development of animal feeding-stuffs was everywhere dependent on the rising prosperity of agriculture, just as this in turn depended on better living standards which enabled customary agriculture to transform itself into a more commercial and scientific industry. The greater security which agriculture in general enjoyed economically and politically made it a better customer for

Unilever. Simultaneously, as other chapters show, the farmer was coming to regard Unilever less exclusively as a rival producer and more as a valuable customer who bought meat and vegetables in large quantities from him and gave valuable advice on such matters as animal breeding, diet and health. All in all, Unilever's relations with Europe's farmers in these years became more complex and flexible. Frictions and prejudices might not altogether disappear, but at any rate they were diminished and modified.

Detergents

As in Britain the post-war Continental soap and detergent industry confounded those Jeremiahs who had prophesied in the 1930s that the soap trade had reached 'a fixed state'. Indeed they had been confounded even before the war. For in Continental Europe even more than in Britain soap consumption had increased remarkably. And just as in the 1930s the increase had been associated with the growing popularity of a new product—the soap powder—in the post-war years it was associated with another new product, the synthetic or non-soapy washing powder.

Before the Second World War these non-soapy detergents were already practicable for use in industry, but not yet for the use of the domestic consumer. It was the early 1950s before a general-purpose soapless detergent was available in European markets, readily soluble in water, mild to the skin, possessing good washing properties and capable of being blended for use in water of all degrees of hardness. These products of an entirely new technology produced something not far short of a market revolution in Europe. The order of importance of Unilever's Continental markets was entirely re-shuffled. In the 1930s the new Unilever organization was selling something like 450,000 tons of soap products in Europe. Well over half this was sold in the United Kingdom. The rest was spread through the Continental markets. Of these the largest was Holland, yet even Holland was only a fifth of the size of the British market. France, Belgium, and Germany followed. The development of soap powders and later of non-soapy detergents enabled still untapped markets amongst the largest Continental countries to be more thoroughly exploited. Another facet of the German economic miracle was the swift rise of the German detergent market. By 1955 Unilever's sales in Germany were twice those in Holland; by 1960 the total German detergent turnover had drawn equal with that of France (so far the largest Continental market for Unilever detergents) and by 1965 it had gone forward by another 18 per cent.

Before the war, Unilever had operated about a dozen relatively small factories scattered through France, especially at Marseilles, Paris, Nantes, and Haubourdin, near Lille. After the war, production and brands were rationalized vigorously. The Marseilles soap trade was old-fashioned, unprofitable, and unpromising. It was abandoned in favour of the trade in branded soaps, made under modern conditions. Haubourdin became the most important centre of production. By the 1960s it employed more than a thousand people and was making most types of soap and detergents. Another factory at Aubervilliers in the Paris suburbs concentrated on detergent powders and liquids. One after another the brands familiar before the war were successfully re-launched. By 1955, for example, Persil sales had reached a peak of over 66,000 tons. But France, being predominantly a hard-water country, offered a promising market for the new non-soapy detergents, and the French chemical industry was now in a position to supply the necessary basic materials. Successively, Omo, a white powder, and Sunil, a blue powder, were launched, while Persil was converted from a soap powder into a non-soapy powder. Between them these three products brought up the annual detergent production in France by 1965 to 145,000 tons.

In pre-war Germany production had already been concentrated in two main factories. One at Hamburg-Wilhelmsburg supplied the north; a second at Mannheim supplied the south of Germany. In the post-war years the main emphasis was on the development of Mannheim, which by the 1960s was producing four times as much as the northern plant, now shifted to Hamburg-Harburg. From the earliest years of the twentieth century, when William Lever had set up his German factory, Germany had been technically advanced in matters of soap production. It had led the world in soap powders and it had been first again amongst the developers of the new synthetic detergents. The German consumer was swift to follow the technical lead of producers. By 1951 detergent sales in Germany were already divided roughly into half soap and half non-soapy detergents. The new products climbed rapidly until, by 1960, they accounted for 95 per cent of the sales as against 90 per cent in France, 84 per cent in Belgium, and 64 per cent in the Netherlands. By the mid-1960s soap powders were virtually eliminated from the Continental markets.

In the Netherlands the main plant was now at Vlaardingen, where Lever had built his original plant. Smaller factories at Amersfoort and at Gouda were shut down. Although it had been heavily damaged during the Second World War,[1] Vlaardingen was completely restored. Production of soaps and non-soapy detergents more than doubled between 1949 and 1965 to nearly 100,000 tons, and this, of course, represented far more 'washing power' than an equivalent weight of soap.

The other smaller markets showed similar developments. In Switzerland the soap factory at Basle was closed down and production concentrated in a new plant at an old centre—Olten, where the original Sunlight factory had existed for many years. Like the rest of the world Switzerland moved over to the new products, though rather more slowly. Amongst the completely new markets, Spain posed special problems for Unilever. Here was a large country with many isolated rural areas, relatively poor communications, and relatively low standards of living. Unilever first entered the Spanish market in 1948, a modest exercise concentrated on toothpaste and Atkinson's toilet preparations, these last a safe bet in Latin Europe. It was 1954 before the first soap was launched and 1956 before the Spanish consumer was offered Omo. After that, sales rose fairly rapidly until by 1965 Unilever was selling over £5 million a year of detergents in Spain. Manufacturing (hitherto done *à facon* at Barcelona) was transferred to a factory near Madrid where the Ibérica Company was purchased in 1964.

The general characteristics of detergent development in Continental Europe were everywhere the same. The new technology called for new relationships with the chemical industry. Unilever on the Continent spent over Fl. 76 million on chemical materials needed for detergent production in 1950. The subsequent rise in this item was as follows:

1955	182,000,000 Fl.
1960	275,000,000 Fl.
1966	393,000,000 Fl.

Everywhere production became concentrated in larger factories employing new processes and heavy capital outlay on spray-towers and other plant indispensable to the new technology. Smaller,

[1] The site was commandeered in 1945 at six hours' notice by the German Army, and used as a V-1 launching base. After some twenty missiles had been launched, the base was bombed and totally destroyed by the R.A.F.

o

now obsolete, factories were everywhere eliminated or made way for new factories on the old sites. A growing measure of economic integration in Europe held out the prospect of even more concentration of production in the future, but for the present the structure of national tariffs limited the onward march of the economies of scale. These had dictated local production within the national boundaries, making international trade in products like soap and detergents largely uneconomic. But even within the limits imposed by continuing economic nationalism, the new technology, partly by reducing the soap-makers' dependence on the old type of raw materials, had made possible the new pattern of factory location within the entire industry.

Thus a new, more concentrated, more streamlined Unilever soap industry was everywhere expanding production and sales of new products in the 1950s and 1960s, facing as it did so ever sharper competition, especially from American rivals, who were beginning to invade European markets everywhere with their own products, which represented the most modern American detergent technology applied in their new European factories.

Chemicals

The chemical industry had played only a modest part in Unilever's Continental operations. This was not because Unilever in Continental Europe was less advanced in its attitudes to science or technology than in Britain: on the contrary. The margarine industry, Unilever's largest interest in Continental Europe, was probably technically more advanced than other branches of Unilever before the war. But Unilever's type of chemical manufacture tended to grow out of soap manufacture and its by-products rather than out of edible oils and fats manufacture. There was nothing in Continental Europe to correspond to the location of Unilever's soap interests in Britain, lying as they did in the geographical area of the chemical industry; nothing to correspond to the connections, part design, part accident, over the years with Crosfield's, Gossage's, Price's, and others, that led Unilever into industrial chemistry in Britain.

Significantly, three of the five Unilever chemical plants on the Continent which supplied Unilever businesses with raw materials developed from factories connected with soap-making. The oldest was at Maarssen in Holland. This was one of the few factories still producing soft soap in 1965, approximately 4,000 tons a year. Its chemical plant manufactured chemicals for the soap factory itself, and for sale to the detergent and other industries. Growing demand for its products suggested that Maarssen's chemical production might well be further extended. At Vlaardingen a chemical plant was similarly attached to the Lever soap factory producing chemicals for other Unilever detergent factories. Unilever, France, likewise produced some of its own chemicals. The chemical plant at Bobigny, not far from the Savonneries Lever factory, was acquired in 1953 to develop the processing of petrochemical raw materials for the new detergents. The knowledge thus acquired was duly distributed throughout all the Unilever detergent plants. In Germany, on the other hand, a different pattern began to emerge. A chemical plant at Emmerich was originally erected as a fat-hardening unit, supplying the Jurgens' margarine factory at Goch. Goch, however, was completely destroyed by bombing during the Second World War, and its margarine production moved to Kleve. Faced by the loss of its parent plant at Goch, the Emmerich plant had to diversify. It chose to do so by undertaking the 'upgrading' of acid oils (that were the by-product of margarine making) for the Common Market just as Price's had done for the United Kingdom market. Emmerich also began to produce technical oils, apart from oils specially prepared for the catering trades. But Emmerich was moving towards a more broadly based manufacturing programme, aimed at capturing trade with third parties.

The boldest move after the war was the decision to set up a joint plant with Emery Industries Incorporated of Cincinnati, Ohio, U.S.A. at Gouda, on the site of Gouda-Apollo, originally a candle works. The aim here was to obtain knowledge and experience of selling specialized chemical products to other industries. Gouda-Apollo produced the raw materials (oleines) for a wide range of chemicals. The new factory (Unilever-Emery N.V.) was designed to supply products of service to many industries, including the plastics industry, the rubber-processing industry, the paint and lacquer industry and the pharmaceutical industry. Here, as in Britain, therefore, Unilever was moving into those processes for 'upgrading' its own by-products rather than disposing of them in less profitable forms.

These chemical ventures on the Continent were not yet on an ambitious scale. They indicated both the possibilities of a profit in a closely related area of technology and the need for more technological knowledge to exploit the possibilities.

Toilet Preparations

If France was sluggish and problematical in some respects as a Unilever market, she was, characteristically, the nerve centre of one important branch of activity: toilet preparations. Here was a trade characteristic of the affluent society. If both the passion for hygiene and the popularizing of fashion were North American, the model was French. Between 1949 and 1965 the total Unilever Continental sales increased from £4 million to over £23 million, and over one-third was accounted for by France.

The main Unilever toilet preparations company in France was Thibaud Gibbs, a company with long Anglo-French historical connections. In 1905 M. Pierre Thibaud was offered the French agency for the products of the English company, D. and W. Gibbs Limited. In the 1920s Thibaud Gibbs built a factory at St. Denis and bought another four near by to give them elbow-room to expand. At the beginning of the Second World War a completely new factory was built at Rennes.

By 1939 Thibaud Gibbs had a turnover of 2,900 million francs,[1] of which about 50 per cent came from toothpastes, 30 per cent from shaving products and 12 per cent from toothbrushes. Subsidiary companies had proliferated in Italy, Belgium, Algeria, Tunisia and Morocco, and agents represented French-manufactured Gibbs's products in South America and the Middle East. Toilet preparations were supplemented by razor blades and razors bearing the Gibbs's trade mark manufactured by Fabrique Nationale des Lames de Rasoirs at Poissy, founded by Thibaud in 1927. The war brought its usual crop of problems for Thibaud Gibbs. Raw materials were unobtainable. What production there was was of very poor quality. The new factory at Rennes was destroyed. It was rebuilt only to be destroyed again. Fortunately the plant at St. Denis was only slightly damaged.

After 1945 Thibaud Gibbs found themselves facing increased competition from the great American manufacturers of toilet preparations deploying very heavy advertising. Colgate rapidly increased its share of the market in toilet preparations. Gillette established itself as the leader in the razor-blade market. Plainly, without considerable capital expenditure on advertising and plant, Thibaud Gibbs would not be able to hold its own. This was the moment when the French shareholders decided to offer their shares to Unilever. Thus re-grouped for the contest, Thibaud

[1] Nearly £14 million sterling.

Gibbs steadily regained and consolidated its position. By 1965 it had recovered half the French home market for shaving soap, 40 per cent for toothpastes, and 11 per cent for razor blades. It supplied its products direct to 50,000 different points of sale and ran a complex storage, handling and despatch system. One of the most important developments was the building of a large-scale research laboratory adjacent to the factory at St. Denis. This was an independent unit, working for the whole of the Unilever group in France, but its work centred on research into toilet preparations and especially their effect on the skin.

The other major toilet preparations business in France was unique within Unilever: Harriet Hubbard Ayer. In 1887 Mrs Ayer, an American in Paris and a matriarch of formidable enterprise, bought the formula of a Crème Recamier. Within six months she was making and selling it successfully both in Europe and America. When Lever Brothers Company, New York, bought this business in 1947 it was a highly fashionable affair, making a wide range of cosmetics: for Unilever a daring innovation but not, at first blush, a successful one. The American side of Harriet Hubbard Ayer was soon disposed of. The European business was kept, however, and its management was sensibly entrusted to French Unilever. It raised many novel problems. More specialized than most Unilever businesses, its character would have been destroyed by any attempt to apply methods of mass manufacture and marketing. No attempt was therefore made to impose either. Instead, its new management built on its high and specialist reputation, adding to its original range of products nail polish, lipstick, eye cosmetics, suntan lotions, bath essences and other *exotica*. The policy was simple and clear: to lead fashion, not to follow it. By 1965 its agents were operating in seventy countries, each agent visiting France once a year and once a year being visited by the managing or technical director. New fashions were released twice a year to coincide with the *haute couture* seasons in Paris, of which Harriet Hubbard Ayer became in fact a part. Here was an unorthodox Unilever operation, but one that showed that it was possible to include a small and highly specialized operation within a world combine, given the right principles and the right management. The company's sales increased impressively: in 1949 their value was about £60,000; in the early 1960s it was up tenfold and still rising.

In Southern Europe Unilever's biggest toiletry business had grown from William Lever's almost accidental acquisition of

Atkinson's after the First World War. The original firm dated from 1799. During the second half of the nineteenth century Atkinson's opened agencies in Spain, Germany, Turkey and Italy. Its best market, however, was in South America, and by 1930 there were factories in Uruguay, Brazil, Chile and the Argentine.[1] Lever Brothers Limited acquired an interest in Atkinson's when its subsidiary, Joseph Crosfield and Sons Limited, bought 90,000 shares in Atkinson's out of a new issue of 100,000. In 1930 this was converted into full control. Oddly ineffective on its home ground, Atkinson's were much more successful abroad.[2] In 1946 manufacture was started in Italy at Affori near Milan. By 1965 the value of the sales of Atkinson's products in Italy had risen some ninefold over the previous fifteen years to a total of nearly £1·8 million.

For toilet preparations, as for other products, West Germany rapidly expanded its demand as economic recovery gathered pace, to become the second biggest market for Unilever toilet preparations in Continental Europe. Starting from a very small base the Elida Company built up a large turnover in such products as shampoos, toilet soaps and toothpastes. In 1955 the value of its sales were under £2 million. But with its sister company, Kleinol, which specialized in hair dyes, it was selling £3·7 million's worth of products by 1960. By 1965 Elida had more than doubled the figure to reach £8·4 million.

Elsewhere in the smaller European markets Unilever's toiletry business varied greatly with local tastes and local climate. In Spain Atkinson's were able to exploit a local liking for eau-de-cologne, needful in a warm climate. In colder Sweden, business was brisker in toothpaste and shampoos. Originally such Unilever toilet preparations were imported into Sweden from England or from Czechoslovakia. Then in 1952 the Swedish company (Vinolia A.B.) was formed, moving after a few years into the factory at Nyköping (the original Lever factory). In Denmark, Vinolia products were made at the Sunlight factory at Glostrup, again a long-established plant. Finland had a factory at Turku. In Belgium, toilet preparations were concentrated on Thibaud Gibbs. (Belgium naturally

---

[1] See page 256.

[2] There is an intriguing sidelight on Atkinson's success in Latin Europe in Giuseppe di Lampedusa's great novel *The Leopard*. At a crucial point in the story (set in the Risorgimento period) Prince Salina, a Sicilian nobleman, 'plastered his hair with *Lemo-liscio*, Atkinson's "Lime Juice and Glycerine", a dense whitish lotion which arrived in cases from London and whose name suffered the same ethnic changes as songs . . .'.

tends to look to France in these matters.) The factory, on the outskirts of Brussels, therefore manufactured most of the products sold in France.

The toiletry trade was a growing trade, highly characteristic of a society where wealth and fashion were percolating downwards. But it was not for that reason an easy trade. It was, on the contrary, highly competitive, a trade as fickle and changeable as its customer, demanding and discarding a large number of new and specialized products with extravagant frequency. Incontestably a 'growth' trade that showed increasing signs of raiding male as well as female purses, it posed elusive problems of management and offered relatively slender profits. To grasp and master its complexities was a problem that might appropriately be compared with the problem of retrieving the bath soap. Unilever had therefore to back up its marketing skill by an increasing research effort into problems of scent, toxicity and skin health to gain the selling edge over competitors.

Foods

'Foods' in Unilever in the 1950s and 1960s meant 'foods other than edible fats'. And until late in the 1950s these interests in Continental Europe were limited in size and scope. One was, by that time, a well-established feature of Unilever's business in the Netherlands: the great meat factory at Oss, formerly belonging to Hartogs, which had become part of Unilever in the late 1920s. Its products—the sausage in an unbelievable number of manifestations, hams, canned meats—were distributed not only in the Dutch market but far beyond the Dutch border into Belgium, Germany, Britain and the United States. But, so far, these were almost traditional kinds of prepared food. The main effort at Oss was directed towards mechanizing production so as to reduce costs and improve quality. The other major interests were in Germany, where as a result of the Schacht currency regulations in the 1930s, Unilever found itself the reluctant part-owner of, *inter alia*, a fishing fleet and several cheese factories. Nevertheless, it was from those beginnings that vastly larger things were to grow. And, between 1954 and 1964 especially, they grew vigorously as Unilever determined its response to the 'food revolution'—that willingness on the part of the consumers to pay for the added degree of convenience represented by prepared and preserved foods. In this single decade Unilever's investment in such enterprises throughout the world rose from £41 million to £158 million. Of this increase about £50 million was invested in Continental Europe.

Some of this expansion was achieved by the steady development of well-established methods. Oss mechanized production formerly done manually. It deployed all the skill of work-study experts. It sold an increasing proportion of its output in new plastic wrappings which gave products a longer life. They could also be sold under brand names more easily, thus following in the wake of other products like margarine, which had long since entered the 'branded phase'. New kinds of foods were added. Learning from Lipton's success in the United States, Hartog's at Oss introduced packet chicken noodle soup for the Belgian market early in the 1950s. New canned soups were added in 1957. Hence a steady increase in sales from Oss through the development of traditional manufacturing methods and the deeper penetration of fairly familiar markets.

These were paralleled by the entry into new but not wholly dissimilar markets by the purchase of existing companies. De Betuwe was an old family business, three-quarters of a century old. Its factory was some twenty miles south of Utrecht and it was famous for its jams and fruit juices. But it was now short of capital and of managerial skill to face the future. In 1960 it joined Unilever N.V.

These were areas where Unilever could move confidently, knowing it had the feel of things. But there was another market where its touch was as yet far less sure. The story of frozen foods in post-war years was new and uncertain—how to make them, how to sell them; above all, who was to eat them. It took time before any of the answers could be clearly given.

Such technical knowledge as was available in Europe was the relic of production for the German army during the war (just as the early knowledge of margarine had come from Napoleon III's plans for feeding the French army in 1870). This German technology, left behind in Holland, Norway, France and Belgium, mixed (somewhat uneasily) with British and American experience derived from Birds Eye via Britain.

Indeed, the name Birds Eye was given to a new Dutch company formed to carry on this business in Holland. It was a failure. Qualities were poor, manufacturing methods unsatisfactory, transport and storage equally so. The public as yet showed little interest in frozen products, especially as they were still relatively expensive by comparison with plentiful fresh and canned food. By 1949 the Dutch Company had lost over a million guilders even on its cautious scale of operations. In the Netherlands—as indeed generally throughout the Continental markets—Unilever withdrew from the frozen-food business.

In the early 1950s, therefore, it seemed that a chapter had been closed. Yet there were those who suspected that the causes of failure were temporary, and redeemable. As Continental prosperity returned, and as the social character of the market in the United States and Britain became apparent, a body of opinion grew in favour of a come-back. By 1957 it was plain that in Europe as elsewhere a potential mass market for frozen foods existed. In that year Unilever was approached by a Leiden firm (Vita). They had considerable expertise of freezing technology dating back to the 1930s. They had developed a network of connections with retailers to whom they managed to sell deep-freeze cabinets—a major key to success in Holland as elsewhere. But all this increase of capital requirements had left Vita short of money. 1957, therefore, brought about a new consortium. It included the experience of Vita in the Netherlands, Birds Eye in Britain, backed by Unilever capital and the knowledge of the Unilever research institute at Colworth. Its brand name, Vita, was changed to Iglo, which possessed the sovereign merit for a brand name that it could be registered, understood and (best of all) easily pronounced in all Continental countries.

Like the Netherlands, Germany even into the 1950s represented for Unilever a market in 'conventional' foods—mainly fish, cheese and ice-cream. Its largest interest was a majority share in a large combined trawling-plus-wholesale and retail fish business, Nordsee. Here again was an interesting example of differing tastes, trends and responses between Western European societies as affluence returned in the 1950s. In Britain, consumers showed a clear preference for meat over fish, and returning affluence and choice saw fish consumption decline. In Germany, fish remained a delicacy and held its own against competing foods as the economic miracle progressed. These differences were mirrored in differing Unilever policies. In Britain, Unilever shed its trawlers and Mac Fisheries ceased to deal exclusively in fish. In Germany, the opposite happened. Nordsee was busy on the intensive development of its trawling fleet. Between 1952 and 1965 Nordsee's turnover rose from a value of £21 to £47 million. By 1960 some 55 trawlers chartered or owned by Nordsee brought in one-third of the total catch by the entire German deep-sea fishing fleet.

But statistics only told half the story. The other half was strictly technology. The trawlers developed by Nordsee were really floating factories. The catch could now be filleted and frozen while the trawler was still at sea. Distance was therefore no object. And though processing firms were established at both Bremerhaven and Cuxhaven (where the catch was landed) more and more of the processing went on at sea. Even fishmeal—a by-product very important to the economics of trawling—was processed on board. Like Mac Fisheries, Nordsee experimented with restaurant and retail innovations; but longer than Mac Fisheries it remained a trawling business supplying the German market with an expanding variety of fresh, processed, canned and frozen fish products.

The story of the ice-cream trade was likewise one of spectacular expansion. The Langnese Company of Hamburg had been acquired in 1936. But until after the war its importance remained purely regional. Even in 1953 Unilever's turnover stood at less than £0·5 million. Thereafter Langnese steadily extended its operations until by 1955 it was represented all over Western Germany. This expanding demand brought into being a second factory at Heppenheim, near Mannheim, in 1960.

Here again, new technology formed the basis of change and growth, for the new Langnese factory, the largest and most modern of its kind on the Continent, embodied all the experience gained by Unilever in post-war years, as did also the Wall's factory which went up at Gloucester only a few months earlier. In support, the marketing organizations for frozen foods and ice-cream were integrated. By 1965, the Langnese turnover had risen steeply to over £11 million.

Quick-frozen food made a late start in post-war Germany and it was 1959 before Unilever Solo-Feinfrost resumed its activities. In a test-market operation in 1959 in the Dusseldorf area Unilever called all its international forces into play. The now formidable marketing and technological expertise of the Birds Eye company in Britain and similar companies elsewhere was made available. In seven months a large quick-freezing plant, embodying all the latest knowledge, was completed at Wunstorf in North Germany on the site of a former margarine factory. It was designed to produce the complete range of quick-frozen foods and it had plenty of reserve capacity to meet bigger demands in the future. By 1963 turnover of frozen foods topped £3·5 million. By 1965 it had more than doubled again.

Unilever in Germany expanded also its turnover of meat products and canned soups. But its other novel contribution to Unilever's food trades was processed cheese. The group of cheese factories had its beginnings in the 1930s when Unilever had been compelled to invest its German profits inside Germany. By 1963 the group had expanded to include, besides the Hamburg and Neu-Ulm factories, another at Kempten in the foothills of the Bavarian Alps, an area celebrated for dairy products.

Unilever's buoyant sales in the German food markets were in contrast to experience in France. It is never possible to pinpoint precisely the reasons why nations differ in their tastes. They are usually a *mélange* in which natural resources, history, ingrained habit and social institutions all play a part. The attitude of French consumers to the new foods accepted so eagerly in Germany would provide material for an entire gastronomic and sociological study. It is enough to say that the rural wealth and traditions of France, perhaps French culture itself, so uniquely continuous and stable where politics were so febrile and fluctuating, were antipathetic to those forces of urban industrialism which formed the general social background to much of Unilever's expansion elsewhere. A country where housewives still made their own soups (though perhaps decreasingly) was not the best market for packet or canned soups. A country where fresh fruit and vegetables were abundant was not an easy market for frozen vegetables. A country where cooking remained a great art was not likely to succumb willingly to convenience foods. Even French tastes in ice-cream proved too varied to be contained easily in the straitjacket of mass production.

There were other difficulties. The farmers' co-operative organizations had their own eye on the future of food processing. If anybody was to produce 'convenience' foods, why not them? Thus there would have been serious difficulties in developing a contractual system of supply from farm to factory such as Birds Eye had evolved in Britain.

Food development was therefore slow. The attempt to launch a national brand of ice-cream had flopped by 1964. Frozen foods had failed to find a footing. The French housewife evidently disliked canned soup: to dried soups she was more tolerant, and thus by

1960 Unilever had captured about a quarter of a market which in all was about equal to that of Belgium (with a population a fifth of the size of that of France).

Such figures and failures showed that thus far French traditional attitudes were proving a tough nut for Unilever to crack. Yet it was too soon to be sure of the future. By 1960 France was only just launching into her own programme of industrialization. This promised not only expansion in the already industrial areas but industrial innovation in areas, especially in the south, where industry had previously never taken root. Only time could show whether France too would provide large markets for the new products as industry and towns grew, and the habits of a rural past became remote and forgotten.

By 1965 the value of sales of all types of foods in Continental Europe was £150 million. Unilever was spending some £40 million sterling on raw materials for these industries—more than ten times the cost of its purchases in 1950. This spectacular expansion was achieved because Unilever generally (though not invariably) succeeded in doing two things. They seized a market opportunity by the forelock, correctly appreciating that social and technological change were inviting a 'food revolution'. Secondly, they brought to bear all their formidable international resources of technical and marketing knowledge and experience. This was indeed vital in view of the very high fixed capital cost involved in the manufacture and distribution of processed foods. The pooling of knowledge reduced the costs of erecting plant and of marketing products. To make such sharing easier, a special executive was set up at Rotterdam to administer the food business throughout Continental Europe. Yet, as in Britain and North America, Unilever on the European Continent had its hesitations, its weaknesses and its outright failures. That they were decisively outweighed by the successes did not mean that they were either negligible or neglected.

Evidently Unilever was most successful when it was dealing with markets that responded orthodoxly to new products; when it was in fact able to extrapolate its experience of rising personal incomes in an industrialized urban society. It was least successful when, as in France, consumers obstinately retained conservative, idiosyncratic—but highly rational—preferences of taste. On the face of it, it might seem possible, if not easy, to avoid mistakes in such markets by a simple appreciation of local traditions and habits. In practice such a verdict would merely reflect the wisdom of hindsight. Propensities might be 'conservative'. How any *particular* group of consumers would react to any *particular* product or innovation remained as difficult to predict as ever. French youth might react as enthusiastically to American popular music as French housewives to refrigerators; but their taste in ice-cream remained as idiosyncratic as ever. Investment decisions were highly particular and increasingly irrevocable. They needed to be grounded on something more secure and scientific than general judgments about national propensities. Yet to convert propensity into prophecy still remained the most difficult of all the operations of business. All Unilever could do was to keep on at the problem, growing more respectfully aware with time that some consumers at any rate remained humanly unpredictable, retaining on occasion their human right to refuse to conform to the manufacturer's idea of what they ought to eat, drink, or like. This might be inconvenient, but it was very good for everybody.

Paper, Printing and Packaging

Few aspects of Unilever's varied activities demonstrated so clearly the expansive logic of its economic growth as its paper and printing industries. Here was a type of diversification that was in itself an exercise in 'the logic of products' that had led Unilever all the way from the simple necessity of supplying its own fundamental needs into large technical and marketing operations that constituted a whole area of new business.

From the beginning the names of the manufacturers who later became known as Unilever were synonymous with the then novel processes of branding and packing products under special marks. The old methods of selling by bulk quantities gave way to small labelled packets and cartons. Thus, just as William Lever had early on set up a printing works at Port Sunlight to make soap cartons and wrappers, Van den Bergh's, round about 1900, put a letterpress plant into their Rotterdam margarine factory. And as time went on many other soap and margarine factories belonging to the Dutch or British groups in Belgium, France, Sweden, Finland, the Argentine, India, Ceylon, Australia and New Zealand set up their printing works. For many years these were regarded as simply an integral part of the soap or margarine factory. Packet or wrapper was—and remains—an indispensable part of the 'convenience' for which the customer was willing to pay. Packaging cost money.

Yet, as the Chairmen pointed out in an address to Unilever shareholders in 1965 (devoted wholly to packaging), 'its cost is justified
if it helps to bring the full economies of mass production and mass
distribution nearer realization.'

Accordingly, as business grew, the printing and packaging
appendages expanded in parallel. It accorded with contemporary
ideas of 'vertical development' when in Germany, as in Britain,
manufacturers bought their way into other printing and packing
businesses in order to supply their expanding needs for these
products. It was no accident that at the same time as William
Lever was buying himself a stake in Thames Board Mills, the
Dutch margarine-makers were doing the same thing in their largest
market in Germany. Thus Jurgens' acquired an interest in Papier-
und Pergamentpapierfabrik Seltmans, while Van den Bergh's
followed with an interest in the Heinrich Nicolaus Pergamentpapierfabrik at Ronsberg. Both these factories were located in the
foothills of the Bavarian Alps.

This was an area where printing had been closely connected
with paper-making since the late Middle Ages. The requirements
for a paper industry were first a plentiful supply of rags made from
vegetable materials. The rough linen that formed the common
clothing of the people over large areas of Germany ensured this.
Secondly, there was the plentiful supply of fresh, clean water.
And finally, the towns of Southern Germany were famous for
accurate craftmanship. This was the home of the famous toy-
makers, instrument-makers and clock-makers who were to be one
of the foundations of industrial Germany. All these were to be
found in an area which formed the geographical and cultural link
between the fading economic glories of Northern Italy and the
rising economic promise of the Low Countries at the end of the
Middle Ages.

In the late sixteenth century at one Bavarian village in the Allgäu,
Ronsberg, was a paper factory, still in existence, and one of the
oldest in the world. It was certainly making paper in 1582. In 1884
it was bought by Heinrich Nicolaus, a young wine merchant from
Lindau. Within a few months, Nicolaus began to revolutionize the
paper-making process, turning to wood pulp as well as rags for
raw materials, and introducing a relatively new British process for
making a vegetable parchment in 1886. This was a greaseproof and
waterproof paper, particularly useful for wrapping fatty goods.
Here was an early technological advance in the history of packaging.

The new parchment swiftly replaced older methods of packing the butter and cheese which formed a principal product of the Allgäu. Business expanded. In 1905 Nicolaus added a printing plant to his Ronsberg paper factory. In 1918 his two sons bought another factory about forty miles away, at Seltmans, and this too began to make vegetable parchment. A new printing works at Kempten was added in 1921. A few years later another factory at Günzach was added to supply raw paper for Ronsberg.

It was this group of four factories in the Nicolaus family owner-ship which attracted the attention of Jurgens' and Van den Bergh's in the early 1920s. In the late 1930s, partly as a result of the currency restriction of those years, the Dutch interest in this paper and printing group expanded again. R. Rube and Company of Weende in Lower Saxony now joined the group, and in 1938 a share was acquired in a factory at Forcheim in Upper Franconia which later became the sixth member of the group. This last was an old factory in the Nuremberg area, long the home of an ancient craft—the hammering of fine gold leaf. In the early twentieth century Forchheim installed machinery to roll aluminium foil, and by the 1950s was making a totally new type of wrapping material consisting of a vegetable parchment covered with layers of aluminium and plastic foil, particularly suitable for preserving food in a variety of climates.

The Kempten factory was bombed and destroyed at the end of the Second World War, but by 1950 it was back in production and by 1962 was the biggest producer of folded cartons in Western Germany. Ronsberg itself went into large-scale printing and laminating of parchment and aluminium foil wrappings. In 1953 modern rotogravure printing machinery was installed and new buildings completed to make it one of the largest and most modern factories in the European packing industry.

In spite of the loss of two paper factories and a board mill in East Germany, the Nicolaus group, strengthened by a newly acquired plastics factory at Neuss, represented an important proportion of West German packaging production. The group produced more than half the vegetable parchment of West Ger-many, exporting 20 per cent of its production outside Germany and specializing in a large number of products designed for in-dustrial use.

The post-war years brought a significant change in the direc-tion of the German paper group's business. Unilever's growing business in Germany itself provided vast opportunities for the paper industry. A single brand of margarine, for example, used eight hundred million wrappers a year. This home trade was the *fons et origo* of the Unilever paper group. At one time four-fifths of the output of Kempten had gone to other Unilever companies. But by 1965, half of Kempten's trade was with customers *outside* Unilever. Here, then, was a compact and tightly organized group of factories representing the most modern technology in the world for conducting all the processes necessary in a modern packaging industry. In a relatively short space of time its technological expertise and marketing enterprise had carried it clean through the barrier that had once fenced it in as a Unilever 'house' industry. It was now also a substantial profit-maker in the open market.

Smaller packaging and printing works operated elsewhere—Pakko-Tryk and Olsen in Denmark, Drukkerij 'Reclame' in Holland. To these established industries were added a brand new printing factory at Beauvais in North France, another (Allpack) in Austria, and Cartitalia near Milan. The rising tide of operations was indicated by the increase of capital investment on packaging plant. Between 1955 and 1960 £2·9 million was approved; between 1960 and 1965 the figure was increased more than tenfold. By 1964 5·6 per cent of Unilever's total capital was employed in packaging and printing enterprises, providing a total turnover of about £67 million. Yet just as these Unilever packaging industries were by no means exclusively tied to supplying Unilever's own needs, so the purchasing industries in Unilever were in no way tied to buying their needs from Unilever packaging factories. Suppliers and purchasers of packaging material in Unilever reserved their freedom to conduct their business in what seemed to them the most efficient and profitable fashion.

CONCLUSION

The Recovery of the Continent 1945–65

The most dramatic feature of these post-war years and especially of the second decade after the war was the miraculous recovery of the Continent, especially of a Germany which had been left devastated in 1945. Unilever contributed handsomely towards the necessary reconstruction and benefited handsomely from the opportunities which returning prosperity offered. The profits derived from the European Continent rose from just under £16 million in 1950 to just over £42 million in 1965, and by this latter year almost half the profits came from the rapidly expanding German market.

Unilever's expansion manifested itself in a number of ways. The manufacture of the great staple commodities like margarine and detergents continued to concentrate itself in a smaller number of larger factories. For the most part such factories grew, or were rebuilt, on traditional sites. Other old factories were provided with new plant and new purpose (as Neuss switched over from making margarine to making plastic bottles). In the newer industries in which Unilever now proceeded to interest itself, entirely new factories in new places were built or acquired. Some, like De Betuwe, were old family businesses now short of capital and management but rich in experience and technical knowledge. In some new markets like Spain or Italy, new factories had to be built for the supply of products traditional to Unilever but new to the country concerned. Italy was a remarkable example of balanced growth: by 1962 Unilever turnover, spread over detergents, edible fats and toilet preparations, had reached £19 million.

Thus Unilever diversified its activities, spread its risks and multiplied its own problems. For throughout these years competition, both from European and American competitors, was growing. Although national boundaries within Continental Europe remained, they were tending to offer less resistance to the flow of goods as supra-national authorities grew in the shape of the Common Market and the European Free Trade Association. These changing conditions of economic progress demanded all the economies of scale that could be provided and suggested that the future might demand even more. New conditions of competition likewise demanded all the streamlined speed of decision that could be devised. The rise of supranational political organization in Europe was therefore mirrored in corresponding trends within Unilever itself. Just as earlier in Unilever history the national managements had gradually taken over certain functions from the individual company managements in different European countries, so, now, newly established central executives were taking over certain functions from the national managements. The new efficiency of communications and transport, the coming of international brands and the growing tendency towards more uniform tastes all demanded a greater degree of central co-ordination of products. Inevitably there was some loss of local initiative,

P

some swing-back towards more centralized control. Yet centralization *per se* was not by any means the whole answer. As previous chapters have shown, Continental markets did not all respond uniformly to new products. Here and there, large groups of consumers would remain obstinately nonconformist. Human society, even in a conformist age, retained a human, if sometimes disconcerting, number of quirks and idiosyncrasies. The local knowledge of local management remained a precious asset to Unilever. And not the least of the lessons which the new products and markets held for Unilever management was that the age of automation still demanded highly individual thinking.

CHAPTER 9

AFRICA

UNILEVER'S interests in Africa in the post-war years were a legacy of the active imagination of William Lever. Haunted by the fear that raw-material shortages might limit his enterprise, he had plunged into the complex economics of the African continent, carving great plantations out of the jungles of the Congo before the First World War and adding the sprawling empire of the Niger Company in the boom that followed. By the 1930s the new Unilever combine found itself in control of the giant trading corporation called The United Africa Company, one of the world's biggest trading companies.

Seldom, if ever, had the African enterprises worked in the way Lever's imagination had originally thought they would. They had never been merely a link in a chain that led 'from the palm tree to the soap kettle'. What had emerged was a vast trading organization operating in its own right. It bought Africa's products—palm oil and kernels, cocoa and coffee, groundnuts and timber, hides and skins—on a vast scale, and re-sold them on the markets of the world. It sold to the Africans many thousands of articles—salt, flour, cotton, textiles, beer, hardware and so on. If world markets for African produce were bad and prices low, African demand for goods imported and sold by The United Africa Company fell. The United Africa Company in fact did well when Africa was prosperous. It did badly when Africa was poor.

In the 1920s and 1930s the affairs of the Company were not prosperous, but the recovery that took place in commodity prices between 1932 and 1936 brought better days and spreading enterprise, not only in Nigeria and Ghana, but in markets adjacent to Africa, like Turkey, the Canaries, and the Middle East, Morocco and the Seychelles. In the Belgian Congo a ten-year programme started in 1935 added another 56,000 acres to the plantations there. They produced better oil at lower costs. Even in British West Africa official opposition to plantations slackened in the face of competition from the palms of Sumatra and Malaya. Model plantations were set up in Nigeria on 99-year leases. Here and in the Cameroons the advantages of systematic planting, harvesting and processing became clear. The old native methods of crushing the oil-fruits by hand gave way to the use of hand presses which recovered a larger percentage of the oil. A power-driven plant which extracted an even higher percentage was developed for the use of African co-operative societies.

The prosperity of The United Africa Company continued after the war. In the early years of peace, when manufacturing in Europe was recovering only slowly, The United Africa Company and the Plantations companies between them were providing between one-third and one-half of Unilever's total profits, and perhaps one-quarter of total turnover. Yet even while profits were at their peak, the whole character of Unilever's stake in Africa was changing fundamentally, and it was to continue to change with spectacular rapidity over the following twenty years. The first manifestation of change was the establishment of the Produce Marketing Boards. The earliest was the Nigerian Cocoa Marketing Board of 1947. In 1949 there followed the Nigerian Oil Palm Produce Marketing Board, the Nigerian Groundnut Marketing Board, and the Nigerian Cotton Marketing Board. Ghana set up Marketing Boards for cocoa and agricultural produce, Sierra Leone set up a Board for agricultural produce, Gambia a Board for oil seeds. These Boards were the result of ideas and policies that had emerged during the Second World War. Produce was to be bought from local farmers, and sold on world markets. The theoretical argument was that the farmers could thereby be guaranteed a minimum price and at the same time the maximum price could be obtained on the world market.[1]

The post-war shortages seemed to reinforce the case for the Boards. High prices, particularly during the Korean War, enabled the Nigerian and Ghanaian Boards to build up enormous sterling reserves. These were no less attractive to the politicians, who were pressing hard for political independence, than the Board's other powers of licensing buying agents. For if the reserves offered financial power that the newly independent governments needed, their licensing rights offered the means of steering towards the African those economic functions like produce-buying which he was well able to perform. Produce-buying, therefore, hitherto in the hands of a few expatriate firms, the biggest of which was The

[1] The case against the Boards is forcefully argued by Professor P. T. Bauer in his book *West African Trade*, 1954.

United Africa Company, began to pass over to African agents. By 1964 the number of agents in many areas of Nigeria had trebled. In Ghana, where the government had acted more directly, the cocoa crop was ordered to be bought solely by the Ghana Farmers Council on behalf of the Cocoa Marketing Board.

By the late 1950s The United Africa Company was thus faced with radical change in Africa and especially in West Africa, where the major part of its business was found. Along with the threat to produce-buying came an equal threat to the import trade and sales of merchandise. For in practice the two were complementary. Everywhere African traders who had acted as middle men and buyers for the Company now began to operate on their own. So did many of the retail shopkeepers, African mammies, market stallholders, and wholesalers. Admirable salesmen of hardware or clothing, they readily took over the organization of the retail trade, assisted by support and guidance from the Company. Legislation, competition and social change combined to demand new policies for The United Africa Company. If it was not to be extruded from Africa, it had to find new functions to perform, new areas of investment in which European money and skill could serve the new Africa that was emerging. Economic and social conditions throughout the areas of Africa where Unilever operated were by no means uniform. There were four such main areas: the Congo; the ex-French territories on the West Coast; the ex-British territories on the West Coast; and the ex-British territories in East Africa.

Of the first it is scarcely possible as yet to write with any certainty.[1] The Unilever plantations in the Congo had from the early days been models of European investment. After nearly twenty years during which Lever and his successors had more than carried out their original contract to build up the productive and welfare resources of these areas, they had at last become not only efficient and prosperous but profitable to the owners. Political independence and the chaos that followed not only halted progress. In spite of the loyalty of the majority of the Congolese staff, wild inflation set in, the real value of wages dropped, the cost of imported goods rose, communications were disrupted, trading stations were isolated and unable to re-stock. By 1964 business ground slowly to a halt, and unless political authority could be re-established the prospects seemed to be that all these fruitful territories would once again steadily revert to the jungle.

[1] Written in 1967.

In the former British and French West African territories and in the East, in spite of local differences of emphasis, a very different story began to emerge. Everywhere the newly established governments of the African independent territories were ambitious to raise the living standards of their peoples by developing their economies beyond the stage where they were merely providers of primary produce to the rest of the world. The new ambition was to see local industries arising to provide from the resources of Africa itself a wide range of commodities that were formerly imported from Europe and America, not least through the agency of the expatriate trading companies. It was this industrial development, aimed at the production in Africa of import substitutes, which offered the most promising avenues for capital redeployment in the 1950s and 1960s. The attitudes of the local governments might differ widely, but many recognized that the technical and managerial skill of expatriates would be valuable for some time to come. Africa still needed outside capital, technical skill and advice. Manufacturing of one sort or another was therefore clearly the new field for investment. The type of manufacturing indicated was something which necessarily had to be decided in the light of local opinion and government opinion in particular. What, first of all, were the imports to be substituted?

At once differences began to emerge in the attitude of governments in the different areas. The list of imports included, for example, a considerable proportion of luxury goods that might well seem dispensable to a 'planning' government. The first need was the provision of basic industries to supply the fundamental wants of the people. Elsewhere a more liberal view was taken. On the Ivory Coast some of the most promising industrial investments were those aimed at producing high-quality goods of a luxury or semi-luxury character. The Nigerian Development Corporations set up in the 1950s likewise took a broader view of what was acceptable in the way of investment programmes by private enterprise. In general, cement manufacture, textile printing, corrugated iron and brewing, were some of the enterprises that emerged as a natural response to local need. The new development programmes demanded tractors, heavy earth-moving equipment, steel girders, and other building materials. The big companies drilling for oil off the shores of Nigeria needed supply boats and off-shore drilling rigs.

But even as these basic changes were being made, the life of the

African people everywhere was changing. Clothes were becoming more sophisticated. Lagos and Accra were as liable to traffic jams as Frankfurt or Chicago. Everywhere along the new highways garages and petrol stations mushroomed, African shops were installing refrigerators to store cold drinks and beer, the radio and even the television set was becoming a normal part of life. In an economy that was thus beginning to be marked by at any rate patches of affluence, capital investment designed to enable Africa to manufacture or at least assemble its own motor cars, refrigerators and radio sets and manufacture its own beer, cigarettes and newspapers, began to compete with the demands for capital for more basic purposes. Each new African state faced in some measure the economic problem long familiar in more developed economies: the problem of priorities for investment. The answer each state gave was determined by many factors. No two gave precisely the same answer.

The French section of The United Africa Company, Niger France, operated in fourteen African republics. Most of these were too small to justify large-scale redeployment of capital into manufacture. The most promising was the Ivory Coast which accounted for a quarter to one-third of Niger France's turnover. Here was a politically stable country with a population of more than three million people and a government well disposed towards France. Niger France was sufficiently attracted by future prospects here to diversify its activities into refrigeration, motor engineering and electrical engineering. But the markets for such things were not yet sufficiently developed to justify total withdrawal from the buying of produce and the selling of imported merchandise. They were, however, large enough to bring good profits. The following table shows the growing part taken by manufacture and the relative profitability of different types of trading.

Compagnie Française de la Côte d'Ivoire
Results, 1965

Turnover			Net Profit
Refrigeration	521M CFA France		20·5%
Motors	633M ,,	,,	16·1%
E.M.E.	357M ,,	,,	22·4%
Textiles	3,817M ,,	,,	11·4%
Gen. Merch.	4,678M ,,	,,	6·6%

Niger France represented an important segment of The United

Africa Company's total business in Africa. It accounted for nearly one-third of total turnover, one-fifth of total capital and nearly one-quarter of total profits. The problems of independence seemed to have been solved in many of the ex-French Territories in a practical spirit remarkably free of doctrine. The old society had adjusted to the new conditions smoothly and rapidly. Living standards were rising, the openings for Western capital promising and capital security reasonably good.

As a milieu for capital investment Ghana posed far greater problems. In some ways Ghana was the most promising of the African states commercially and industrially. By 1965 its average population density was amongst the highest in West Africa—87 people to the square mile. It enjoyed a national income higher than that of any neighbouring territory—£94 per head. But its public expenditure was in post-war years very heavy. Ghana spent a greater proportion of her income on defence than any other ex-British African country as well as investing enormous sums in grandiose projects, and the large sterling reserves which were stored up at independence were rapidly reduced. This in turn led to restrictions on imports and on the repatriation of profits earned by foreign firms.

These and other discouragements had not been foreseen when the United Africa Company's investments programme was accepted by the Ghanaian Government in 1958, and when the restrictions were imposed in 1961 the company were already fully committed to this investment programme. It was accordingly completed. The largest enterprises were those which had a natural link with those agricultural and planting activities where the Unilever experience was traditionally deepest. At Samreboi a complete township was carved out of the dense forests of the Amenfi Awowin region. When the new £700,000 ply mill was added in 1961, Samreboi became Ghana's largest timber business, responsible for a significant proportion of the country's exports. But there were many other smaller enterprises, mostly in partnership with government or other businesses. The brewery at Kumasi was a joint enterprise for which the leading Dutch brewers, Heinekens, provided technical advice. Outside Accra on a large industrial estate at Tema, Unilever opened a large new detergent plant in which the Ghanaian government took a 49 per cent interest. Nearby was the Ghana (Government) Textile Printing Company's new works, in which The United Africa Company, with other members of the Anglo-Dutch African Textile Investigation Group, in which it had an interest, took up a 49 per cent share by countervailing right. The Tema estate was also the site of a vehicle assembly plant which designed and built a bus specially tailored for African use. The entire body was built in Africa, but the Bedford engine which powered it was still imported. In Ghana, as elsewhere in Africa, the sale and repair of motor vehicles and bulldozers proved profitable. The Caterpillar tractor, for which The United Africa Company was agent, was used throughout Ghana in large building projects, including the Volta River project. The United Africa Company moved also into a new kind of retail investment as its old-fashioned retailing businesses dwindled. The Kingsway Stores now operated in all sixteen modern department stores. (Four were in Ghana, eleven in Nigeria and one in Sierra Leone.)[1] Thus, in one way or another redeployment of capital and resources went on as Unilever came to terms with the new order in Africa.

On a very much larger scale were the new operations in Nigeria, geographically the largest single market in Africa with a population comparable with that of the United Kingdom by 1965. By 1961 The United Africa Company had withdrawn from produce-buying with the exception of a few isolated purchases of ground-nuts and rubber and some buying of hides and skins in the Nor-thern Region. With the produce-buying went most of the old merchandise businesses as the company's former clients set up as independent agents. But favoured by a generally sympathetic political atmosphere redeployment into new activities went ahead fairly rapidly.

Some of the developing enterprises were those which The United Africa Company could supply from its own capital and skill. As in Ghana, timber was the major enterprise. The largest single manufacturing plant was that of African Timber and Plywood (Nigeria) Limited at Sapele. Sapele's output was comparable with

---

[1] As with many other developments, this one had been foreshadowed half a century earlier by William Lever. The late Mr W. K. Findlay, a former West African merchant and director of Lever Brothers Limited, recalled the following incident: 'One day, it must have been about 1912, Lever asked me to lunch with him at his club in Liverpool. On the way there we came to Woolworth's and he went in, so I followed. We walked around and when we came out again he asked me if I thought it would be a good idea to set up stores like Woolworth's in Africa. I had to tell him that Africa wasn't yet ready for anything like that. That was far-seeing. I admired Lever for thinking about that, but he was thinking away ahead of Africa as it was then.'

the Samreboi plant in Ghana and the mill became one of the largest employers of African labour in Nigeria, with over 3,000 employees. As in Ghana, the other manufacturing enterprises were by comparison small. The West African Cold Storage operated a new factory producing meat, sausages and pies. Wall's nearby turned out vanilla ice-cream.

In many other ventures, while The United Africa Company could supply the capital, and management and invaluable knowledge of local marketing conditions, it had to call upon manufacturing skills of which it knew little. Beer and stout were a case in point. In a growing but still limited African market a Unilever stout would have been hard put to it to prove its goodness. Hence a partnership with Guinness which founded at Ikeja (the industrial estate of Lagos) one of the most modern breweries of its kind, producing a brew which was popularly held not only to possess the characteristic taste of Guinness but also to render its drinkers more virile than before. Throughout Nigeria another chain of breweries, the Star breweries, were operated as a joint partnership by the Dutch brewer Heinekens and The United Africa Company to produce an inexpensive lager. Chilled for tropical consumption, this proved an ideal drink for Africa. These examples are characteristic of the new trend: where previously Unilever had acted as commercial agent or distributor for a product, they now became partners with the manufacturer of that product in a joint African enterprise.

The West African Portland Cement Company, jointly financed by the Portland Cement Company, the Western Region Development Corporation and The United Africa Company, had achieved an output by 1965 of nearly 330,000 tons of cement at its works at Ewekoro, Nigeria's 'city of stone'. Niger Motors, operating with a staff trained in motor engineering at the Vauxhall works at Luton, ran a nationwide car-hire business; by 1965 its business had a turnover of £4·25 million. The United Africa Company of Nigeria owned a vehicle assembly plant at Apapa. Vono, in which U.A.C. had a small interest together with the Western Region Development Corporation, produced beds, chairs, and other metal products locally designed.

A similar pattern of development emerged in the much smaller state of Sierra Leone. Here again the partnership with Heinekens set up a modern high-capacity brewery outside Freetown in 1957. The transformation of the West African economy promised to become more rapid as the operations of the oil companies grew. By 1963 Nigeria was producing three million tons of crude oil; by 1965, 13 million tons, and it was estimated that the figure would continue to rise steadily. Burutu, until recently an all-British colony poised in the roadless swamplands of the Niger Delta, resounded in the 1960s with the accents of Californian oil men. All this industrial growth changed also the nature of Unilever's transport enterprise. Niger River Transport, which once carried only raw materials along the involved tributaries of the Delta to the Nigerian coast, now operated for a variety of government agencies and other firms beside its parent, The United Africa Company. The old method of working by which the company's own ships would bring out its merchandise and take back to Europe cargoes of cocoa, coffee, palm oil and peanuts, had long since disappeared. The formation of the Palm Line symbolized the passing, here as elsewhere, of the concept of vertical integration. Palm Line ships plied independently as common carriers, taking their share of the competitive freight trade in timber products from Sapele and Samreboi, and carrying cargoes of raw materials to Europe and elsewhere for the Marketing Boards.

In East Africa, the 1960s saw the ex-British territories of Kenya, Uganda and Tanzania in a transitional phase. The United Africa Company in 1937 had acquired here the businesses established by two young railway engineers in the Edwardian age, James Hamilton Gailey and D. O. Roberts. Even before it was acquired, Gailey and Roberts had launched into the provision of heavy equipment for road making, land clearing and house building. In the 1950s and 1960s the process was pushed a stage further. Gailey and Roberts were assembling and servicing Caterpillar tractors, Parker crushing machinery, Nuffield tractors, Austin and Guy vehicles, Raleigh bicycles, Avery weighing machines, and electrical machinery.

By the 1960s the United Africa Group had succeeded in re-deploying a sizeable proportion of its capital. The operation had not been carried out without encountering serious technical and personnel problems. The first was the switching of employees from the old to the new types of job. In the late 1950s, as bush stations closed down, and the whole produce-buying and merchandise business shrank, many old employees had to be turned off. In Nigeria alone 2,500 Africans employed in lower grades lost their jobs. Many European staff also found themselves redundant. Try

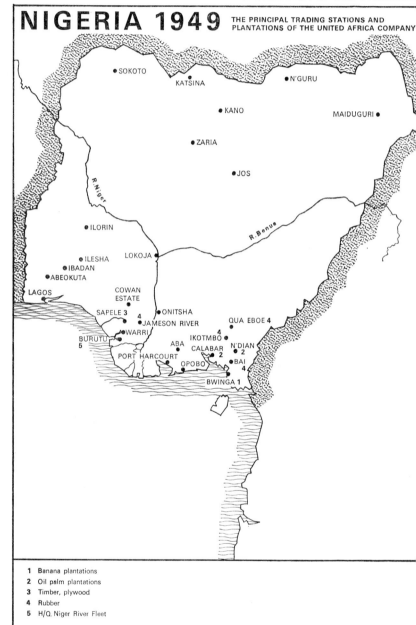

NIGERIA 1949

THE PRINCIPAL TRADING STATIONS AND
PLANTATIONS OF THE UNITED AFRICA COMPANY

1 Banana plantations
2 Oil palm plantations
3 Timber, plywood
4 Rubber
5 H/Q. Niger River Fleet

Figure 14

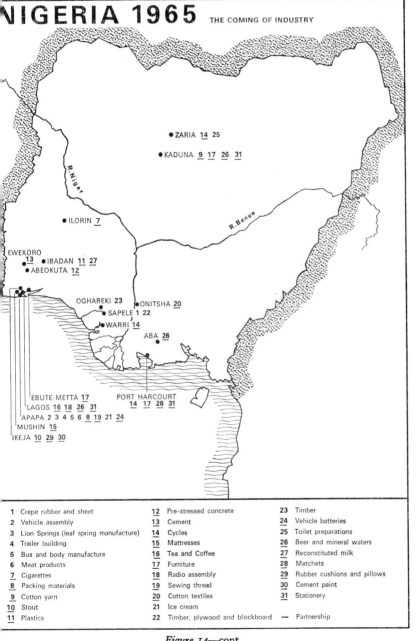

NIGERIA 1965

THE COMING OF INDUSTRY

●ZARIA 14 25

●KADUNA 9 17 26 31

R.Niger

R.Benue

●ILORIN 7

EWEKORO
13
●IBADAN 11 27
●ABEOKUTA 12

OGHAREKI 23
●ONITSHA 20
●SAPELE 1 22
●WARRI 14

ABA 26

EBUTE-METTA 17
LAGOS 16 18 26 31
APAPA 2 3 4 5 6 8 19 21 24
MUSHIN 15
IKEJA 10 29 30

PORT HARCOURT
14 17 28 31

1 Crepe rubber and sheet	12 Pre-stressed concrete	23 Timber
2 Vehicle assembly	13 Cement	24 Vehicle batteries
3 Lion Springs (leaf spring manufacture)	14 Cycles	25 Toilet preparations
4 Trailer building	15 Mattresses	26 Beer and mineral waters
5 Bus and body manufacture	16 Tea and Coffee	27 Reconstituted milk
6 Meat products	17 Furniture	28 Matchets
7 Cigarettes	18 Radio assembly	29 Rubber cushions and pillows
8 Packing materials	19 Sewing thread	30 Cement paint
9 Cotton yarn	20 Cotton textiles	31 Stationery
10 Stout	21 Ice cream	
11 Plastics	22 Timber, plywood and blockboard	— Partnership

Figure 14—cont.

as it might, the company could not always find new jobs for those dispossessed by change. Yet it was at the same time heavily involved in programmes of education, training and retraining to meet growing shortages which were developing as a result of these new enterprises. While the old kind of labour was becoming redundant, there was a growing shortage of African engineers, electricians, and mechanics for the new Africa. For these, all employers—government agencies, armed forces and private business—were in competition. The United Africa Company, with many other firms, joined in the new investment in higher education. Its first technical training school dated back to 1934 and was established at Burutu. Now another one was set up at Sapele. In Ghana a training school in Accra specialized in mechanical technology as did a second in East Africa. Niger Motors set up a training school for its employees at Kano in Northern Nigeria. Yet these African institutes could not do everything that was required. In the joint ventures with European partners, African trainees were sent back to the parent companies in Europe for training periods. Guinness, Vauxhall and Heinekens among many others all provided training courses for African technicians.

Technical training was itself only one of the steps on the ladder of management. Here the way to the very top demanded a whole range of educational processes, some of them already provided in Africa through such institutions as the business school at Ahmadu Bello University of Zaria in Northern Nigeria. For managers as for technicians Unilever in Africa found itself in intense rivalry with other employers—including government itself—all in desperate need of men to fill the most responsible appointments. Here again it had the advantage of being able to bring back to Europe for training the most promising candidates. But it developed in Lagos its own training college at Igbobi. Igbobi concentrated on the severely practical aspects of management, especially on developing in the young African manager a sense of responsibility not only to those above him but to those below him too. By one route or another the flow of managers had increased until by 1965 40 per cent of all African managerial posts were held by Africans. If the programme could be maintained according to plan, that percentage would have doubled by 1980.

There were other more obstinate hindrances to rapid redeployment in Africa which slowed down the pace and were more difficult to overcome. One was the state of communications and the limited size of many of the markets to be served. Quite apart from political uncertainties many of the new states were too small to offer by themselves attractive markets for Western capital. Roads and railways often led only from the interior to the coast, reflecting the economy of earlier times when all trade gravitated to the points where imports came in from Europe and from which exports to Europe were embarked. Until communications could be improved, markets were sometimes too small to warrant the establishment of highly expensive modern plant which could only be run economically at full capacity. When the Sierra Leone diamond boom collapsed in the late 1950s and the demand for beer fell, for example, the new Star brewery outside Freetown proved temporarily to be too large for its market.

This relationship between productive capacity and the capacity of the market to absorb it put an added premium on the kind of service which The United Africa Company could bring to the varied industrial partnerships in which it was involved. From long experience of selling in markets spread throughout the African continent, it not only had an intimate knowledge of existing African tastes and habits, but it also had a shrewd idea how those preferences were likely to develop as rising incomes and changing social conditions enabled the African to buy more, and more expensive, goods. While The United Africa Company gained the technical skill that its partners brought into the new industrial ventures, it was able to offer them its own unique commercial experience of these African markets.

The problems of redeployment, political, economic and social, and the complete overhaul of management organization which was its essential prerequisite, meant that growth in Africa was necessarily slower than in more advanced economies. Thus, as the post-war boom subsided in the last fling of its old-style merchanting business, The United Africa Company's *proportionate* share in Unilever's total activities inevitably declined. In 1955 27 per cent of Unilever's total capital was employed on the African continent. By 1965 the proportion had sunk to 15·3 per cent. (Allowing for the tremendous increase in total Unilever capital, Africa's share in *absolute* terms remained roughly stable.) But for this redeployment into industrial investments vital to the emerging nations of Africa something could be claimed. Unilever had in all invested in 72 factories in tropical Africa, providing commercial management for 55 and technical management for 34. It had contributed towards lifting the double curse of African economies—chronic unemployment and over-dependence on peasant agriculture. It divided the economy more rationally into those functions that Africans could perform and those which demanded European knowledge and skill. To Unilever it had brought a new sense of purpose in an awakening continent and a new range of legitimate opportunities for profitable investment. It had not been achieved without great cost in effort and in money, but by the mid-1960s it was evident that a new future had been won for Unilever in the new Africa.

CHAPTER 10

OVERSEAS MARKETS

PREVIOUS chapters have made it plain that Unilever's largest base is in Europe, including Britain. Yet the extra-European world provided an actual basis for business on a large scale and a potential base for even larger enterprises. From 1949 to 1965 the American continent and other territories overseas (excluding The United Africa Company's business in Africa) accounted for a fairly stable proportion (23–24 per cent) of total world sales which increased from some £556 million to some £1,850 million during this period. The overseas areas' share therefore rose from approximately £128 million to nearly £420 million.

The firms which operated under the aegis of Unilever in these areas covered a very wide spectrum. They had one thing in common: most of them stemmed from roots put down by William Lever towards the end of the nineteenth or early in the twentieth century. During the two decades with which this enquiry is concerned, they everywhere developed along lines in some respects similar. Their management passed largely, sometimes almost exclusively, into the hands of nationals of the countries in which they were situated, and this produced most striking results in countries like India, where until recently business of this kind was largely administered by Europeans. Secondly, all shared in improving standards of living for either the whole of society or part of it. Upon this improvement Unilever's business depended and to it Unilever made a creditable contribution. Everywhere business expanded and diversified.

There the similarities ended. All else was disparity. The markets varied in size from the vast areas of North and South America or India to relatively tiny areas such as Ceylon—smaller even than it appeared, since two-thirds of the population were crowded into one-third of the island. The societies comprised within such areas varied from the affluent peoples of the United States of America or Australia to the still desperately poor peoples of India and South-East Asia. Incomes were rising in India but the disparity between the Indian situation and that of the Western world remained glaring.

In each territory, however, the Unilever system worked on the same principles, though the application varied enormously with local conditions. The economic basis of the business remained the original capital, invested by Lever or his successors. This fructified by the application of skill, trained and provided in the past from the resources of the Unilever concern. More recently capital began to come from the reinvested profits of the local businesses themselves. Yet though management passed into local hands and capital was likewise provided partly from local profits or borrowing, skill and knowledge were drawn ever increasingly from the central reservoir of Unilever itself. Into this reservoir each local organization returned its own contribution of ideas, knowledge and experience. Such was the new division of labour between the centre and the perimeter. Management must be familiar with both its local problems and the total volume of current commercial and industrial knowledge. The local problems were everywhere different. The South American countries almost all faced rampant inflation. In North America a highly complex equilibrium of private capitalism and public checks on monopoly called for specialized management. In Asia, as in Africa, political problems ranging from taxation to nationalization, or rumours of nationalization, called for steady nerves at the top. Everywhere the competition of new products and new technologies increased, sharpening the need for utmost intelligence in management, the best and swiftest decisions based on the best and swiftest communications that could be devised.

United States of America

In the United States, the Unilever enterprises comprised Lever Brothers Company, New York, and since 1937 the former American business of Thomas J. Lipton. From the 1940s other food businesses had been added to the original Lipton tea business. The two enterprises, with their entirely different history and problems, were organized and managed separately.

Lever Brothers Company in the United States were always *sui generis*. From the start, Lever himself had been fascinated by the American scene. Many of his ideas on technology and marketing—more especially advertising—were the by-product of his observations on his American journeyings. After a difficult start the American business had taken off under the leadership of Francis A. Countway. By the 1920s it was a bright spot in an often dismal picture. Countway himself was a man after Lever's own heart, a man who, as he said, got results and met competition. Lever, not as a rule a good delegator, was wise enough to let Countway run the American business in his own American way. He had negotiated its progress out of its original 'prison' in New England into the expanding economy of the Middle West. He had chosen those kinds of soap, like Lux, which Americans liked, and had soft-pedalled those like Sunlight, which they did not. By 1929 he had pushed up Boston's sales of soap to over 91,000 tons, making this the second largest market after the United Kingdom; he added, in 1936, a lard substitute, which bit hard into the business of competitors like Procter and Gamble. Under Countway's vigorous rule the sales figures of the American business had gone up from less than $1 million in 1913 to $19 million in 1925. Ten years later turnover stood at $52 million, and twenty years later at $143 million. To serve this expanding market, Countway had set up a new plant at Edgewater on the Hudson, to produce his new 'shortening', and to serve the expanding trade of the Middle West a new model factory at Hammond, Indiana.

The immediate post-war years saw the American economy carried along on a wave of optimism and expansion, in which Lever Brothers Company shared. It was not difficult to sell almost anything that was made. At the end of 1945 Lever occupied a powerful position in the detergent field. Procter and Gamble had more brands and a slightly larger total share of the market, but Lever marketed the premier brands in each field. Rinso was the largest-selling packaged soap powder; Lux Toilet Soap was the largest-selling toilet soap and Lifebuoy was the largest-selling deodorant soap; and Lux Flakes ranked first among the fine fabric soap products.

In February 1946 Mr Countway, who had reached the age of 68, left the business. He was succeeded by Charles Luckman. At the end of 1946 Procter and Gamble introduced a new synthetic detergent product Tide, which was to precipitate a revolution in the detergent industry in the United States. Procter had seized the initiative, and it supported Tide with large-scale advertising and promotion expenditures. By 1949 Tide had become the leading family laundry detergent sold in the United States, a position it has retained.

In 1949 Luckman moved the centre of the Lever Brothers Company business complex from Boston into the brisker air of New York. Luckman left the business in January 1950, and he was succeeded by Mr Jervis Babb. Babb reorganized the top echelons. The new headquarters on Park Avenue, a milestone in the architectural history of America and indeed of the twentieth-century world, was finally opened in 1952. But in the new battle for the detergent market, Lever were still undergunned, especially in technical matters. In 1955 William H. Burkhart became president of the company, and in 1958 he was elected chairman of the Board. Significantly, the new chief was by training a technical man, but with a thorough understanding of the vital links between technology and marketing. The years between 1946 and 1955 were difficult and anxious ones when the whole future of the business was at stake. It was the second half of the 1950s before growth and confidence returned. By 1954 the sales figures had risen to $235 million. By 1965 they stood at $456 million.

Within this context of new growth lay a story of the remodelling of the entire business complex in modern terms, the incorporation of new technologies and the 'transformation [in Mr Burkhart's phrase] of what had been a trading company into a marketing company'. In the synthetic detergent market Lever had made up some of the lag in the 'heavy duty' detergent, though in sales volume they remained a long way behind their chief competitor. In other types of detergent, however, they had made remarkable progress and in some cases had given the lead, as with liquid detergents.

They had likewise developed the edible fat trade, building here on the acquisition of the Jelke Margarine Company in 1948. At the time it was bought, this was not a prosperous business, but, skilfully managed, it had seized the new opportunities in the margarine market. The post-war years had seen a remarkable expansion of margarine consumption, and a corresponding decline of the 'natural' dairy market in the United States. Fiscal penalties against margarine had been reduced, largely because technological progress had made it possible for farmers and manufacturers to turn an old enmity into a new alliance through the use in margarine of American-grown oil-bearing seeds, like soya and cottonseed. So that while the old market for lard substitutes had given way to a new preference for liquid oils, the prospects for the margarine trade and especially for Lever's premium brand, Imperial, seemed excellent.

The new patterns of marketing and production could be discerned from the geographical location of the various Lever Brothers Company manufacturing plants. To the original plant at Cambridge, Massachusetts, had been added a second, acquired at Baltimore in 1938, the vegetable-shortening plant at Edgewater in 1931, the factory at Hammond, Indiana, in 1928; and to these in more recent years were added the acquisitions of the Pepsodent factory at Chicago in 1944 and a new model plant at Los Angeles in 1951. Since the end of the Second World War, the plant layout had been rationalized as follows: the Cambridge plant had been closed and soap and detergent for the eastern United States moved to Baltimore and Edgewater. This type of production for the Middle West and South centred on Hammond and St Louis, while the explosion of population in the West brought into existence the new plant at Los Angeles. Chicago became the national centre for dentifrice production. The whole of this production passed through some fifteen distribution warehouses where stocks could be built up for the retailers. From this vast market, enjoying the highest standard of living in the world, local differences of habit and preference were steadily disappearing. The manufacturer therefore enjoyed the *entrée* to a homogeneous market, offering unique opportunities for experiment which in turn could serve as a base for further aggression into foreign markets. In no other country in the world did the manufacturer have such opportunities deriving from mass consumption at a uniquely high level of prosperity.

The value of the United States business was not merely the $26 million worth of net profit which, for example, it was able to contribute in 1965. It lay even more in the unique experience of marketing and technological progress, which had contributed to the growing reservoir of Unilever knowledge. After the sag of the late 1940s, the United States business had once again resumed its position as the spearhead of technical progress in a number of respects. This position Lever Brothers Company in America had seized and held largely through its apprehension of what is increasingly the central problem of all modern consumer businesses, the need for continuous and close liaison between the marketing expert on the one hand and the technical and research experts on the other. Such liaison was not limited to merely the top ranks of management. It needed to be a liaison right through the entire organization of the business. Possibly the reason why the problem had forced itself on American attention earlier than elsewhere was fundamentally a sociological one. Where immigration had played an enormous part in the national history, where geographical and social mobility were both characteristic of a new society, consumers were uniquely responsive to innovation. The frontier took longer to disappear commercially than in almost any other way. This was a market highly receptive to advertising. The North American response to any new product was swift. It was easier to sell something the first time than in almost any other country in the world. But it was correspondingly harder to hold the market you had, for there was less of that 'consumer loyalty' to older products which characterized more conservative markets. Consumers were generally ready to co-operate in market research into their preferences. And this in turn had encouraged manufacturers to use techniques for finding out what consumers wanted, of making products that would satisfy their wants and of letting the consumer know that you possessed the answer to his wants. These techniques of marketing had become paramount in the achievement of business success.

Correspondingly, technology and research were often highly conditioned, highly applied. There was little disposition to regard either as entitled to an expensively independent existence. True, technological changes of fundamental importance still happened. One was the change from natural to synthetic detergents. Another, more recent, that from synthetic powders to liquid detergents. Liquid detergents for dish washing had in turn made it possible to produce the cold water washing product, and this in turn was valuable to a society which was increasingly using synthetic fabrics, which were best not washed in hot water for their basis was thermoplastic which tended to wrinkle. There could still, therefore, be a complex interweaving of market technology and laboratory technology. An indefinite future might still offer revolutionary technological changes which might strike at the whole organization of a detergent business, for example disposable clothing might eliminate the need for a whole range of detergents and suggest the need for future diversification into entirely different types of product. But this was in the unforeseeable future. The more immediate future suggested a range of minor or marginal refinements. The main thrust, therefore, of such a business must be a *marketing* thrust; the object, to exploit the consumer's desire for satisfaction in a world where all the competitors were doing the same. The increasing expense of launching new products made it vital that risks should be reduced to the minimum. Out of the small percentage of new ideas accepted, one or two would survive to the stage where they were put to test amongst a sample body of consumers and then finally to the marketing test in a particular area under all the real conditions of competition.

In such a context American management had seized at an early stage on the fact that *measurement* was the essence of the managerial problem in the present age. The new generation of managers needed to be able to defend their decisions to their colleagues, their superiors, the stockholders, the consumers and the government. A large variety of systems designed to test products, to test individuals and to test the opinions of groups of individuals, largely developed in wartime, had been extrapolated into civilian life after the war. The object in each case was prediction—to predict the capabilities of individuals as managers, to predict the reactions of consumers to new products. It was calculated recently that to maintain the level of business conducted by Lever Brothers Company some 46 people needed to reach and take off the shelf of one shop or another one package each of a Lever product every second of every shopping hour.

A market so vast and so volatile invariably stimulated the demand for information on the part of the entrepreneur. And in spite of the gaps in knowledge and the possibility of epic mistakes, Mr Burkhart could commit himself to the belief: 'An intelligent company does not nowadays have many failures in the market place.' Tests applied to television advertising, for example, could indicate whether a particular television commercial film had or had not changed the preference of the consumer for a competing product. To hold and develop markets in American conditions required increasing co-ordination of almost all the sciences, from the physical sciences through the work of mathematical, statistical and computer experts down to the economists and sociologists.

The nature of Lever's research and technological development in the United States had been itself sharply conditioned by the market situation. The co-operation between marketing, research and production was as close as it could be made. Little in the way of undirected research was encouraged. The scientist was largely, though not exclusively, guided in his research programme by the indications passed to him from the market. For the investigation

of social and technical conditions eliminated in advance a good deal
of research on which money might otherwise be wasted. For
example, there was less cause, in American conditions, for spending research money on dehydrated vegetables since refrigerators
were known to be large, cheap and virtually ubiquitous. On the
other hand, there remained a large field of work between research
and production. Most of the products which Lever's dealt in
were not pure chemical entities. Impurities and baffling differences of performances were apt to arise. A product which worked
in the laboratory or pilot plant might work differently in full
production. Thus, although research throughout the Unilever
world organization was increasingly and successfully co-ordinated,
there was still room for all kinds of local investigations. The
Edgewater research organization steadily became a model of
tightly applied research. This did not eliminate a minority interest
in fundamental problems. Edgewater's research on detergents led
to contracts from public authorities for investigations into skin
problems which produced important discovery and progress in the
field of germicidal drugs. The industrial scientist, like other
scientists, was trained to observe phenomena which, though
accidental, might have consequences far outside his own immediate
field of interest. As a distinguished academician recently remarked,
the lines dividing basic and applied research and applied research
and application itself have never been entirely clear, so that 'much
new knowledge has been generated at the borders of basic and
applied research, and even of applied knowledge and its application'.[1]

Quite separately managed, yet sharing many of the characteristics and problems of the Lever business, was the Lipton
business. Originally an offshoot of the enterprises of the ebullient
Thomas Lipton himself, the American Lipton business had
become an independent enterprise operated from 1931 under the
terms of a trust. Six years later Unilever N.V. acquired an interest
in it and completed their control in 1946. The situation they had
inherited was chaotic, for though Lipton might have claimed to
convert America to tea drinking, he had certainly done it at great
cost. The business Unilever acquired was running downhill
rapidly. From 1939 the new management moved boldly to bring
in new men and new methods and build a consumer franchise for

[1] Clark Kerr (President of the University of California), *The Uses of the
University*, Harvard, 1963, page 117.

the business. Diversification into other foods began almost at once. A Chicago dehydrated soup manufacturer was acquired and by 1941 had added $2 million worth of turnover in a highly competitive market. In 1956 Lipton's went into pet foods, only to meet with dismal failure. The following year they had better luck with a salad-dressing business and in 1961 they acquired an ice-cream business with wide coverage in the Eastern and Middle West areas of the United States. (Ice-cream in the United States is not so much a food as a way of life.) Meantime, the tea business had been reconstituted. The American housewife found tea leaves a domestic nuisance. The tea manufacturer in the United States had therefore early provided tea in a small paper bag. Lipton's had improved on this by obtaining exclusive supplies from 1950 of a tasteless and neutral container. In 1958 came 'instant tea', but to a slow start. New products are apt to be expensive, but instant tea, which could be prepared iced for a hot climate, produced in the end excellent results. Thus the diversification into foods was pursued through a company with long experience of consumer habits, sharpened and systematized by the same new techniques of marketing as were simultaneously helping to focus the aims of Lever Brothers Company.

Receptive as American society might be to innovation, and sympathetic to capitalist enterprise, the management of private capitalism in the United States bristled with its own peculiar problems. Few people outside the United States realize how conditioned is the progress of enterprise there by the existence of anti-trust legislation. Fewer still understand how deeply rooted is such legislation in the history and attitudes of the American people. Its roots lie in that particular kind of radicalism which attempted in the late nineteenth century to return to the early simplicity of Jeffersonian democracy. The objects of the creators of anti-trust law were comprehensive, political as well as economic. On the face of it, nothing could seem more paradoxical than the distrust of a people who enjoy a uniquely high standard of living through the efficiency of private capitalism for the implications of this very form of economic organization. Yet popular opinion in the United States remains distrustful of the implications of capitalism. Hence a belief in the maintenance of competition which has become an article of almost religious faith. The requirements of economic efficiency took second place in the last resort to suspicions that great aggregations of wealth could strike at the roots of democracy. Under a political system which leans heavily on lobbying, it is theoretically possible for a lobby to become so powerful that it can outbid other lobbies. This suspicion, that monopoly might jeopardize the democratic system itself, explains why any business of size must be continually on guard, aware that if it transgresses in any matter of mergers, agreements or trade practices, it will be subject to legal action. Anti-trust law forms in fact a kind of economic planning by remote control.

Such a situation posed special problems for an international business like Unilever. American law in no way inhibits foreign ownership of business within the sovereignty of the American federal government, but in anti-trust matters it applies the same rules which it would apply in the case of a fully American-owned business. The problem was aptly and vividly illustrated when in 1958 the Anti-trust Division of the Department of Justice challenged the purchase by Lever Brothers Company, New York, of the trade-mark and rights of a detergent belonging to the Monsanto Chemical Corporation, a low-suds detergent called 'all'. An anti-trust suit was instituted against Lever's on the grounds that this purchase would reduce competition in the detergent industry. Lever's defence was bold and direct. They contended that the purchase would not reduce competition but would increase competition in a line of business where both Lever Brothers Company and Monsanto had been losing money and were both faced by business failure. Ultimately, following a trial, the Federal District Court in New York ruled in 1963 in favour of Lever Brothers Company that the acquisition of 'all' did not threaten to lessen competition. The Justice Department subsequently chose not to appeal to the United States Supreme Court, and Lever's thus ultimately prevailed in the case.

The case illuminated several aspects of the management problem in the United States. In particular it underlined the fact that one reliable defence against an anti-trust action is proof of an increase and not a decrease of competition.

Empirically, the American approach to the managerial problem has worked its way towards a theory of equilibrium. The social justification does not lie merely in increased efficiency (which monopoly can sometimes claim) but in increased efficiency balanced against the safeguards of continued competition. Many progressive industrialists accept that some such restraint on the powerful logic that may lead to monopoly must be accepted.

India and her Neighbours

There could be few more striking contrasts than that between the affluence, the sophistication and the unique type of competition of the North American market and the economic conditions of the great Indian continent. Here was a country of 438 million people— nearly ten times the population of the United Kingdom, and more than twice the population of the United States—yet of this total some 360 million were country people, living at a level which afforded nothing more than the bare necessities of life and frequently less. Another 78 million or so lived in towns, but many of these too had nothing beyond the income required for their immediate needs. Even before India achieved independence, the British Raj had devised plans for the economic future of India and from 1951 these were put into force by the new government. By 1961 national income had gone up by about 42 per cent, but more than half of the benefit had been absorbed by the increase of population which followed ineluctably on the heels of improvement. The average income per head in India therefore remained about £25 per annum, one of the lowest in the world. Industry and urbanization still remained thinly spread. The Indian economy was agricultural, and agriculture was still dominated by the monsoon. Consumer industries of the kind associated with Unilever had therefore a limited market to which to turn in India, and beyond the problems of poverty lay the problem of illiteracy, apathy and a system of communications which paralysed many of the techniques of business progress as they are understood in societies which 'took off' at an earlier stage and are now able to spread their increments of wealth downwards throughout the lower ranks of society.

Against such a background of economic obstruction, the progress of the Unilever enterprise in India (from 1956 known as Hindustan Lever Limited) was one of the phenomena of economic progress in the developing economies. In the sector of private industry Hindustan Lever could claim to occupy a highly strategic position in the modernizing of India. Even before government pressure was exercised towards handing over the management of Indian enterprises to Indian nationals, the process had gone on for some time in Unilever's Indian companies, so that only a handful of the 400 or so managers of Hindustan Lever were expatriates. The progress of Hindustan Lever was the product of a partnership between a truly Indian national management and a European parent organization able to supply technical guidance, knowledge and advice.

The Unilever association with India was an old one. William Lever started to export Sunlight soap to India in the 1890s. This was followed by Lifebuoy, Lux, Vim and so on. In the 1920s the first local company was acquired in the shape of the North Western Soap Company at Garden Reach, Calcutta, situated in a former harem. Another export office opened in Bombay in 1930 and soap production in Bombay began in 1934. By 1935 Bombay and Calcutta were producing 11,000 tons of soap per year. Meantime, the Dutch margarine manufacturers, beginning by exporting vegetable ghee into India, had gone into local manufacture by 1932 in Bombay. To these staple lines were added in the 1960s various diversified food enterprises specially associated with the new plant at Etah in the western part of Uttar Pradesh state. Between 1944 and 1956 all these various enterprises, covering the Indian market by manufacturing plants based on or around Bombay in the west, Tiruchirapally in the south, Calcutta in the east, and Ghaziabad in the north, had been grouped and rationalized under a single management, Hindustan Lever Limited, with 10 per cent of the shares quoted on the Indian stock exchange. The progress in turnover is shown from the following figures:

	Edibles (tons)	Detergents (tons)	Toilet Preparations (value)
1949	38,000	35,000	£220,000
1963	95,000	90,000	£1,170,000

Shortages of oils seriously affected Indian sales of edible fats in 1964 and 1965, but detergents sales made further progress (to top 100,000 tons in 1965) whilst in 1965 Indian sales of toilet preparations exceeded £1·5 million.

This remarkable measure of progress was achieved in spite of formidable natural obstacles to which were often added the unavoidable burdens arising from India's political and financial situation. Communications in India remained mostly primitive so that one of the biggest problems facing the consumer industry remained that of reaching the customer. The market fair on appointed days was still one of the established methods by which buyers from the surrounding villages come to the 'mandi'. Lever's long ago pioneered nation-wide distribution by company salesmen, and more recently they have gone out to most of the smallest towns and largest villages with motor vans carrying stocks and salesmen. Even now many of the villages remain beyond their reach.

In a society still poor and illiterate, advertising could have only a limited appeal, reaching perhaps only less than one-tenth of the population. In all, perhaps 50 or 60 million people in India can afford more than the bare necessities of life and it was to them that Hindustan Lever must appeal. Prejudice and superstition combined to check the growth in the sale of the main vegetable fat—called *vanaspati*—which sells at about half the price of real ghee (a kind of boiled, clarified butter). Most Indians are now satisfied that *vanaspati* is not actually harmful to human beings, but the progress has been slow.

To the natural poverty of India had to be added the inevitable problems caused by the early stages of planned industrialization. Opinion remained divided about the relative weight that should be given to the promotion of industry and the improvement of agriculture in the Indian Five-Year Plans. In so far as such planning might increase and distribute more widely the wealth of India, consumer industries stood to benefit. But in the early stages their problems were often made more serious. To conserve India's supplies of foreign currency as well as to stimulate her own industry, it was held necessary to control the imports of oil-bearing seeds. So that while the edible-fat business of Hindustan Lever was able to secure the necessary supplies of home-produced raw materials without too much difficulty, import controls created difficult problems for the soap and toilet preparations industries. Here, Hindustan Lever were in a strong position to tap a growing market amongst the more affluent sections of the Indian population. Climate and social habit combines to create a potentially good market for toilet preparations whose use came naturally to people long accustomed to the use of various unguents, hair oil, powders and the like. Yet expansion was inhibited largely by the shortage of raw materials. In the edible-fat trade, where raw materials were more easily obtained, there was proliferating competition from vast numbers of small manufacturers and also from the makers of natural ghee. To protect the ghee manufacturer, there were laws which prevented the *vanaspati* manufacturer from adding any colour or flavour to it that would make it resemble natural ghee.

For this and other reasons, therefore, Hindustan Lever branched off into other diversified activities similar to those which were being explored in other parts of the world. The Etah ghee factory was designed to produce (in addition to ghee) some 2,500 tons of skimmed milk powder and 1,500 tons of baby food. In Ghaziabad a pilot plant was put down in 1958-9 to produce dehydrated peas. This project was developed in conjunction with the Unilever food research laboratory at Colworth House. In five years the 40 acres of peas grown in the Uttar Pradesh had become 4,000 acres. Ultimately Hindustan Lever aimed to produce 300 tons of de-hydrated peas a year.[1] In time spinach, carrots, cabbage and other vegetables would be added to peas. Ghaziabad made cattle food too. In Bombay a plant would be installed for the manufacture of a catalyst which would be sold to industry to replace the catalyst at present imported. Another new plant at Bombay manufactured compound animal feeds; in 1965 sales of these products amounted to 28,000 tons. The cattle population of India is probably the highest in all the countries of the world, but the animals are generally poorly fed and milk yields very low. The plan was for the Bombay factory gradually to extend its sales from the greater Bombay district to the important dairy districts in the hinterlands and the up-country as well. Intensive poultry-raising seemed to offer a market for compound poultry feeds. But, again, in the animal-feed business the manufacturer was up against the shortage of raw materials, many of which were still needed primarily for human consumption. These new ventures were nevertheless evidence, slow as yet, but full of promise, that the vicious circle of Indian poverty was at last being broken. Unilever's entry into foods opened up a new and potentially fruitful mutual relationship with the farmer. This relationship, which involved Unilever as a buyer and seller in the agrarian community, was to be a significant omen for the future. Once the ascending spiral could be established, the prospects in India were limitless.

Many of the problems of India were shared by her neighbours in Pakistan. Yet here, too, were the beginnings of industrialization, and in 1953 Unilever opened a factory at Rahim Yar Khan in Western Pakistan, a town built round the cotton textile industry, and producing also oil as a by-product of the seed. Here, on a 30-acre site amongst a rapidly growing population was a factory

[1] An acre produced a little over half a ton of natural peas but there is massive loss of weight during dehydration.

producing soap, *vanaspati*, glycerine and animal feeding-stuffs. It soon became evident that it was not economical for the Rahim Yar Khan unit to try to supply all the needs of West and East Pakistan in the mid-1960s. Another plant was therefore developed at Chittagong in East Pakistan, a thousand miles away, for making household soap and refining glycerine.

Southwards in Ceylon was a peasant society of mixed races and religion, mostly living in one-third of the island territory, the area around Colombo in the south-west. The Singhalese were relatively literate, voraciously reading newspapers from cover to cover and passing them round amongst their friends. They were a civilized and friendly people, good at talk. Ceylon has often been called 'the Ireland of the east'. Here, too, the business was gradually turned over to local management. By 1964, 53 out of the 59 managers were Singhalese.

The business in Ceylon was much less hampered than most of its neighbours by religious problems, and *per capita* income was twice that of India. It was, on the other hand, even more heavily burdened by taxation. Facing a total taxation of just over 70 per cent the Ceylon business was probably more highly taxed than almost any other Unilever company. In addition, it faced strong competition in its varied products of soap, margarine, toilet preparations and foods.

South-East Asia

To the east and south of Calcutta lay another four eastern markets, each with its separate problems and destinies: Malaysia, Burma, Thailand and Indonesia. Of these, Malaysia seemed in the immediate post-war period the least promising, racked as it was by banditry and lawlessness. But by a bold stroke which was later admirably vindicated, Unilever moved over in 1952 to local production. The new State had a population of just over ten million. Its standard of living was, for the east, very high, especially amongst the Chinese, who represented 38 per cent of the population in Malaya and 76 per cent in Singapore itself. Behind this, however, lay the usual problems for a business of this kind—widespread illiteracy especially. 'If the elite minority of our customers are disregarded [said a report in 1956] then the market can be compared to nineteenth-century England and our problem is further complicated by the fact that we must overcome illiteracy in four languages.' Nearly half the advertising expenditure therefore went on making direct contact with consumers by the well-established methods developed in India in earlier days— van demonstrations, house-to-house canvassing, and competitions.

Malaya went on improving through the 1950s. Unilever here was one of the first companies to entrust management to Malayan executives. The new policy was not only popular, it was also successful: '. . . our first experiments in Malayanization have proved to be most successful and if anything have added to, rather than detracted from, the efficiency of our organization.' In the decade between 1952 and 1962, a management formerly entirely European had become preponderantly Malayan. Unilever could be well pleased with its initiative. A visiting director wrote in 1960: 'Malaya is a delightful place to visit. The country is green, the economy is booming, the rebels have been put to flight and the people are happy.'

Further north, on the Asian mainland, Burma presented a less satisfying picture. Territorially vast, Burma has a relatively small population of less than 22 million people. 85 per cent of these people are rural. The economy depends to an overwhelming extent on the production of rice. *Per capita* income is low— perhaps some £18 per annum, a lower figure than the pre-war figure. A Unilever visitor in 1960 recorded his impressions: '. . . the country has a run-down appearance . . . Rangoon and Mandalay . . . are unkempt towns. . . . Altogether one cannot feel a real energizing force in the country; although there is strong nationalism it does not express itself in a whole-hearted determination to improve the country's economy.'

A series of governments of different shades of opinion, but all of them rather sceptical and parochial, had pursued policies since the war which aimed at security rather than progress. Burma had witnessed little in the way of economic expansion, and the general temper of the country, strongly influenced by Buddhism, was not favourable to the ideas of an affluent society.

This was obviously not an ideal setting for a consumer industry. The bazaar, with its stalls, and a few co-operative stores and government chains were the typical outlets for washing soap, mainly of the old-fashioned kind. (Cold water is still very generally used for washing clothes in Burma.) Communications were poor, newspapers few and printing standards low. It was not easy in such circumstances to counter competition, often of an imitative kind, from local manufacturers, and official controls were not calculated to encourage much in the way of investment. Neverthe-less, the Unilever Burma management pushed ahead, and in the late 1950s was struggling to develop a local factory site in face of a good many frustrations such as having to pay import duties on machinery and building materials, and delays by the government in granting the lease of the factory site itself. Later it found itself facing a tax of 99 per cent on all profits over £22,500. The enter-prise that emerged in 1960 was a joint venture between the govern-ment of Burma and Unilever for the 'manufacture and sale of soap'. Under the agreement Unilever was guaranteed against nationaliza-tion for fifteen years, and the government participated to the extent of 25 per cent of investment. In spite of this undertaking the Burmese government announced in 1965 that it proposed to nationalize the joint business. The entire agreement with Unilever was thus unilaterally denounced and dishonoured.

Unilever's experience in Thailand was much happier. Here too they faced similar difficulties of communication and distribution; income *per capita* was lower than in Malaya and the very low monetary unit was a further disadvantage. The *baht* was worth about 4*d.* In the way that monetary units have of dominating consumers' habits, this accordingly became the upper limit to what people would pay for, for example, an ice-cream or a Coca-Cola. On the other hand, Thailand enjoyed political stability and rising living standards, and business benefited from low taxation, favourable incentives, absence of controls and a fully convertible currency. Unilever had a particular advantage in an excellent management team. A visiting marketing adviser summed up Unilever's position in 1965: 'This business has been pulled off the floor by the introduction of first-class products, by some very sound marketing appraisal, planning and execution and by a lot of very hard work especially in the upper levels of management.' In spite of a disastrous start their main products, a detergent, Breeze, and Lux Toilet Soap, had done well and the company now felt that the market was ready for a wider range of products in the soaps and detergents field and also, at a slower pace, in edibles. An important problem for the continuity of the business was the recruitment of Thai management; here too Unilever were com-peting in a very tight market. The burdens of life for a senior manager were not avidly sought by the Thais; nevertheless, there were signs that prestige born of success was strengthening Unilever's position here.

R

Apart from India and Pakistan, the largest market of the East was to be found in Indonesia. In 1935 Unilever had built the Batavia (now Djakarta) factory, battling against Japanese and American imports and the products of local Chinese soap manufacturers. A start had been made with margarine and edible fats too. Here was a market of between 70 and 80 million people, in numbers potentially twice the size of the United Kingdom. Ravaged by the war, and by the disorders which followed, the Dutch East Indies had given place after three centuries of Dutch rule in 1949 to the Independent Republic of the United States of Indonesia. The demand for soap, margarine, cooking oil, far exceeded supply. But the labour situation was chaotic. Of Unilever's force of some 2,000 workers, for every one that moved into a factory, another as swiftly moved out. So that at Unilever's large factories at Djakarta and Surabaya less than half the workers had been there as long as a year.

Nor was the external context any better. Strikes, government restrictions, attacks by brigands, all combined to make life unpleasant for managers and employees. A visiting director described the conditions in 1950: 'We are working with a great number (over 50) of employees, who have been sent out from their home country to Indonesia. These people have been working under a very severe strain these last few years. Small luxuries, which make life more pleasant in other countries, have been lacking or have sold, even before the monetary measures, at impossible prices. Imports of motor cars have been restricted to such an extent that at present hardly any transport is available to take them to the hills, as used to be done before the war. Electricity is cut sometimes for days on end, putting out of action refrigeration, air-conditioning, radio, not even mentioning the fact that one has to read by candlelight or oil-lamps. Water supply is inadequate and the flow of water in the houses during the dry season does not reach higher than the ground floor and even there is reduced to a trickle. Our sales inspectors travelling up-country were often in danger of their lives, although this situation has now much improved.'

The managing director faced every kind of problem, including midnight arrest by the military police, yet contrived to remain, in the eyes of government as well as his commercial colleagues, the spokesman of industry in general. The situation was, therefore, a series of question marks. The economic potential of Indonesia was vast, yet economic apathy was widespread. Productivity and exports had declined and this had meant a drastic cut in imports. By 1960 almost all industries were operating at only a fraction of their capacity, and the need to fall back on local raw materials had led to poor-quality products. The status of the business itself was still in doubt. It depended on whether the government decided that Unilever in Indonesia was a Dutch organization, in which case it would be nationalized, or whether it was an international company, which would enable it to operate independently within the 'guided economy'.[1]

From the experience of Unilever in India and the East, several conclusions emerged. Its local companies had to be prepared to share the problems and privations of the society of which they were part. Controls, taxation, even discriminatory laws made heavy demands on human patience. For the consumer-goods industry, the transition from a customary to an industrial society was usually burdensome. The returns on the investment—at first anyway—were often small. Continued investment was often as much an act of faith as a matter of rational calculation. Yet in the long term it could bring gains to the lenders and borrowers of capital. To the developing country, the advanced techniques of technology and marketing meant more employment and expanding supplies of food, necessities and in due course luxuries, better distributed over an ever-widening proportion of the population: to the investing business, a fair return on an expanding and diversified enterprise. The mutual gain was essentially long-term. Before the investment could fructify risks and losses might have to be faced. Only a strong and stable concern could face such risks, and thus enable the Old World to help sustain the New. It is doubtful whether any form of private enterprise other than a self-financing concern under a professional, non-owning management would feel free to take such a long view. For though the resources committed to the developing economies may be only a small proportion of Unilever's total resources, they represented absolutely an enormous capital commitment. In older days it was an exceptional capitalist indeed who had the foresight to take such a plunge. Referring in 1906 to his relatively new overseas ventures—and they were still mainly in European countries or English-speaking

---

[1] The business was put under Government control in 1964 but was handed back to Unilever early in 1967 by the 'New Order' regime of General Suharto.

settlements—Lever described the critical attitude of his share-holders: '. . . the only comment we have ever had upon them at these [shareholders'] meetings has been, "Don't put too much money in these associated companies". Well, we have got to help these children, they are growing, and it would be a little difficult to follow this advice with them.'[1]

There spoke the voice of the sole Ordinary Shareholder to the cautious owners of the Preference capital. Times have changed in the succeeding half-century, yet in many ways Lever (himself an owner-manager but already a largely self-financing one) was prophetic in his attitude to investment. By 1965 the Common-wealth enterprises that seemed so risky and precarious to the Preference shareholders of half a century or more ago seemed gilt-edged by comparison with the perils of Africa and South East Asia.

Canada, Australia, New Zealand and South Africa

The three Commonwealth nations of predominantly European settlement, Canada, Australia and New Zealand, and the Republic of South Africa, have sufficient economic and social similarities to justify considering them as a group, at any rate so far as Unilever is concerned. In the first place, they had all presented the same problem to the industrial entrepreneur in the early stages. They all comprised vast areas of territory containing relatively small populations largely collected in relatively scattered urban pockets. Even in the 1960s their total populations did not add up to as much as the total populations of the United Kingdom, Indonesia or Pakistan.

In Canada, Australia and South Africa, therefore, Lever, in his explorations on the eve of the First World War, had concluded that each of these markets required a sizeable number of local factories to supply its widely spread markets. A string of factories, partly Lever-built, partly acquired, stretched across Canada from east to west. Some ten factories encircled the coastline of the whole southern half of Australia from Townsville in the north-east to Fremantle in the south-west, all of them part of the Lever–Kitchen–Burford federal structure. New Zealand was likewise served by a Kitchen factory. In South Africa, Lever had decided that distances required the presence of three major manufacturing centres: Cape Town, Durban and Johannesburg. Contemporary

---

[1] *The History of Unilever*, vol. I, page 110.

manufacturing methods and transport costs probably justified his decision to maintain supply from a series of local factories spread over these large territories. For one thing, animal fats were plentiful in all these areas. As time went on, some degree of rationalization took place (especially in South Africa), but it was limited by the economics of transport and contemporary technology.

Another feature common to them all was that patterns of consumption and social habits in these societies reflected to a greater or lesser degree those of Britain, Continental Europe, or North America. That is to say, they enjoyed a relatively high *per capita* income, they looked for high standards of living, and they demanded high-quality products. Although they lagged behind Europe and North America in social sophistication, they were in some degree adaptable to methods of marketing, distribution, advertising and the like, invented in the first place in Britain or North America. In spite of local, though usually temporary, financial difficulties, they represented a pretty solid and reliable investment over a period of time, though one which was hardly likely to throw up startling innovations of either product or method.

The problems of Canada had early thrust themselves upon Lever's attention, even before 1914. In the 1930s they were still exigent. Larger in area than the United States, Canada could only count one inhabitant where America could count fourteen. The problem of distances has already been described.[1] Canada also had one special problem as a result of its juxtaposition with the United States. Its manufacturers, and Lever's in particular, felt the sharp edge of competition from some of the world's most efficient manufacturers just across the border. Even so, the years before the Second World War saw Unilever in Canada making measurable progress. During and after the war, the Canadian management was the first of this group to rationalize production on a radical scale. By 1943 Calgary had ceased to operate and by 1945 Vancouver, Winnipeg and St. Stephen were only in part production.[2] From 1944, therefore, the future production areas for Canada were being investigated intensively. Some sixteen possible plans were considered. The main question was obvious. Where was production to be centred: Vancouver, Winnipeg, Toronto or Montreal? In the end the lot fell upon Toronto, which

[1] See *The History of Unilever*, vol. I, page 12, vol. II, pages 357–8.
[2] See page 86.

accordingly developed two plants: one for margarine and shorten-
ings and another for detergents and toilet preparations. To a
visiting director from London in 1955 the new detergents factory
was a paragon: 'Automatic operation and control has gone further
than in any other Unilever factory, and while it may cost a little
more initially and require some fairly high-skilled maintenance,
the results are impressive both in the reduction of manpower and in
the uniform quality of the production. We should do more of this
in our factories.'

Non-soapy detergents were introduced in Canada in 1948 and
afterwards. Diversification followed fairly swiftly into frozen foods
(Birds Eye) and cosmetics (Harriet Hubbard Ayer and Shadow
Wave Home Perm). Lipton's tea had become part of Unilever in
Canada in 1938, and since 1960 had been a separate Lipton Company. The broad outline of demographic and social change all
seemed favourable to Unilever in Canada. The plans of 1944
predicted a population of 13 million for the 1960s. This turned
out to be 5 million short of reality. Standards of living were on the
American level. Almost everybody owned radio, television,
refrigerators, washing machines. Everybody was on the telephone
and nearly everybody owned a motor car. Yet, as so often, it
proved there was a fallacy in arguing from general prosperity to
particular profits. The story of the 1940s and 1950s in Canada was
not all it might have been. The frozen-food industry was making a
loss in 1950, and indeed Birds Eye in Canada was sold in 1955.
Declining sales brought about the decision to liquidate Harriet
Hubbard Ayer and the Shadow Wave Home Perm businesses in
1954. In 1951 the entire Unilever group in Canada made a trading
loss of nearly £500,000. By 1953 the profits were up to £1·3
million, but they fluctuated in subsequent years.

The reasons for these vicissitudes were not far to seek. United
States competition forced Canadian manufacturers to spend
heavily on advertising and promotion in a society where the housewife was less ready than her southern neighbour to rush in and
buy a new product simply on the grounds of novelty. The edible-
fat industry suffered from legislative restrictions. A federal act for-
bade margarine until 1949. In that year it was withdrawn, but most
provincial governments retained laws against colouring margarine,
and taxation against it remained stiff. Even so, margarine turnover
increased rapidly down to 1962, but as late as 1964 a Unilever
expert observer was not happy about either the quality of the

Canadian product or the Canadian housewife's attitude to it. Amongst the new food industries of Unilever, Lipton's had done well, but more because they had managed to capture a very large part of the dried-soup market than because of any success of the product for which Thomas Lipton had originally been famous. Lipton's tea had not conquered the heart of the Canadian housewife as it had that of her American neighbour. In 1963 a new Lipton plant went up at Bramalea, thirty miles from Toronto, to take care of most of its products, though its ice-cream continued to be made at Simcoe, Ontario. Diversification had not stopped at foods. In 1960 Hart Products, a producer of highly specialized chemicals, was acquired, and in 1961 Success Wax Limited, a producer of household waxes and polishes.

In all, a variable picture. With all its superficial similarities to the United States, the Canadian market contained some obstinate problems. Space, distance, competition—these were basic, and to these must be added another far from negligible problem: the existence of two societies in Canada, one French-speaking, the other English-speaking, separated not only by language but also fairly clearly geographically and frequently also in such matters as cooking and methods of home-washing. This presented two marketing problems instead of one for the Canadian management; none the less in the 1960s they were in good fettle, reckoning on a steady increase in profits.

Like the Canadian market, the Australian market, as we have seen, had demanded a series of factories right from the beginning. Again, transport costs and plentiful supplies of local fats for manufacture had all pointed in the same direction. In spite of some degree of rationalization, the picture remained similar, even in the 1960s. A few small factories had been closed down, particularly in the north-east, on the coast of Queensland, but from Fremantle in the west, via Adelaide, Melbourne and Sydney, up to Brisbane, Unilever maintained a ring of factories. Little radical concentration had taken place, and diversification had merely added a considerable number of new companies to the family, mainly food manufacturers. Keen observers saw here a prosperous future for consumer industries such as those Unilever was interested in. The post-war story was one of rapid industrial expansion and diversification, industrial self-confidence was high, profits at record levels. The Australian business itself was well managed. 'The management team,' said a visiting director in 1958, was 'happy, aggressive, vigorous and forward-thinking.' Consumption and distribution seemed to be developing on American lines, with community shopping centres, huge parking spaces, self-service shops and supermarkets. There seemed to be overwhelming justification for further intensive investment in this evidently prosperous economy. Even in the 1950s common sense suggested that diversification was essential to reduce Unilever's excessive dependence in Australia on detergent sales, for these produced by far the largest part of the profits.

In the early 1950s diversity had meant Lipton's tea and soup, and Birds Eye frozen foods. Alas, neither tea nor frozen foods prospered, and both were sold. To make up for this, other food businesses were acquired. In 1959 the ice-cream business of McNiven Brothers and two table margarine manufacturers in South Australia and Western Australia joined the group. Street's Ice Cream of Sydney and the Gardiner Refrigeration Company in the same area both came in. J. P. Sennitt's ice-cream business followed in 1961, the Golden Nut Margarine Company in South Australia in 1962 and the Rosella Preserving and Manufacturing Company in 1963.

Business in Australia had its problems. The Australian population of some 10·5 million was spread over large areas. The management of a widely dispersed collection of factories of varying age, character and efficiency, and their relations with the market, presented problems of unusual difficulty. American competition, though less fierce than in Canada, was nevertheless formidable. The diversification into frozen foods failed. Amongst the mistakes was the fatal one of giving insufficient attention to quality. The failure was disturbing in a country where the frozen food industry was one of the newest and fastest-growing segments of the economy, heading rapidly towards rationalization.

In spite of the rapid growth of the economy, government attitudes were not consistently helpful to economic growth. Price controls remained for a long time after the war, and balance of payments troubles more than once meant disturbing interference with the flow of raw-material imports. Maybe also the observer who thought that Australians were temperamentally inclined to bite off rather more than they could chew, had something of an argument: 'In general, if there is a prevailing weakness, it is not lack of initiative, enterprise or hard work, but that the desire to use the most advanced and modern methods and emulate what a large country can afford, sometimes leads to more cost than the size of the business can really afford.' Even so, profits went on expanding, doubling between 1955 and 1960 from £1 million to £2 million. With the revolution in the technology of oils and fats described elsewhere,[1] it seemed fair to suppose that some more radical rationalization of the productive structure in Australia must represent the next phase of Australian development. Against a background generally favourable to this kind of industry, the era of modernization and rationalization of production seemed to offer every prospect of greater efficiency, lower costs and larger profits.

From William Lever's first incursion into the Australasian market until very recently, affairs in New Zealand came under the wing of the management in Australia. Yet in many respects New Zealand was a different society from that of Australia. 'New Zealand,' wrote a visiting director in 1949, 'a comparatively wealthy country, has chosen to apply part of its wealth to the acquisition of social security, to the levelling of incomes and to increased leisure. . . . There is no poverty. The necessities of life are abundantly and plentifully available to all, but most definitely they tend to be of a rather . . . homespun nature—what is called "utility" in England.' Wealth was indeed evenly spread through-out the population and a generally high level of living standards was rising. Wages were high, unemployment non-existent. Indeed, labour was everywhere short. In a world where the delights of affluence and the speed of progress were already causing some people at any rate to wonder nervously whether this could go on much longer or, if it did, whether it should, New Zealand might well seem a haven of peace, where life pursued an agreeable but placid way, sensible and above all free from extremes of wealth or poverty.

There was much to be said for such a view, and in 1949 Unilever had no reason to grumble: '. . . the soap and toilet preparations we manufacture are counted amongst the necessities which every New Zealander buys in quantity—so we can rely on further, and I believe appreciable, expansion in our trade. Our business has grown solidly for years, and is now very soundly based.' The business produced reasonable though not exciting margins of profit; it expanded, but not in any spectacular fashion. For against steady sales in a market where no consumer was very rich

[1] Chapter 4, pages 76 et seq.

but nobody very poor had to be set some undoubted difficulties. The total population of New Zealand was, after all, only small. At 2·5 million it seemed pretty static. The labour shortage meant that workers had little reason to stay put. '. . . even the prospective alteration in a bus route near our factory is giving cause for concern lest a walk of a few hundred yards will put staff off.' Company taxation was high, working on a progressive system somewhat analogous to progressive rates of income tax. A prevalent egalitarianism had led internally to a system of price controls which tended to check expansion and profits. Customers stuck to traditional methods of retailing. Chain stores and self-service were slow to make progress in this generally conservative community, cradled in an economy which, though prosperous, was heavily dependent on agricultural exports, especially to the British market. Any upset of the balance of payments, therefore, led immediately to measures to reduce imports, especially of manufactured goods.

This was a serious matter for Unilever, which, in spite of local factories at Petone and Wakefield Gully (both near Wellington) was still importing its synthetic detergents from Australia or England. Thus in 1958, when a payments crisis arose: '. . . we can no longer count on importing finished products like Surf, which means we will have to think of still further investment in a country where our investment per head is higher than in any other overseas country and where the yield has never been very satisfactory.'

The implication was plain: sooner or later New Zealand, like all other developed countries, would manufacture its own needs. This, and the slow rate of expansion, together suggested a further move. It would be better if New Zealand were less dependent on Sydney for decision and direction. It '. . . would gain in self-confidence, initiative, and verve were it on its own', as two visiting directors suggested in 1956.

In one respect New Zealand had already launched out. During the Second World War, quick-freezing equipment had been brought in from America to provide 'fresh' foods, particularly green vegetables, for American hospitals. The plant was located in Auckland, and later moved to Hastings after the war. Birds Eye, New Zealand, secured an immediate and resounding success. New Zealand housewives took eagerly to frozen foods, perhaps because there was virtually no daily help available in New Zealand. Peas, beans, asparagus, sweet corn, mixed vegetables, and fish, all sold like hot cakes. 'It is remarkable', as the visitors said, 'that the business has grown so quickly and so soundly on such "shoe-string" arrangements as we have for processing at the two factories at Riccarton [near Christchurch—South Island] and Hastings [North Island]'. Alas, it was not to last. Competitors were swift to seize their chance. By 1957 there was over-production and a price-cutting war. Successive losses pointed to a merger with Butland, a local New Zealand firm, in a joint operation to combine all their food interests except edible fats. Birds Eye were to specialize in frozen foods, Butland Industries in canned and non-perishable products. Unilever was to sell its Pukekohe factory in the North Island, retaining the factory at Mutueka.

However, by 1965 a visiting director was able to report that both the country and the business had changed, much for the better. The benefits of independence from Sydney were evident; the business had 'developed not only in volume and profitability, but in competence and morale'. In spite of increased taxation the trading profit in detergents after tax had risen to £255,000 by 1965 as compared with £28,000 in 1955 and it was felt that the organization would be well able to adapt itself to increased competition. In foodstuffs the smallness of the market remained a basic problem, but with a more organized administration than previously the business had expanded greatly as a result of the Butland amalgamation and the eventual purchase of the Butland food interests.

Of this group of markets, the most remarkable was South Africa. Of a total population of some 16 million, just over 3 million were white. The income per head in 1949 was some £69 per annum, perhaps twice what it had been in 1939. By 1964 it had doubled again. This was largely the result of the growing element of manufacturing in the nation's economy which had been stimulated by government measures aimed at promoting new investment and general economic diversification. In earlier days South Africa had been a problematical market for Lever Brothers. As in Australia and Canada, the vast distances had suggested a proliferation of plants, and these had been increased by the policy of buying up a number of smaller competitors. By 1936 production had been concentrated and with concentration came greater efficiency and prosperity in the late 1930s.

The progress begun then continued, with interludes created by the war and shortages since, down to the 1960s. The progress that had been made with the older manufactured staples in soaps and edible fats was maintained, and to these were added new ventures in food—dried and canned soups and ice-cream, especially. The traditional products were still concentrated at Durban (Maydon Wharf), Johannesburg (Auckland Park), and Cape Town (Salt River), but to these was added a new plant at Boksburg, Transvaal, for margarine and detergent production. Wall's Ice Cream put up a separate factory on the Boksburg site, while the Rondi ice-cream business, acquired in 1963, contributed a factory at Cape Town (two other Rondi factories at Johannesburg and Durban were closed). Another line of diversification in South Africa was chemicals. Early in 1963 a controlling interest was acquired in Silicates and Chemical Industries, with factories in the Transvaal and at Durban, producing sodium silicate, ammonium chloride and sodium sulphate.

These vigorous policies were designed to tackle the traditional problems of the South African market. South Africans had been slow to take to the new detergents in the 1950s, as they had been slow earlier to move from hard soaps to soap powders. Now the latest products were available. Margarine had been hampered by the influence of the farmers' groups in both major political parties. But now butter shortages forced the government to allow margarine to be made, and Stork margarine soon gained a dominant share of the market. Ice-cream was another successful addition to Unilever's business and, long before the acquisition of Rondi, the Wall's management had been building up goodwill. But otherwise foods were slow starters. For one thing there was no product which either appealed to the Africans or was within their means. They were, on the other hand, big buyers of margarine and soap, especially in the new self-service shops, which became a source of endless free entertainment to visiting African customers.

In the early 1950s there were fears that a trend away from expansion and towards consolidation might set in so far as government economic policy was concerned. This would create difficulties, especially for secondary industries in securing permits and government co-operation. Yet the expected slow-down did not take place. In spite of controls, of stronger competition from American competitors, and of all the social and political problems of South Africa, the Unilever management continued to expand production and sales. In 1960 a visiting director could write home: 'We have a splendid business, well-led and well-run.'

Equally satisfactory seemed to be the affairs in the Federation of the Rhodesias and Nyasaland in the decade between 1953 and

1963, when the Federation was dissolved. Here, too, local manufacture was beginning to replace former imports from South Africa, and Unilever was buying its way into other and more varied businesses. By 1963 the factory in Salisbury, Southern Rhodesia, was itself manufacturing new synthetic detergents. In spite of a shortage of educated Africans, the business was going forward. 'I previously visited Rhodesia in 1953. At that time no visitor could fail to get a feeling of excitement at the rapid development, the wealth of the country, and the good prospects for our business, and indeed for trade and commerce in the territory generally. The changes seen in Salisbury on this visit, however, surpassed any expectations in 1953. Building of shops, offices and European and African flats and houses has progressed at a quite remarkable speed and is continuing.' With the dissolution of the Federation, Unilever activities in Southern Rhodesia, Zambia and Malawi were necessarily separated once more. The effect this would have on operations was a problem for the future.

South America

As potential markets for the kinds of products Unilever makes and sells, the Latin American countries differed in every respect from the other economies of the world, developing or developed. They also differed markedly from each other. For one thing, they were the most recent markets to be explored. This was in a way curious, for South America—especially the Argentine—was supplied generously with British capital throughout the nineteenth century, and trade links were at one time strong. Perhaps the explanation was that those links weakened, British confidence was sapped, and British leadership in South America gave way to North American leadership, just about the time that Lever was expanding his business on a world scale. At any rate, whatever the reason, South America was one of the few places William Lever did not contemplate as another field in which to deploy his enterprise and capital. Anton Jurgens did. But in the 1930s his oil mill at Rosario[1] still stood empty, a total white elephant and a solemn warning against over-confidence.

It was not through the development of the great staples of household soap or margarine that Unilever finally slipped into South America in the 1930s. Local conditions and local competition were against them. Toilet soap and edible oils did a little

[1] See *The History of Unilever*, vol. II, page 205.

better in the Argentine, but here, as in Brazil, the business grew up through perfumery sales, and the spearhead was a business acquired by Lever in the hectic boom after the First World War (and not conspicuously successful in Europe), J. and E. Atkinson. Through one of those historical quirks which frequently leave agreeable corners of mystery in economic history, Atkinson's were as successful in South America as they were unsuccessful in England. On these somewhat tenuous bases larger things were to be built, but not without a struggle.[1]

Argentina presented, on the face of it, the most obvious market in South America for Unilever products. Standards of living were good amongst a high percentage of its 17 million people. It had a large middle class, rich resources, and relatively little poverty. These general considerations had produced a Lever soap factory at Buenos Aires by 1928 and a large modern perfume factory by 1934. Yet the high expectations which such an ambience might arouse were never really fulfilled, and from time to time were to be bitterly disappointed. The two main enemies were political instability and inflation.

Until 1955 the Perón regime made business a hazardous affair in Argentina, as a visiting director observed in 1951: 'Living conditions arising from the methods and politics of the Perón regime are most disconcerting, as one would expect in a police state—the atmosphere is very reminiscent of pre-war Germany and Italy. . . . The difficulty of obtaining exchange permits for raw materials and the dictatorial government decrees—aimed to appeal to the electorate and issued apparently without any regard to their economic consequences—combine to stifle initiative . . . I doubt if the outside observer can have a true picture of [Argentina's] atmosphere.' As a foreign business selling partly luxury products, dependent on imported raw materials, to a mass market, Unilever firms were necessarily vulnerable. The growing caprice and corruption of the regime made management increasingly difficult, until late in 1955, when Perón was forced to flee the country.

The early optimism that followed soon fell away. Even in 1959 another visiting director could remark that 'Argentina seems a country still suffering from a hangover.' The economy was stagnating, labour unrest was widespread, there were serious deficiencies of transport and power, and the cost of living rose steeply and continuously. (Between 1948 and 1965 the cost of living index rose

[1] See supra, page 200.

by 5,420 per cent.) Raw material prices and rates of exchange followed suit. Yet, between 1950 and 1957, soap sales almost doubled. Edible oil went down and was given up in 1955. The most profitable side remained toilet preparations—dentifrices, shampoos, hair dressings, talcum powders, toilet waters and colognes.

Unilever also diversified, introducing dried soups and building a synthetic detergent plant in 1960. Even so, political conditions continued to make life difficult. A decade after Perón disappeared, his Communist opponents remained, complicating all labour relations and threatening go-slow action without notice. The Argentine currency remained under heavy pressure. A firm like Unilever, which needed to import raw materials, was faced with import regulations erratically imposed and no less erratically lifted. (Another was clamped down on 10 January 1965.)

By contrast, Chile was one of the most politically stable of the South American countries, though heavily dependent economically on exports of copper and nitrates, nearly 75 per cent of its total exports. It was therefore highly sensitive to world prices, and, like the Argentine, a victim of runaway inflation. The standard of living of its population ($5\frac{1}{2}$ million in 1948, 8 million in 1964) was below that of Argentina. For Unilever, the main problem was to distribute its products through a long, narrow country, geographically isolated, economically backward and lacking local supplies of oils. But the water of Chile is hard, and the prospects for synthetic detergents were therefore good. As in the Argentine, the Unilever spearhead was Atkinson's. But from their first entry in 1929 they had to face fierce competition from the great French perfumery manufacturers, price cutting and small profits. Atkinson's therefore made an agreement in 1954 with a local company, Compania Industrial (Indus), to set up a department in their factory at Santiago for the manufacture of toilet preparations (including Lux Toilet Soap) and also detergents. In spite of the successful launching of non-soapy detergents (Rinso) in 1957, this partnership did not enhance the fortunes of Atkinson's. It was not until 1962 that the business really began to expand, when, chastened by rumours of American competition, a new company was formed from the same partnership but with Unilever equally sharing the responsibilities of management. Indus Lever S.A.C.I. acquired a local soap manufacturer, Perlina, partly American owned, where they successfully developed their detergents and toilet preparations and then planned to extend their margarine and foods. Chile was a small market, but against a background of pretty hard-headed national economic policies and steadily improving relations with local partners, Unilever could look forward by the mid-1960s to a steady if unspectacular improvement in its Chilean fortunes.

In Peru, one of the poorest of the South American countries, progress was slow. Maybe a quarter of its 8 million people were potential customers for Unilever products. Unilever's business started in 1951 in partnership with two local companies, Pacocha (manufacturing) and Ferreyros (distribution). A visiting director in 1951 was cautiously optimistic: 'Altogether an attractive little business with a sound tie-up with a local house for local manufacture and sale without investment by ourselves. There still remains the smallish market, many of whom are of very low purchasing power, and I rather feel we are using some high-powered machinery for a rather light haul.' However, as in their earlier experience in Chile, Unilever found that partnership with a local (and often competing) company was not always an unmixed blessing. To be properly competitive Unilever had to feel free to operate by its own methods and to its own standards: an expensive investment was often in the end more profitable than a modest participation. After various and mainly unsuccessful experiments at coming to grips with a difficult market, by 1964 Unilever had bought out all but one of its partners (Bunge y Born) and operated mainly through Lever Pacocha S.A. In 1965 a visiting technical adviser admitted that operating in Peru was still not easy. 'Price control, intensive competition and arbitrary governmental decisions based solely on political considerations, all combine to make matters for our Company extremely difficult. In addition industry is now facing a heavy bill to finance social services, which promise to be about the most comprehensive and advanced in the world.' However, despite considerable losses and little prospect of immediate profit, there was now some confidence that the market was better understood and that long-term success could be achieved, not least through 'sound, thorough analysis of consumer trends and needs'.

Far the largest and most promising market of South America lay in Brazil, approximately four-fifths the size of the whole of Europe, with all its 66 million people concentrated in one-fifth of the country. The spread of wealth was far more uneven than in Argentina, transport problems enormous, but the natural resources vast. The assessments of Brazil's future were regularly confident and optimistic. 'No one can fail' wrote a visitor in 1952, 'to be favourably impressed by the general vitality and energy of the Brazilian people today. The tangible size of the progress and prosperity that has taken place in the country in recent years can be well seen in the great civil engineering projects of roads, petrol pipe-lines and building construction in the three cities we visited —Rio, São Paulo and Santos. . . . Generally speaking, both our businesses are alive, their products are good and there is a good chance of expansion on both sides.' This kind of comment was repeated at regular intervals by later visitors. 'Brazil' it was later noted, 'has a vigour and horizon far greater than other South American republics.' Business was expanding, sales increasing, profits rising: 'Our business is essentially sound, the goodwill of our products has steadily improved, and our overheads are not excessive.'

Of course, Brazil presented problems. Unilever, here as elsewhere, suffered from problems of continuous inflation, of import restrictions, too great a dependence on too small a number of products, and ferocious competition from both local and North American competitors. Welfare contributions demanded by the government were high, and the needs of working capital burdensome.

From 1955, therefore, the business was reorganized. The perfumery side of Atkinson's was purged in an attempt to reform the 'hotchpotch of smells, labels and lines, some of which are vigorous, many of which should have been ruthlessly excised long ago.' New products were introduced—Rinso, talcum powder, hair cream, toothpaste, household cleaners, and so on. The reform and the expansion both proved successful. Unilever had no choice: 'It was either getting out of Brazil or spending considerable amounts in trying to make our business profitable.' The policy had raised morale, strengthened confidence and stimulated the natural optimism of the local management. With improvement in the general standard of living more and more people were becoming potential customers for Unilever products. A visiting director remarked in 1959: 'There is now a middle class in Brazil.'

It was against this hopeful background that Unilever decided in favour of a merger with their largest local competitor. The Gessy business, based on a large factory at Valinhos, was a much larger business than that of Unilever. The merger was completed in December 1960 and under a subsequent reorganization the old

s

Lever factory at São Paulo took over the production of all washing powders, the former Gessy factory made toothpastes, toilet soaps, talcum powders, and so on, while its remaining free space could be reserved for manufacturing margarine and foods. The importance of the merger was not only that it increased sales and raised profits, but that it gave a new stimulus to the local management. Throughout the 1950s Unilever had pursued a policy of putting Brazilians in charge of the local management. When the Chairman of Unilever Limited visited Brazil in 1964 he was able to tell the local board that their products 'as a range are as good as anything we have got in Unilever'. Edible fats, and to some uncertain extent foods, unquestionably had a future in Brazil. With industrialization going forward at a spanking pace, Brazil seemed to offer a bright prospect. A visiting director had remarked in 1954: 'The only things which could really decide us to quit Brazil would be if the Americans stopped drinking coffee or the Brazilians went Communist. I don't believe either of these will happen.' It still seemed fair comment on Unilever in Brazil ten years later.

The Rest of the World

In Asia as in Europe the Second World War and its aftermath spelt the end of what had seemed at one time to be promising ventures as well as the beginnings of new ones. Even in 1937 a director visiting China had seen here one of 'the two great eastern markets' of the future. The other one—India—had lived up to its expectations. China, for obvious reasons, had disappeared, just as Unilever's markets east of the Iron Curtain had disappeared also.

Against this could be set progress in Japan. Alert as ever to the promise of an industrializing society, William Lever had set up a soap factory in Japan. Alas, it was one of his less successful ventures, and in 1929 it fell victim to D'Arcy Cooper's programme of economy. In the post-war years Japan entered a new and rapid phase of economic expansion. Here were all the conditions for a successful investment, and in 1963 the Japanese government approved a joint venture between Unilever and the Hohnen Oil Company. The company, Hohnen-Lever, was registered in 1964 and a new factory with capacity of some 26,000 tons annually of margarine, shortening and other edible fats, was officially opened in October, 1965.

Away in the Philippines were the progeny of one of William

Lever's more carefree adventures in the insouciant early 1920s. *The History of Unilever* has described how Lever purchased shares in the Philippine Refining Corporation and the optimism with which he regarded the future of the company. Its history in the 1920s had been one of continuous disappointment. In the 1930s its affairs had improved, only to be overtaken by the Second World War. Its mills had been heavily damaged and the work of reconstruction was slow and difficult. Even in 1949 the Philippines business was still losing money, still far from competitive.

That year Roger Heyworth,[1] the director responsible for this area, made a report to the Special Committee which proved to be the foundation of a new phase of expansion. He did not mince his words about the problems '. . . I see a rough time ahead for us in the Philippines, and we shall require all our skill to weather the storm. The immediate priorities are to improve our own efficiencies and organization, cut our expenses wherever we can and build up our domestic business. Whether we can find some way to improve the difficult milling situation is the greatest problem of all.'[2] In the event the storm was weathered, efficiency raised, costs cut, the Philippines business went forward, and from being a milling company developed into a fully rounded organization—and producing profitably and competitively everything from raw materials to edible fats, soap and the latest non-soapy detergents.

Turkey, half Asiatic and half European, was another market which attracted Unilever's attention. They were, in fact, by no means strangers to Turkish markets. The United Africa Group contained a company, G. and A. Baker Limited, who had been selling merchandise in Turkey for over a century—they had begun by selling silk to the ladies of the Imperial Palaces. The Turkish business proved an uncovenanted success. Shortly before the Second World War, two directors whose plane had been forced down in Turkey had remarked that the Turks were great eaters of bread but were short of anything to spread on it. This casual observation was deepened by methodical enquiry after the war when Unilever became one of the first companies to respond to the Turkish government's offer of special terms for foreign investors.

[1] Of the three Heyworth brothers, all of whom became directors of Unilever, Roger was the youngest. Asia and the East were his special responsibility. His early death while on a journey through Ceylon in 1954 was a great loss to the business.
[2] Report by Mr R. H. Heyworth on his visit to the Philippines, 20 January/ 4 February 1950.

Changing social conditions suggested a modest but worthwhile market for margarine and possibly for artificial ghee for cooking. Unilever already had an antique oil mill (acquired from The United Africa Company which in turn had acquired it as part payment for an outstanding debt). A factory was established in 1952 in partnership with a leading Turkish Bank, Türkiye Iş Bankasi. Production rapidly outran all expectations. In fifteen years Unilever's Turkish market for edible fats rose to a size where it was comparable to the French market.

Turkey was a classic instance of a society going through the early phases of modernization—industrialization, population increase, rising living standards: for Unilever a favourable setting, but not without problems. Demand constantly outran capacity. That could be remedied. But it also outran the supply of local raw materials. That was less easy, for it meant importing raw materials in a situation where the balance of payments was a perennial weakness. Hence a delicate politico-economic balance. But in spite of successive problems Turkish Unilever walked its tightrope skilfully. By the mid-1960s it was well advanced with plans to develop its detergent and perfume business, thereby contributing not only to the growth of domestic manufacturing industry but opening up possible avenues for export trade.

Conclusion: Unilever and the Developing Economies
The companies that came under the surveillance of the Overseas Committee comprised the most varied group of all Unilever's investments, ranging as they did from the more or less orthodox patterns of Canada and Australia to the novel and exotic experiments of India and South America. Indeed, one is tempted to suggest that almost the only common factor between them was that they were located 'overseas'. Yet this would be to exaggerate. All of them manufactured and sold products for which Unilever in Europe was well known. All of them benefited by capital, skill and knowledge developed in older or more advanced economic areas.

As regards the 'developing' countries, probably more people would be found to agree on the value of *government* aid than would agree on the value of *private* investment in such countries. The private investor of capital has come to be associated in the minds of many people in former colonial territories with 'exploitation', with disregard of local welfare, with the supposed 'drain' of profits and dividends and a dozen other evils of colonialism, real or imagined. Such suspicions have in turn led the newly independent governments of such territories to take popular but ill-conceived action against foreign private enterprises. Expropriation, often without notice or compensation, has been an experience that Unilever, in common with other international businesses, has had to accept as a matter of *force majeure*.

The result of these mutual suspicions has been a falling away of private investment in the developing economies just at a time when its contribution was most needed and its advantages more apparent. Worse still, the governments of Western and developed economies have added to the problem by a clamp-down on the export of private capital, without always distinguishing between those kinds of capital export which may embarrass the exporter in the short term and those which can be reasonably said to benefit both capital exporter and capital importer in the longer term.

Without entering into any detailed discussion as to the value of government-to-government aid, we can say without fear of contradiction that *historically* it was private international investment which first fertilized the 'new' countries in the past. Government aid is a newcomer. The United States, the South American States, Australia, New Zealand, Canada and South Africa were all developed, provided first with systems of transport, communications, public works and later manufacturing industry by British and European private capital. Nor was this different in more than degree from experience within Europe itself. Large quantities of British capital went into Continental railways and utilities in the course of the nineteenth century. France, Germany, Italy, Spain were then still relatively 'backward' compared with Britain. Lever's, Jurgens' and van den Bergh's as we have shown, invested British and Dutch capital in a number of Continental countries as the difficulty of lifting a growing volume of manufactured products over rising tariff walls inescapably made local factories the only solution of their problem. Those who exported capital in this way faced criticisms very like those still being voiced today—they were 'giving away knowledge', 'creating unemployment', 'sowing dragon's teeth', and so on. British shareholders still viewed such faraway places as France, Holland and Germany as dangerous jungles better avoided by prudent company directors.[1]

Such arguments applied to the *developed* economies, though

[1] See *The History of Unilever*, vol. I, chapter VII, especially pages 110–11.

occasionally resuscitated in politically or economically obscurantist corners of society, would generally receive short shrift today. But joined to the political risks already mentioned—the risk of expropriation without compensation, savage taxation deriving from xenophobia, or the denial of the right to repatriate profits—they still help to bedevil the future of private investment in the *developing* economies. Yet, as William Clark, Director of the Overseas Development Institute, has said, the alternatives to recognizing the value of economic interdependence between the developed and the developing world, including private international investment, are grim. 'For the poorer countries it means draconian laws of austerity to ensure that savings are wrung from the poor, so that the country can pull itself up by its bootstraps. For the richer countries it means the political danger of a world divided by an abyss of income differences, and economically it means the end of hopes of a really expanding world economy with trade bringing into play the two-thirds of the world's population who at the moment sit on the sidelines.'

Where does the international company fit into this scheme of things? What is the justification for these vast aggregates of capital which spill into one country after another?

The first answer (which begs some questions that will be dealt with later) is that the international company, with its unique range of experience, technological skill and capital resources, can and does bring to the developing country the fruits of the developed economy—new and better manufactured products and services, greater wealth, more employment, higher living standards, a diminishing—though often very slowly diminishing—fear of poverty and starvation. Previous chapters have shown how Unilever, through the links between its factories and laboratories in the developed countries and its companies in Asia, Africa and South America, has exported not so much *products*—for governments everywhere have conspired to ensure by fiscal measures that export trade in consumer goods like soap, margarine and foods is made uneconomic as rapidly as possible—but the *skill* and the *processes* for producing those products in the developing countries. There are relatively few problems in transmitting methods of producing non-soapy detergents, edible fats or convenience foods to Asia or Africa. The serious question which faces the international company is whether it is (*a*) profitable or (*b*) socially desirable to do so.

Profitability may raise the question of physical conditions. If the water in, say, Malaysia, happens to be specially soft, will it be worth while to try and convert consumers from ordinary soap to synthetic products? The answer may depend on conditions of competition. If consumers show signs of responding to advertising campaigns by *other* international concerns, it will be difficult not to compete. Where foods are concerned, the edible-fats producer is always running to catch up with the population explosion. Where raw materials are concerned, for example palm oil, the experience gained over half a century in plantations in the Solomons and the Congo cannot fail to bring positive results. Here, as in many agricultural fields, Western capital, knowledge and research have helped to raise yields to an extraordinary degree. The African forests used to produce modest quantities of three kinds of timber for export. They now provide twenty or more kinds of higher-quality timber.

Thus Western capital can help to produce more quantities and better qualities of raw materials, both for local consumption and for export; new and improved manufactured products, again for domestic consumption and/or export.

So far as products and services are concerned, however, the operations of the international company raise questions of culture as well as of economics. Many of those concerned with the destinies of the developing countries believe they need the material progress their developed neighbours can offer; others are more doubtful whether the culture of the West is what they want. Are better detergents and mass advertising the goal to which Africa and Asia should turn? It is easy to say yes or no. The answer must in reality be a compromise. A business must operate in reasonable tune with the values of the society in which it is situated. But it must also operate with reasonable regard to the realities of economic life. It cannot operate at a continuous loss, or without regard for industrial discipline, productivity or efficiency. It must, in short, evolve some sort of compromise between the standards of an economically developed and a developing society. Ideally, it ought to allow the maximum flexibility to the society in which it is placed to express its own preferences and desires.

Inevitably, the technological superiority of the Western world will, for the time being, impress local opinion. In so far as the Western world has, in the last century and a half, demonstrated its ability to conquer famine, poverty and to a large degree disease, this is fair and reasonable. The societies of the developing economies could hardly be blamed for wanting the means to produce not only the basic needs of man, but the means of affluency itself. International firms certainly have helped to meet consumers' demands locally, sometimes also to boost a country's exports. Through higher levels of salaries and wages, and the higher yield of taxes these have made possible, they have helped to create new purchasing power. For example, United Africa Company (Timber) adds £1·2 million annually to the national income of Ghana and £2 million to that of Nigeria.

Just as in the past, private investment has created wealth. It has done this by bringing together an economically creative process, capital, managerial skill and labour. Through this process local or other resources could be made to fructify, new products created or old ones upgraded, industrialization be made to replace an economic void or a primary economy. It has worked, that is to say, in exactly the same way as domestic investment had worked in developed countries from the Industrial Revolution onwards and private capital export since, say, 1815. Of these processes, private 'aid' is a natural extension. Its efficiency is governed by the same mechanisms and devices which measure its profitability.

One difference began to emerge in recent years. In earlier periods the capital and the management were invariably imported *in toto:* the labour was recruited locally. Now it was seen increasingly that if the suspicions so common in this area of development were to be dispersed, nationals of the capital-importing country must be trained to carry on every aspect of the business, from top to bottom. Numerous examples of the progress in Unilever companies of what became known as 'ization' have been given. After 1945, and with gathering pace, responsibility for the day-to-day operation of most of Unilever's companies in Africa, India and elsewhere has been gradually assumed by local managements. This has not been merely a political gesture. It has been part of the fundamental change in economic climate. 'Economic growth' Dr Kuin has said, 'is largely a spontaneous process and international firms can do much to bring it about. The modernization of an economy is not a question of machines and methods alone, it also requires a change in mental make-up and values.'[1]

The training of a manager, invariably given partly in Europe

[1] In a paper read to the 13th International Management Congress in New York in 1963 by Dr P. Kuin, a director of Unilever.

or one of the developed areas, is an expensive business. There can be no guarantee that when trained he will stay in the business that has trained him. Yet by and large the creation, by international businesses, of a *cadre* of skilled managers is one of the basic social and economic changes such businesses can inaugurate. For only through this class can local human talent and resources be turned into much-needed supplies of food, goods and services, and living standards thus raised.

Similarly, a change took place with regard to the provision of capital. In Unilever's overseas enterprises, it was often provided out of local profits. In Ghana, for example, half the profits earned in the last decade were ploughed back voluntarily to create new investment. But here again, a sense of local participation and involvement could only be created if nationals themselves were given an opportunity to share in the ownership of the business. A number of examples has been given of joint enterprises where Unilever has entered into partnership with local banks or governments. (Although, as the case of Burma showed, this did not necessarily prevent a government from unilaterally repudiating an agreement.) Elsewhere nationals have bought shares in the company, and local businesses given freedom to re-invest a fair share of profits in the country of origin. Unquestionably, the opportunity to buy shares in a company increases local interest and a local feeling of participation. The new shareholders have (as in India) eagerly followed the fortunes of their company. They are vocal, sometimes critical, at shareholders' meetings. But that has not diminished the conviction among many Unilever managers that local shareholding is a beneficial move in the right direction.

The debate over the merits of private investment such as that of Unilever in the developing countries has been bedevilled by another controversy: the balance of payments. Opinion in the developing country has often been hostile to private industrial investment on this ground alone. President Nasser of Egypt declared in 1960 that he preferred foreign loans to equity investment because dividends were an eternal strain on Egypt's balance of payments. Others have demanded that the amount of profit to be transferred overseas should be fixed by agreement. Of course, the governments of developing countries are not the only ones to allow themselves to overspend and run into balance of payments crises: but they are specially prone to do so, partly through lack of experience, partly because their situation often justifies heavy spending abroad. The fundamental truth here should not be lost sight of. Foreign investment in a country expands that country's economic equipment. If it yields profits, it must increase the country's national income. Those profits cannot therefore be a net burden on the local community. It must be for the government of the community to see that facilities are normally provided for the transfer of dividends as an accepted charge against the national balance in recognition of the services provided by the capital investment.

The proportion of Unilever's total capital invested in the developing countries is small compared with that invested in Europe. Even so, in absolute terms, the volume is large. From the earliest days Lever Brothers invested capital in plantations. In the decades under review, larger and more productive plantations continued to evolve from the commingling of Unilever capital and new scientific knowledge. By 1965 a total of 224,217 acres had been planted, and in that year 37,000 people were employed. As against this, the politically less-settled plantations still told a story of disturbance and loss. William Lever's favourite child, the Congo plantations, lost £1·5 million through loss and damage of stocks and assets by continuing civil strife. Deeper knowledge of the technology of oils and fats enabled more of the products of plantations in Africa and Asia to be turned into human food. In Africa capital earlier invested in trade was now re-deployed into manufacturing industry. New processes of food preservation were transmitted from Western laboratories to developing countries, as the Surprise pea process was extended to India, with benefit to consumer and farmer alike. Everywhere a widening range of manufactured products—detergents, foods, chemicals—was made available by local manufacture, replacing former imports from the West. Teams of skilled managers were trained and economic leadership provided.

Many of these ventures have attracted mutually contradictory criticisms. Some critics thought the effort was too puny; others thought it was dangerously ambitious. One thing is plain. It could have been larger had it been possible to feel more confidence that private investment would be somehow insured against capricious and irresponsible action. Here it is impossible to feel any great optimism about developments in the near future. To remove the suspicions that obstruct private investment in the developing countries, action by governments in the capital-exporting and in the capital-importing countries is urgently needed. The former have a duty to encourage the private investor to complement government aid by removing fiscal obstacles and giving tax incentives to potential investors. The receiving countries need to reciprocate by giving all the assurances they can, fiscally and politically, to those who can help them with capital, skill and knowledge.

It would be satisfactory to be able to say that the two decades covered in this study showed some appreciable advance in the understanding of these issues. Except perhaps at the academic or administrative level they did not. The year 1965 ended with many governments in developed and developing countries more concerned with measures to hinder, diminish and restrict international private investment than to extend it. Only as the grim consequences of these actions become clear does there seem to be any hope of real progress towards that free flow of capital without which further material improvement in the developing countries must be hobbled if not halted.

LEVER BROTHERS AND UNILEVER LIMITED

List of Directors at 1 January 1945

	Date of ceasing to be a Director
Harold Hall Bagnall	1950
Croudson William Barnish	1948
James P. Van den Bergh	1965
Sidney J. van den Bergh	1963
Johan Willem Beyen	1946
Charles Hugh Clarke	1953
Sir Herbert Davis (Vice-Chairman)	1956
John Henry Hansard	1956
Arthur Hartog	1951
Geoffrey Heyworth (later The Lord Heyworth) (Chairman)	1960
James Laurence Heyworth	1957
Ralph Estill Huffam	1959
Rudolf G. Jurgens	
The 2nd Viscount Leverhulme (Governor)	1949 (died)
Rowland Huntley Muir	1951
J. L. Polak	1946
Paul Rijkens (Vice-Chairman)	1955
Frank Samuel	1954 (died)
Georg Schicht	1946
Arthur Godfrey Short	1946
James Lomax Simpson	1946

The following, who were Directors of Lever Brothers & Unilever N.V. at 1 January 1945, were appointed Directors of Lever Brothers & Unilever Limited on 14 June 1945:

P. D. H. Hendriks	1946 (died)
Rudolf Jurgens	1946
M. G. de Baat	1957

LEVER BROTHERS AND UNILEVER N.V.

Extract from Directors' Report of Lever Brothers & Unilever N.V. (dated 27 May 1946) for the year 1944:

'On 11th June 1945, the Military Commissioner for Legal Rehabilitation exercising the powers of the Council for Legal Rehabilitation, decided that the Board of Directors of N.V. should consist of the persons whose names appear in front of this Report together with Messrs. Rudolf Jurgens, Georg Schicht and James Lomax Simpson who have since resigned and whose many years of service to the organisation are gratefully acknowledged. All these persons were members of the Board of Directors of LIMITED or were nominated to be members of that Board, so that the identity of the Boards of Directors of N.V. and LIMITED which was abandoned in 1939 owing to the imminence of war, has been re-established.'

The persons whose names appeared in front of the Report are listed below:

Paul Rijkens—Chairman

P. D. H. Hendriks ⎫
Geoffrey Heyworth ⎬—Vice-Chairmen

M. G. de Baat	Arthur Hartog
Harold Hall Bagnall	James Laurence Heyworth
Croudson William Barnish	Ralph Estill Huffam
James P. Van den Bergh	Rudolf G. Jurgens
Sidney J. van den Bergh	The 2nd Viscount Leverhulme
Johan Willem Beyen	Rowland Huntley Muir
Charles Hugh Clarke	J. L. Polak
Sir Herbert Davis	Frank Samuel
John Henry Hansard	Arthur Godfrey Short

Subsequent appointments to the Boards of Limited and N.V. and dates of ceasing:

	From	To
R. H. Heyworth	1947	1954 (died)
A. E. J. Simon Thomas	1947	1957
F. J. Tempel	1947	1966
G. J. Cole		
(later The Lord Cole)	1948 (LIMITED) 1949 (N.V.)	
W. A. Faure	1948 (,,) 1949 (,,)	1959

H. S. A. Hartog	1948 (LIMITED)	1949 (N.V.)	
F. D. Morrell	1948 (,,)	1949 (,,)	1961
A. H. Smith	1948 (,,)	1949 (,,)	
A. M. Knox	1952		
A. D. Bonham-Carter	1953		
J. F. van Moorsel	1953		1967
J. A. Connel	1954		1961 (died)
G. D. A. Klijnstra	1955 (LIMITED)	1956 (N.V.)	
R. H. Siddons	1955 (,,)	1956 (,,)	
A. C. C. Baxter	1956		1966
A. F. H. Blaauw	1956		
F. J. Pedler	1956		
E. G. Woodroofe	1956		
M. M. van Hengel	1957		1966
J. F. Knight	1958		
A. W. J. Caron	1960		
D. J. Mann	1960		
J. P. Stubbs	1960		
A. J. C. Hoskyns-Abrahall	1961		
P. Kuin	1961		
S. G. Sweetman	1961		
E. Smit	1964		
J. G. Collingwood	1965		
J. J. H. Nagel	1966		
J. M. Goudswaard	1967		
D. A. Orr	1967		
The 2nd Viscount Trenchard	1967		

LEVER BROTHERS AND UNILEVER LIMITED

Advisory Directors at 1 January 1945

	Date of ceasing to be an Advisory Director
Horatio Ballantyne	1956
The Marquess of Carisbrooke	1956

Subsequent appointments	From	To
L. V. Fildes	1946	1956
J. L. Polak	1947	1948
The 3rd Viscount Leverhulme	1949	
Sir Robert Hall	1961	
Milton C. Mumford	1965	

LEVER BROTHERS AND UNILEVER N.V.

Advisory Directors at 1 January 1945

	Date of ceasing to be an Advisory Director
R. J. H. Patijn	1947
Th. A. Fruin	1945 (died)
K. P. van der Mandele	1966
J. M. Honig	
H. L. Woltersom	1960 (died)

Subsequent appointments	From	To
Rudolf Jurgens	1946	1954 (died)
Jhr. J. A. G. Sandberg	1946	1966
J. L. Polak	1947	1948
H. M. Hirschfeld	1952	1961 (died)
T. J. Twijnstra	1953	1959 (died)
Paul Rijkens	1956	1965 (died)
A. E. J. Nysingh	1961	
J. E. De Quay	1964	1965
G. E. van Walsum	1965	
F. J. M. A. H. Houben	1966	
F. J. Tempel	1966	

Secretaries at 1 January 1945

	Date of ceasing to be a Secretary
L. V. Fildes (Limited)	1946
E. A. Hofman (N.V.)	1967

Subsequent appointments	From	To
H. N. Saunders (LIMITED)	1946	1956
P. A. Macrory (LIMITED)	1956	
P. A. Macrory (N.V., jointly with E. A. Hofman)	1962	
E. A. Hofman (LIMITED, jointly with P. A. Macrory)	1962	1967
A. A. Haak (LIMITED, jointly with P. A. Macrory)	1967	
A. A. Haak (N.V., jointly with P. A. Macrory)	1967	

INDEX

Aberdeen, research unit at, 85

Accra, 217; training school at, 224

Acton, ice-cream plant at, 169, 170

Adelaide, S. Australia, Unilever factory in, 249

Adhesives, 73, 98, 176; synthetic, 177

Advertising: on television, 19, 99–100, 101–5, 107; William Lever's comment on, 92; promotion, 98–9; expenditure, 99, 106; Lintas, 100; linked with total marketing process, 101; of detergents, 101–4; of frozen foods, 104; 'introductory', 104–5; of margarine, 105; soap and soap powders, 105–6; objectives, 106–7; tests, 107

Advita Limited, 180

Affori, Milan, Atkinson's factory at, 200

Africa: William Lever's enterprises in, 213; Produce Marketing Boards set up, 214; political, economic and social changes, 216–17; technical training in, 224; hindrances to rapid deployment, 224–5 *See also* Belgian Congo; British West Africa; Burutu; Cameroons; Gambia; Ghana; Kenya; Nigeria; Sierra Leone; Tanzania; Uganda; United Africa Company; West Africa

African Textile Investigation Group, 219

African Timber and Plywood (Nigeria) Limited, Sapele, 219–20

Ahmadu Bello University of Zaria, Nigeria, 224

Agricultural research, 66

Ailort, Loch, experimental fish farm at, 175

Alaska, 169

Algeria, 198

Allpack printing works, Austria, 210

Amersfoort, Holland, detergent factory at, 195

Animal feeding-stuffs trade, 165, 192, 240

Animal nutrition, research in, 65

Antwerp, margarine factory at, 186

Apapa, Nigeria, vehicle assembly plant at, 220

Argentina, 207; Atkinson's factory in, 200, 255; Unilever market in, 256–7

Arkwright, Richard, 132

Ashford: Batchelor's factory at, 174, 175; perfume factory at, 180

Asnières, France: margarine factory at, 188; oil mill, 191; animal feeding-stuffs production, 192

Associated Feed Manufacturers, of Belfast, 164

Atkinson's, perfumers, of Bermondsey, 160, 195, 200, 256, 257, 259

Aubervilliers, soap factory at, 194

Auckland, New Zealand, quick-freezing plant at, 252

Aussig, Czechoslovakia, 10

Australia, 168, 207, 227, 262, 263; use of divided pan unit, 84; nature and problems of the market, 246, 247, 250–1; chain of Unilever factories, 246, 249; Unilever market in, 249–50

Austria, recovery of Unilever business in, 10

Avonmouth, oil and cake factory at, 164, 165

Ayer, Harriet Hubbard, 199, 248

Babb, Jervis, 230

Bahrenfeld, Germany, margarine factory at, 185, 186

Baker, G. and A., Limited, of Turkey, 261
Barcelona, 195
Barlby, Yorks., breeding research at, 165
Basle, soap factory at, 195
Batavia (Djakarta), Unilever factory at, 244
Batchelor's, 73, 85, 172–5
Beauvais, printing works at, 210
Belgian Congo, 14; plantations in, 213
Belgium, 8, 198, 202, 207; Unilever factories in, 9; margarine plants and trade, 186; detergent market, 193, 194; toiletry market, 200–1; food market, 201, 206
Benelux Pact, 7
Bentley, Thomas, 7, 91
Bertrand Frères, of Grasse, 180
Besigheimer oil mill, Bremen, 190
Béthune, France, margarine factory at, 188
Betjeman, John, 162
Bilbao, margarine factory at, 184
Birds Eye, New Zealand, 252, 253
Birds Eye Foods Limited, 166, 175, 202, 203, 204; subsidiary of Unilever, 104; early history, 171; rise in output and sales, 171–3
Birdseye, Clarence, 171
Birmingham Chemical Company, of Lichfield, 180
Blaauw, A. F. H., 77
Blue Band margarine, 105, 162
Bobigny, France, chemical plant at, 197
Boksburg, Transvaal, Unilever factory at, 254
Bombay, Hindustan Lever export office in, 238
Bordeaux, animal feeding-stuffs production at, 192
Boulton, Matthew, 7, 91
Bracknell, Mac Fisheries headquarters at, 175
Bramalea, Ontario, Lipton's tea plant at, 114, 249

Brazil: Atkinson's factory in, 200; Unilever market in, 256, 258–60
Breeze detergent, 243
Bremen, Besigheimer oil mill at, 190
Bremerhaven, fish processing firm in, 204
Breweries, in Nigeria and Sierra Leone, 220
Brisbane, Queensland, Unilever factory at, 249
British Extracting Company, 156, 164
British Oil and Cake Mills, 163, 164, 165, 169
British Soap Makers' Association, 102
British West Africa, Kingsway stores in, 22
Bromborough, British Extracting Company's oil mill at, 161, 164
See also Price's Limited
Bromborough Dock, 159
Brough, E., 90
Buenos Aires, Lever Soap factory at, 256
Bulgaria, loss of Unilever trade in, 10
Bulk packaging, 21
Bullard, Professor Sir Edward, 78n.
Burkhart, William H., 230, 233
Burma, Unilever market in, 111, 242–3
Burutu: oil production in, 221; technical training school, 224
Butland Industries, New Zealand, 253
Butter: competition with margarine, 105; French preference for, 188
Butter flavours, added to margarine, 71–2, 80

Calgary, Lever factory in, 86, 247
Calvé-Delft oil milling company, 191, 192
Cambridge, Massachusetts, Lever manufacturing plant at, 231
Cambridge University Appointments Board, 48

Cameroons, 214
Canada, 42, 168, 262, 263; chain of Lever factories in, 86, 246, 247–8; nature of the market, 246, 247, 249; Lever's market in, 248–9
Canary Islands, 213
Canned foods, 84, 168, 173–4
Cape Town, Unilever factory at, 246, 254
Capital Gains Tax, 125
Capital Issues Committee (U.K.), 123
Cardboard manufacture, 98
Caron, A. W. J., 52, 54, 91
Cartitalia, near Milan, printing works at, 210
Catalysts, 176
Cattle food, 165, 192, 240
Ceylon, 207, 227; Unilever market in, 241
Cheese, 162, 165, 205
Chemical Group, 181, 182
Chemicals: research in, 65, 75; for soap production, 176; Unilever's diversified investment in, 176–82; total sales in 1952 and 1965, 182; the industry on the Continent, 196–7; South African industry, 254
Chicago, dentrifice production at, 231
Chicken Noodle soup, 84
Chile: Atkinson's factory in, 200; Unilever market in, 257–8
China, disappearance of Unilever market in, 260
Chittagong, East Pakistan, Unilever plant at, 241
Clark, William, 264
Cole, Lord, 3, 10, 17–18, 25, 26, 27, 32, 117
Colgate, U.S.A., 103
Colgate-Palmolive, U.S.A., 96
Collingwood, J. G., 67, 77
Colworth House, Bedfordshire, food research laboratory, 65, 72, 85, 165, 172, 174, 175, 203, 240
Commercial Plastics Industries, 178

Common Market, 8, 9, 10, 11, 38, 135, 189, 197, 211
Compagnie Française de Nutrition Animale, of Tours, 192
Compania Industrial (Indus), Chile, 257
Competition, 132–6, 139
Compound feeds, for cattle and poultry, 165, 192
Computers, use of, 73, 78, 95, 142
Congo, 213, 215, 268; research establishments in, 65; decline of Unilever plantations in, 215
See also Belgian Congo
Connel, J. A., 25
Consumer demand, prediction of, 91, 92
Consuming organizations, 133
Contact Director, 42
Cook, Edward, of Bow, 156
Copra, 77
Cooper, Francis D'Arcy, 22, 48, 51, 117–18, 260
Co-ordinators of product groups, 41
Co-partnership, 55
Corporation Tax (U.K.), 125
Cosmetics, 248
See also Perfumery trade; Toilet preparations, 248
Cottonseed oil, 11, 12, 230
Countway, Francis A., 229
Craigmillar, ice-cream plant at, 169
Crema, near Milan, margarine factory at, 188
Crème Recamier, 199
Croix-Sante: oil mill at, 191; animal feeding-stuffs production at, 192
Crosfield, Joseph, of Warrington, 83, 84, 98, 155, 156, 158, 176, 196, 200
Cumbernauld, near Glasgow, board mill at, 177
Cuxhaven, fish processing firm at, 204
Czechoslovakia: loss of Unilever market in, 10, 184; toiletry trade, 200

Davis, Sir Herbert, 24, 51
De Betuwe company, 151, 202, 211
de Blank, Joost, 51
Dehydration: of peas and beans evolved from research, 72; freeze-drying process, 84–5; of soups and vegetables, 84, 174; of complete meals, 174–5
Deniston, Robert, 168
Denmark, Unilever margarine factories and market in, 187–8
De-No-Fa, fat-hardening plant of, 151
Dentabs, 87–8
Detergents, synthetic, 17, 18; American competition, 37; research in, 65–7; development of synthetic products, 81–3; essentially chemical character of the industry, 86; marketing of, 97; advertising, 101–4; Unilever share of U.K. total sales remains static, 1923–62, 155–6; reorganization at Port Sunlight, 156–9; vast increase of production, 159; synthetic products reduce output of glycerine, 178; factories and markets in Europe, 193–6; Procter and Gamble's 'Tide', 229; Lever market in U.S.A., 230; liquid detergents, 232; Indian market, 238; Canadian market, 248; South African market, 254
Deverall, W. J., 59n.
Divided pan unit, in soap production, 84
Djakarta. See Batavia
Domestos, of Newcastle-upon-Tyne, 159–60
Dove (synthetic toilet soap), 83
Dried foods. See Dehydration
Drukkerij 'Reclame', Holland, 210
Duiven, research laboratory at, 66
Durban: Unilever factory at, 246, 254; chemical plant, 254

East Africa, 15, 215; United Africa Company's interests in, 221, 224
East Germany: loss of Unilever market in, 10, 184; paper factories and board mill in, 209
East India Company, 132
Eastbourne, frozen food plant at, 173
Echo margarine, 162
Economic diversification, resulting from research, 74
Edgewater, New Jersey: research laboratory in, 66, 70; vegetable-shortening plant in, 229, 231
Edible fats: research in, 66, 67; solvent fractionation process, 80–1; a static market but improvement in quality, 161–3; Lever market in U.S.A., 230; *Unilever markets*: India, 238, 239; Canada, 248; New Zealand, 253; South Africa, 253; South America, 260; Japan, 260
See also Margarine
Edible oils: hydrogenation process, 64; research in, 66; sources, and extraction process, 78–9; refining, etc., 79–80; Unilever's markets in S. America, 255–6, 257
See also Oil milling
Edwards, Professor H. R., *Monopoly and Competition in the British Soap Industry*, 103–104n, 133
Egypt, 14, 267
Elida Company, West Germany, 200
Emery Industries Incorporated, of Cincinnati, 197
Emmerich, Germany, chemical plant at, 197
Emulsifier, 73
Engineering, 77
Englewood Cliffs, New Jersey, Lipton's research laboratories at, 66, 114
Equalization Agreement, Unilever's, 121
Erith Oil Works, 163
Etah, Uttar Pradesh State, food plant at, 238
European Atomic Energy Commission, 7

European Coal and Steel Community, 7
European Economic Community, 7
See also Common Market
European Free Trade Association, 8, 211
Ewekoro, Nigeria, 220
Expellers, used in oil extraction, 78–9

Fablon, 178
Fabrique Nationale des Lames de Rasoirs, of Poissy, 198
Fats. *See* Edible fats
Fatty acids, 72, 81, 83, 179
Ferreyros company, Peru, 258
Field, C. W., of Liverpool, 180
Findlay, W. K., 219n.
Finland, 207; Unilever margarine factories and market in, 188

Fishing and fish canning, 166–7, 203
Foods: dehydrated, 72, 84–5, 174–5; frozen, 18–19, 104, 165, 166 171–3; research in, 65–7; methods of preservation, 84; extension of Unilever interests in, 165–6; fish, 166–8; meat, 168; ice-cream, 169–71; canned, 173–4; further increase of products, 175; investment total by 1963, 184; markets on the Continent, 201–7
Food Groups, 41
Forcheim, Upper Franconia, paper-making and printing works at, 209
Formaldehyde, 180
Foundation of Labour, 56
France, 8, 11, 202, 207, 263; Unilever factories in, 9; scent industry, 180; detergent market, 184, 193–4; margarine factories and market, 188, 189; oil milling, 190, 191–2; animal feeding-stuffs, 192; chemical industry, 197; toiletry market, 198–9; food market, 205–6

Freeze-drying process, for food, 84–5, 173
Fremantle, Western Australia, Unilever factory in, 246
Frosted Foods Limited, 171
Frozen foods, 18–19, 165, 166; television advertising of, 104; Continental market, 202–3, 204–5; Canadian market, 248; Australian market, 250; New Zealand market, 252–3

Gailey, James Hamilton, 221
Gambia, 214
Gardiner Refrigeration Company, of Sydney, 250
General Foods Corporation, U.S.A., 104
Germany, 7, 8, 11, 200, 263; Unilever factories in, 9; self-service stores, 19; labour relations, 56; ice-cream market, 85, 114; Unilever's fishing vessels in, 114; and the Common Market, 134–5; frozen food market, 171; Unilever's problems in this market in 1930s, 183; margarine plants and market, 184, 185–6, 189; oil milling, 190–1; detergent and soap market, 193, 194; chemical industry, 197; foods market, 201, 203–5; paper, printing and packaging, 208–10; Unilever contribution towards recovery of, 210
See also East Germany; West Germany
Gessey company, Brazil, 259
Ghana, 213, 266; detergent factory in 114; sets up Marketing Boards, 214; United Africa Company's interests in, 218–19; Unilever ploughs back half its profits, 267
Ghana (Government) Textile Printing Company, 218
Ghaziabad, Hindustan Lever factory at, 85, 238, 240
Ghee, 239, 240
Gibbs, D. & W., 160, 198

Gibbs Pepsodent Limited, 160

Gillette company, 198

Glostrup, Denmark, Sunlight factory at, 200

Gloucester, 175; ice-cream plant at, 85, 170, 204; oil mill, 164

Glue business, 157
See also Adhesives

Glycerine, 83-4, 176; output of reduced by synthetic detergents, 178; central company for refining and sale of, 180

Glycerine Limited, 180

Goch, Jurgens' margarine factory at (destroyed), 185, 197

Godley, Cheshire, Thomas Wall's factory at, 169

Golden Nut Margarine Company, S. Australia, 250

Gossage's, of Widnes, 155, 158, 196

Gouda, Holland: ozonization plant at, 114; detergent factory, 195; chemical plant, 197

Gouda-Apollo company, 197

Great Yarmouth, 172; frozen food plant at, 173, 175

Greece, 10, 168; new Unilever enterprises in, 184

Green, Richard B., and Company, 168

Greenock, oil and cake factory at, 164

Grimsby, frozen food plant at, 173, 175

Guinness: their brewery at Ikeja, Lagos, 220; provides training courses for African technicians, 224

Hamburg: research laboratory at, 66; margarine factory, 185; oil mill, 190, 191; cheese factory, 205

Hamburg-Harburg, detergent factory at, 194

Hamburg-Wilhelmsburg, detergent factory at, 194

Hammond, Indiana, spray-drying plant at, 82, 231

Handley, W. A., 160

Harburg, Thörl's factory at, 190

Harris, T. H., of Stratford, 156

Hart Products, Canada, 249

Hartog, Harold, 25n., 41

Hartog meat factory, of Oss, 59, 152, 201, 202

Hastings, New Zealand, quick-freezing plant at, 252

Haubourdin, near Lille, soap factory at, 194

Hay, William, of Hull, 180

Hayes, Thomas Wall's factory at, 169

Health. *See* Industrial medicine

Heavy-duty detergent, 82

Heinekens, Dutch brewers, 218, 220; provide training courses for African technicians, 224

Heinrich Nicolaus Pergamentpapierfabrik, of Ronsberg, 208

Helsinki, margarine factory at, 184, 188

Henkel, German chemical firm, 103

Heppenheim, Germany, ice-cream factory at, 170, 204

Hertonäs, Finland, margarine factory at, 188

Heyworth, Geoffrey (later Lord), 22, 23-5, 29, 30, 32, 33, 51, 96, 103, 150, 155, 178; on introductory advertising, 105; and Frosted Foods Limited, 171

Heyworth, Roger, 261

Hindustan Lever. *See* India

Hoboken, New Jersey, research laboratory at, 66

Hohnen-Lever, Japan, 260

Hohnen Oil Company, Japan, 260

Holland. *See* Netherlands

Holloway, E. R., Limited (later Holpak Limited), 177-8

Holpak Limited (formerly E. R. Holloway Limited), 178n.

Hudson and Knight, 98, 158

Hudson's, 155

Hull: oil and cake factory at, 164; frozen food plant at, 173, 175

Hume, William and George, 168

Hungary, 184; loss of Unilever market in, 10

Huntingdon, Batchelor's factory at, 174, 175
Hydrogenation process, 64
Hytox, 160

Ibadan, departmental store in, 114
Ibérica Company, 195
Ice-cream, 66, 85, 166, 169–71, 204, 205, 220, 235, 249, 250, 254
Igbobi, Lagos, training college at, 224
Iglo (formerly Vita), 203
Ikeja, Lagos, brewery at, 220
Imperial margarine, 230
India, 15, 207, 227–8, 242, 245, 260, 262, 268; Hindustan Lever Limited, 13, 85, 237–40; economic obstruction in, 237; planned industrialization, 239
Indonesia, 14, 77; Unilever market in, 244–5
Indus Lever S.A.C., 257
Industrial medicine, 60
Inflation, 4
International Package Design Committee, 97
Introductory advertising, 104–5
Ireland, Republic of: detergent market in, 156; edible fat factory, 161
Is-Bank of Turkey (Türkiye Is Bankasi), 111, 262
Isleworth: research laboratory at, 66; Thomas Wall's factory at, 169
Italy, 7, 8, 11, 168, 198, 263; Unilever progress in, 184; toiletry market, 200; new factories built, 211
Ivory Coast, 216

Japan, 168; Unilever market in, 260
Jelke Margarine Company, 230
Johannesburg, Unilever factory in, 246, 254
John West Foods Limited, 168
Joint Workers' councils, 58–9
Jurgens, Anton, 255
Jurgens, Anton, firm of, 27, 99, 152, 163, 176, 190, 263; paper-making and printing interests, 208, 209
Jurgens, R. G., 77

Kalmar, Sweden, margarine factory at, 184, 187
Kano, Nigeria, training school at, 224
Kempten, Germany: cheese factory at, 205; paper and printing works at, 209, 210
Kenya, 221; Unilever partnership in, 111
Keynes, Lord, 24, 116, 125
Kingsway Stores, West Africa, 22, 219
Kirkby, near Liverpool, frozen food plant at, 173
Kleinol company, 200
Kleve margarine factory, Western Germany, 40
Klijnstra, G. D. A., 77
Knight, John, of Silvertown, 58, 152, 156–9, 176, 177
Kuin, Dr P., 266
Kumasi, Ghana, brewery at, 218
Kunerol factory, Vienna, 79

Labour, Ministry of, 58
Labour conditions/relations in Unilever: management and labour relations, 55–7; personnel manager's responsibilities, 57–8; technological innovations, reorganization and redeployment, 58–60; industrial medicine, 60–1; pension schemes, 61–2
Lagos, 217; Igbobi training college, 224
Lahti, Finland, margarine factory at, 188
Lamiaco-Lejona, Spain, margarine factory at, 189
Langnese Company, of Hamburg, 204
Langnese-Iglo ice-cream factory, 85
Lard substitutes, 229, 230

Laubardemont, near Bordeaux: oil mill at, 191; compound foods production at, 192

Leeds. *See* Watson, Joseph

Leicester University, 69

Lever, William Hesketh (first Viscount Leverhulme), 3, 6, 13, 17, 21, 22, 25, 45, 47, 50, 55, 61, 91, 95, 99, 106, 110, 132, 134, 138, 156, 163, 166, 168, 176, 183, 190, 199, 207, 208, 226, 228, 238–9, 246, 255, 260; on the development of Lever's, 108, 109; acquires Thames Board Mills, 176; African enterprises, 213, 215, 219*n.*, 268; American interests, 228, 229; and the Dominions, 246, 251; and the Philippines, 260–1

Lever Brothers and Associates, 158

Lever Brothers Company, U.S.A., 66, 168, 199, 235; research by, 66, 70; develop synthetic detergent, 82; synthetic toilet soap, 83; Anti-trust Division proceedings against, 135, 236; beginnings, and development, 228–9; move from Boston to New York, 230; edible fat trade, 230; new patterns of marketing and production, 231; value of the business, 231; use of technology and research, 232–3; close co-operation between marketing, research and production, 233–4

Lever Brothers Limited, 22, 27, 48, 92, 100, 106, 109, 112*n.*, 156, 163, 171, 176, 200, 253

Lever Brothers Ltd., Canada, 82

Lever Pacocha S.A., 258

Leverhulme Trust, 112 and *n.*

Lever's Feeds Limited, 164, 165

Lidingö, near Stockholm, margarine factory at, 187

Lifebuoy soap, 105, 229, 238

Lintas (Lever's International Advertising Service), 92, 100

Lipo-proteins, 66

Lipton, Thomas J., 66, 114, 228, 234–5, 248, 249

Liquid detergents, 232

Lisbon, margarine factory in, 184

Loder's, of Silvertown, 164

Los Angeles, Lever Brothers model plant at, 231

Lowe, Charles, and Company, of Manchester, 180

Lowestoft, frozen food plant at, 173

Luckman, Charles, 229–30

Lux Flakes, 229, 238

Lux Toilet Soap, 105, 229, 243, 257

Luxembourg, 8

Maarssen, Holland, chemical plant at, 196–7

Mac Fisheries, 21, 97, 166, 172, 175, 203, 204; retail fruit and vegetables, 167–8

McNiven Brothers, Australia, 250

Macrory, P. A., 119

Malawi, Unilever market in, 255

Malaya, Malaysia, 168, 213, 265; Unilever market in, 241–2

Management: achievement of D'Arcy Cooper, Paul Rijkens and Geoffrey Heyworth, 22–5; divorced from ownership, 27; responsibilities, 27–9; delegation of powers to committees, 290–31; major problem of top management, 31; three instruments of basic control, 31–2; growth of advisory departments, 32–3; other departments, 33, 37; responsibility for co-ordination of products, 37; and dangers of centralization, 37–9; political problems of local managements, 39–40; and product co-ordination, 41; contact directors, 41–2; connection with the processes of social change, 42–4; changes in nature of the manager's function, 46–7; policy on managers, 54–5; relationship with labour, 55–7; and new forms of competition and technology, 139–40; increased responsibilities for local managers, 140–1

Manchester, oil and cake factory at, 164

Mannheim: oil mill at, 190, 191; detergent factory, 194

Margarine: Dutch research laboratories, 65, 71; production revolutionized, 71–2; and research into microbiology, 72; preparation of emulsion, 80; marketing, 97, 101; a static market but improved quality, 161–3; rising production leads to increase of fatty acids, 179; markets and plants in Europe, 184–9; U.S.A. trade, 230; Canadian market, 248; South African market, 254; Japanese market, 260

Margarine Union, 61, 112n., 163, 190

Marine Harvest Limited, 175

Marketing, market research: increasing range of specialized activities, 90–1; market research, 92–5; American influence, 95–6; streamlining of products, 96–7; supermarkets, 97–8
See also Advertising

Married women, number at work, 104

Marseilles: oil mill at, 191; compound foods production, 192; soap factory, 194

Marshall, Alfred, 90

Meat, 168–9; Continental market, 205

Medical officers, 60

Melbourne, Victoria, Unilever factory at, 249

Merksem, near Antwerp, margarine factory at, 186

Merseyside Power Station, 114, 159

Microbiology, research on, 72

Mill, John Stuart, 145

Mill Bay Company, of Plymouth, 155

'Model village' schemes, 55

Mond, Ludwig, 6

Monopolies Commission (U.K.), 136

Monopolies and Mergers Act (U.K.), 136

Monopoly, 132–6, 139, 150

Monsanto Chemical Corporation, 135, 236

Monsted, Otto, 169

Morocco, 198, 213

Mutueka, New Zealand, Unilever factory at, 253

Nantes: oil mill at, 191; compound foods production, 192; detergent factory, 194

Napoleon III, 202

Nasser, President, 267

Nazis, 183, 190

Netherlands, 8, 202, 263; and the Common Market, 10; self-service stores, 19; low trade union membership; 56; Lintas Agency in, 100; statutory limitation of dividends, 123; margarine plants and market, 186–7; oil milling, 190, 191; animal feedings-stuffs production, 192; detergent and soap trade, 193, 194–5; chemical industry, 196–7; failure of frozen foods, 202–3

Network analysis, 88–9

Neuss, Rhineland: margarine factory at, 152; plastics factory, 186, 209, 211

Neu-Ulm cheese factory, 205

New Jersey, tea plant in, 114

New Pin factory, 155

New York Stock Exchange, 111

New Zealand, 168, 207, 263; nature of the market, 246, 247, 251–2; Unilever factories, 246, 252; Unilever market, 252–3

Newcastle-upon-Tyne.
See Domestos

Nicolaus, Heinrich, 208, 209

Niger Company, 118

Niger France, 217–18

Niger Motors, 220, 224

Niger River Transport, 221

Nigeria, 213, 219, 266; tobacco factory in, 14; sets up Marketing Boards, 214, 215; Development

Nigeria—*cont.*
Corporations, 216; crude oil production, 221
Nigerian Cocoa Marketing Board, 214; Cotton Marketing Board, 214; Oil Palm Marketing Board, 214
Nordsee fishing/trawling company, 21-2, 167, 203-4
Normann invention, for hardening liquid oils, 79
North America, 9, 11, 37, 82, 227, 228, 237, 247
See also Canada; United States
North Western Soap Company, of Calcutta, 238
Norway, 168, 202; Unilever company in, 84; margarine factories and market, 187-8
Nucoline, of Silvertown, 164
Nurses, 60
Nyasaland, Unilever market in, 254-5
Nyköping, Sweden, Vinolia factory at, 200

O.A.T.S. (On Air Testing Service), 94
'Off flavours', 80
Oil, 64, 213; Nigerian crude oil production, 221
See also Edible oils; Oil milling
Oil milling: in the U.K., 163-5; in Europe, 190-2
Oleo-chemicals, 81
Olsen company, Denmark, 210
Olten, Switzerland, soap factory at, 195
Olympia Oil and Cake Company, of Selby, 163
Omo, 194, 195
'On-the-job training', 52
Oslo, margarine factory at, 187-8
Oss, North Brabant; meat factory at, 201, 202
Ozonization plant, at Gouda, 114

Pa$$ Technique in marketing, 94
Packaging, 176, 177, 184, 207-10
Pacocha company, Peru, 258

Pakistan, Unilever market in, 111, 240-1
Pakko-Tryk company, Denmark, 310
Palm Line ships, 221
Paper industry: research, 66; manufacture, 98, 207-10
Papier und Pergamentpapier-fabrik Seltmans, 208
Paris, soap factory at, 194
Parkinson, Professor, 38, 116, 117, 139
Parsons, Cumming, of Manchester, 180
Paternalism, 55
Pear's, of Isleworth, 160
Peas: dehydrated, 72, 73; frozen, 173; canned, 173-4
Pelling, Stanley, 168
Pepsodent factory, Chicago, acquired by Lever's, 231
Perfumery trade, 180, 256, 257, 259
Perlina, soap manufacturer, Chile, 257
Peron, President, 256, 257
Persil soap powder, 83, 105-6, 194
Personnel manager, responsibilities of, 57-8
Peru, 168; Unilever market in, 258
Peteri, Ir H. B., 74
Petone, New Zealand, Unilever factory in, 252
Philippine Refining Corporation, 261
Philippines, the, 77; Unilever market in, 260-1
Pig breeding, 169
Planta margarine affair, 189*n.*
Plastics: research on, 66; manufacture, 98, 177-8, 186
Poland, loss of Unilever market in, 10, 184
Polymer resin, 73
Port Harcourt, departmental store at, 114
Port Sunlight, 3, 47, 83, 100; works laboratory at, 64-5; research on detergents, chemicals and timber, 65, 66, 72, 73, 74-5, 76; detergent production,

Port Sunlight—*cont.*
152; soap production, 155–7; reorganized for detergent production, 157–9; 'explosive expansion' of 1959–62, 159; acquires Domestos, 159–160; oil mill, 163; printing works, 207
Port Sunlight Village, 159
Portugal, 8, 168; margarine factory in, 189
Premier supermarket chain, 97
Preserved foods. *See* Foods
Price's Limited, of Bromborough, 55, 81, 156, 176, 179, 196, 197
Price's Patent Candle Co., of Battersea, 160, 179
Printing industry, Unilever's, 98, 184, 207–10
Processed foods. *See* Foods
Procter and Gamble, U.S.A., 37, 96, 103, 158, 229
Produce Marketing Boards (Africa), 214
Product co-ordination, 41
Product groups, co-ordinators for, 41
Product refinements, 94–5
Programme Evaluation and Review Technique, 73
Promotions, 98–9, 103
Proprietary Perfumes Limited, of Ashford, 180
Public relations, 33, 37
Pukekohe, New Zealand, Unilever factory at, 253
Purfleet: edible fat factory at, 161, 162; board-making factory, 177
Puritan Soap, 156, 159, 160

Quick-frozen foods. *See* Frozen foods

Rahim Yar Khan, Western Pakistan, Unilever factory at, 240–1
Rama margarine, 186
Raw materials: situation revolutionized for margarine, 71; transport problems, 77–8; for detergents, 113; investment risks, 114
Refinements of products. *See* Product refinements

Renfrew, oil and cake factory at, 164
Rennes, Thibaud Gibbs' factory at, 198
Research: laboratories, 64–6; size of staff, and outlay, 66–7; problems and organization, 67, 69–76
Retailing system, changes in, 19–21
See also Supermarkets
Rhodesia, Unilever market in, 254–5
Rijkens, Dr Paul, 22–5, 42, 51, 105, 178
Rinso soap powder, 229, 257
Roberts, C. O., 221
Robinson, Professor Joan, 132, 137, 138
Rome, Treaty of, 7, 8
Rondi ice-cream company, S. Africa, 254
Ronsberg, Germany, paper factory at, 208, 209
Rosario, Argentina, Jurgens' mill at, 255
Rosella Preserving and Manufacturing Company, 250
Rotterdam, 11; margarine factory at, 59–60, 186, 207; research in microbiology, 65; headquarters of special food executive for Continental Europe, 206
Rube, R., and Company, of Weende, 209
Rumania, loss of Unilever market in, 10, 184

S.P.D. Limited (Speedy Prompt Delivery), 100, 172, 173
St. Denis: research laboratory at, 66; Thibaud Gibbs' factory, 198, 199
St Louis, Minnesota, spray-drying plant at, 82, 231
St Stephen, New Brunswick, Lever factory at, 86, 247
Salmon breeding, 175
See also Tinned salmon
Samreboi, Ghana, timber business at, 218, 220

Santiago, toilet preparations factory at, 257

São Paolo, Brazil, Unilever factory at, 259, 260

Sapele, Nigeria: timber plant at, 219–20; technical training school, 224

Scandinavia, 8; Unilever factories in, 9; labour relations, 56; progress of Unilever trade, 184 See also Denmark; Finland; Norway; Sweden

Schacht, Dr Hjalmar, 27, 201

Schichts, of Vienna, 10, 27, 99, 176, 184

Self-financing, system of, 123–6, 138

Self-service stores. See Supermarkets

Seltmans, Germany, paper-making at, 209

Sennitt, J. P., ice-cream business of, Australia, 250

Seward's, of Vauxhall, 160

Seychelles, the, 213

Shadow Home Wave Perm, 248

Sheffield, Batchelor's factory at, 172–4

Shop, Distributive and Allied Workers, Union of, 58

Sierra Leone: Board for Agricultural produce, 214; United Africa Company's interests in, 220; collapse of diamond boom, 225

Silcock, R., and Sons Limited, 164, 165

Silicates, 176

Silicates and Chemical Industries, S. Africa, 254

Silvertown Soap Works. See Knight, John

Simcoe, Ontario, ice-cream plant at, 249

Singapore, 241

Skippers, 166

Smit, Dr E., 77

Smith, Adam, 27, 29, 133, 138

Soap, natural: improvement in manufacture, 83–4; advertising of, 105; increase of sales, 155; competition of synthetic detergents, 156; competition between Unilever and Procter and Gamble, 157–8; increased production at Port Sunlight and Warrington, 159; and chemicals, 176; demand for hard soap, 179; factories and markets on the Continent, 193–6; U.S.A. sales, 229; S. African market, 253; S. American market, 255–6

Soap powders, 105–6, 229

Soap Trust, 156

Soapless detergents. See Detergents

Sodium silicate, 176

Soft drinks, 162

Solomon Islands, research establishment in, 65

Solvent fractionation, 81

Sønderborg, Denmark, margarine factory at, 187

Soups: dried, 84, 174, 202, 249, 254; canned, 202, 205, 254

South Africa, 168; nature of the market, 246, 247, 253; Unilever factories, 246–7; Unilever market, 253–4

South America, 17, 42, 227, 228, 262, 263; toiletry market, 200; nature of the market, 255 See also Argentina; Brazil; Chile; Peru

South-East Asia. See Burma, Indonesia; Malaya; Thailand

Southall, Thomas Wall's factory at, 169, 172, 173

Soyabean oil, 11, 12, 71, 191, 230

Spain, 18, 19, 263; new Unilever enterprises in, 184; margarine factory, 189; detergent market, 195; toiletry market, 200; new factories, 211

Spray-drying plants, 81, 82

Spyck, Germany, oil mill at, 191

Square Deal Surf, 102–3

Star breweries, Nigeria and Sierra Leone, 220, 225

Stergene, 160

Stockholm, margarine factories at, 184, 187

Stoke Mandeville, experimental farm at, 169

Stork margarine, 162, 254

Stork Margarine Works, 156

Street's Ice Cream, of Sydney, 250

Strikes: at Hartog meat factory, 59; in Indonesia, 244

Sumatra, 213

Summer County margarine, 162

Sunil, 194

Sunlight soap, 229

Supermarkets, 19–21, 97–8, 252; and promotions, 98–9

Surabaya, Indonesia, Unilever factory at, 244

Surf (detergent), 102

Surprise brand of vegetables, 73, 85, 174

Sussex Wax Limited, Canada, 249

Sweden, 19, 177; Unilever market in, 18; wood pulp from, 77; margarine factories and market, 187; toiletry market, 200

Switzerland, 8; margarine factories and market, 187; soap and detergent market, 195

Sydney, N.S.W., Unilever factory at, 249

Synthetic products. See Adhesives; Detergents; Toilet soap; Tanning agents

Tanning agents, synthetic, 179–80

Tanzania, 221

Tavistock Institute of Human Relations, 50

Tea trade: U.S.A., 235; Canada, 248, 249; Australia, 250

Technical training, in Africa, 224

Technology: closely associated with research, 76; increasing importance of, 76–7; expansion of Unilever dependent upon technologies related to manufacturing process, 77; and oils and fats, 78–81; and synthetic detergents, 81–3; and natural soap, 83–4; and dried foods, 84–5; influence on production and management, 85–9; in relation to market situation, 142–3; chemical, 176–82, 195, 196; in U.S.A., 232

Television advertising, 19, 100–5, 107

Tema, Ghana: detergent plant at, 218; vehicle assembly plant, 219

Tempel, F. J., 25, 103

Test marketing, 94

Thailand, Unilever market in, 243

Thames Board Mills, 176, 177, 208

Thibaud, Pierre, 198

Thibaud Gibbs company, of Rennes, 198–9, 200

Thomas, Christopher, of Bristol, 156, 160

Thomas, J. L., of Exeter, 155

Thörl's Hamburg factory (destroyed), 190

Tide detergent, 229

Timber, research in, 65; United Africa Company's interest in, 65, 219–20

Tinned salmon, 166, 168

Tiruchirapally, India, Unilever food plant at, 238

Toilet preparations: research on, 65–7; concentration of production at Leeds, 160–1; the European market, 198–201; Indian market, 238; S. American market, 257

Toilet soap, synthetic, 83

Toothpaste, 87, 231

Toronto, Lever factories in, 86, 247–8

Tours, headquarters of Compagnie Française de Nutrition Animale, 192

Townsville, Queensland, Unilever factory in, 246

Trade unions: negotiation with, 56; in the Netherlands, 56

Transport problem, with raw materials, 77–8

Transport company, Unilever's. *See* S.P.D.

Trawlers, 167, 203–4

Trout breeding, 175

Tunisia, 198

Turkey, 10, 200, 213; Unilever partnership and market in, 111, 261–2

Türkiye Iş Bankasi. *See* Iş-Bank

Twijnstra company, 192

Uganda, 221

Unilever-Emery N.V., 197

UNILEVER LIMITED/N.V.: rise in number of operating and administrative companies 1948–65, 4; application of scientific methods in 1950s and 1960s, 5–7; a European-based business, 8; welcomes the Common Market, 8; Common Market conferences, 9; losses beyond the Iron Curtain, 9–10; and the Common Market agricultural policy, 11–12; food processing, 12; trade in animal feeding-stuffs, and technical assistance to farmers, 12–13; and post-war conditions in former colonies, 14–16; and overseas investment, 16–17; and rising standards of living, 17–18; improvement and increase of products, 18–19; and the new retailing system, 18–22; achievement of D'Arcy Cooper, Rijkens and Heyworth, 22–5; George Cole and F. J. Tempel, 25–6; the two parent companies, 29; number of people employed 1938 and 1965, 46; the managers, 46–7; and local aspirations, 47; proportionate increase of skilled workers, 47–8; recruitment of university graduates, and the selection and training system, 48–54; policy on managers, 54–5; labour relations and conditions, 55–61; pension schemes, 61–2; and the Welfare State, 62–3; research (*see* Research);

technology (*see* Technology); network analysis, 88–9; transition from private partnership to public company, 108–9; changes in capital structure 1929–1965, 109–13; major projects, 114–15; turnover 1949–1965, 115; return on capital employed 1954–1964, 115–17; the Finance Committee's report, 117–18; problem of depreciation of fixed tangible assets, 118–19; economies of new investment, 119, 121; dividends declared 1949–1965, 121–3; self-financing system, 123–6; government restriction and overseas investment, 126; taxation, and contribution to social benefits, 126–7; streamlining the organization, 140–1; question of size, 141; growth in relation to Gross National Product, 144–5; acquisitions of businesses, 149–52; motives behind merger of 1929, 183; and the recovery of the Continent, 210–12; investments in Africa, 225–6; and problems of trade in the East, 245–6; and the developing economies, 262–9.

Special Committee, 25, 30–2, 42, 67, 69, 117, 172, 261

Articles of Association, 29

National Management, 31

The Annual Operating Plan, 31

The Annual Capital Expenditure Budget, 31–2

The Annual Review of Remuneration and Selection of Top Management, 31

Information Division, 33, 37

Product Committee (for Continental Europe), 41

Unilever Companies Management Development Scheme, 49

Technical Division, 85

Finance Committee, 117–18, 121

Capital Depreciation Committee, 119, 121

Unilever Margarine Group, 162
Unilever Merseyside Limited, 158–9
Unilever N.V., 22, 29, 44, 110, 111, 121–3, 202; its problems in the German market in the 1930s, 183; and the Planta margarine case, 190n.
Unilever Oil Milling Group, 79, 165, 175
Unilever Solo-Feinfrost, 204
United Africa Company, 13, 15, 16, 22, 30, 227, 262, 266; timber interests, 65, 219–20; lean times, 213; prosperity, 214; French section (Niger France), 217–18; interests in Ghana, 218–19; department stores, 219; withdraws from produce-buying, 219; brewery interests, 220; East African interests, 221; decline of proportionate share in Unilever activities, 225; Turkish subsidiary, 261
United Kingdom: labour relations, 56, 57; use of bio-degradable detergents, 83; supermarkets, 97; Unilever's advertising in, 100; Capital Issues Committee, 123; legislation on restrictive practices, 135; *Unilever markets:* detergents, 155–60; toilet preparations, 160–1; margarine and other edible fats, 161–2; oil and cake industry, 163–5; foods, 165–75
United States, 37, 42, 46, 69, 116, 189, 202, 203, 249; relaxes discriminatory laws against margarine, 11, 230; Lever Brothers research laboratories in, 66, 70–1, 85; development of synthetic detergents, 81; market research, 93–4; anti-trust laws, 134–6, 235, 236; salmon canning industry, 168
See also Lever Brothers Company
Uruguay, Atkinson's factory in, 200

Valabrègue, France, 191
Valinhos, Brazil, 259
Vanaspati, 239
Vancouver, Lever factory in, 86, 247
Van den Bergh, Albert, 61
Van den Bergh, Sam, 91
Van den Bergh, firm of, 27, 99, 105, 109, 152, 162, 176, 190, 263; pension scheme, 61; paper and printing interests, 207, 208, 209
van Marken, 55
Vauxhall Motors, 224
Vegetables: dehydrated, 72–3; frozen, 173, 205; canned, 173–4
Victoria, Lever factory in, 86
Vik Brothers, Norway, 175
Villastellona, Italy, Unilever margarine factory at (destroyed), 188
Vim, 238
Vinolia A.B., Sweden, 200
Vinolia Company, 160
Vita company, of Leiden, 203
Vitamins, 64, 180
Vlaardingen, Holland: research laboratory at, 66, 71, 76, 162, 187; detergent factory, 195; chemical plant, 197
Volta River project, 219
Vono, 220

Wakefield Gully, New Zealand, Unilever factory at, 252
Walker Chemical Company, 179–80
Wall, Thomas, and Sons, 85, 166, 168–71, 204, 220, 254
Walton-on-Thames: Birds Eye headquarters at, 175; Advita headquarters, 180
Warrington, soap and detergent production at, 152, 159
See also Crosfield, Joseph
Washing powders. *See* Detergents; Soap powders
Watson, Angus, and Company, of Newcastle, 166, 168
Watson, Joseph, of Leeds, 156, 158, 160–1
Watt, James, 7

Wedgwood, Josiah, 7

Welfare State, 62

Welwyn, Herts., research laboratory at, 66

Wembley, Thomas Wall's factory at, 169

West, John. *See* John West Foods Limited

West Africa, 15, 65, 77, 151; research establishments in, 65; United Africa Company's interests in, 215
See also British West Africa

West African Cold Storage, 220

West African Portland Cement Company, 220

West Germany: Unilever factories in, 8; labour relations, 56–7; margarine market, 185–6; toiletry market, 200; foods market, 204; paper industry, 209

West Indies, 42

Western Region Development Corporation, 220

Whale oil, 113

Willesden, Thomas Wall's factory at, 169

Winnipeg, Lever factory at, 86, 247

Wisk (detergent powder), 82

Wood pulp, 77

Woodroofe, Dr E. G., 6, 25, 67, 69, 77, 157

Woolton, Lord, 24

Workington, pulp and board mill at, 177

Worksop, Batchelor's factory at, 174, 175

World War II, recovery from, 4–5

Wunstorf, Germany: margarine factory at, 186; quick-freezing plant, 204

Yarmouth. *See* Great Yarmouth

Yugoslavia: Labour relations in, 56; loss of Unilever market, 184

Zambia, Unilever market in, 255

Zwijndrecht: health research laboratory at, 65; hydrogenation plant, 115